THE GOALS OF PSYCHOANALYSIS

Identification, Identity,
and Supervision

León Grinberg

THE GOALS
OF PSYCHOANALYSIS

Identification, Identity,
and Supervision

León Grinberg

translated by
Christine Trollope

Karnac Books

London　1990　New York

First published in 1990 by
H. Karnac (Books) Ltd.
58 Gloucester Road
London SW7 4QY

Distributed in the United States of America by
Brunner/Mazel, Inc.
19 Union Square West
New York, NY 10003

British Library Cataloguing in Publication Data
Grinberg, León
    The goals of psychoanalysis: identification, identity,
    and supervision
    1. Psychoanalysis
    I. Title
    150.19'5

    ISBN 0-946439-83-4

Printed in Great Britain by BPCC Wheatons Ltd, Exeter

ACKNOWLEDGEMENTS

I would like to thank the following for their kind permission to use material from their publications:

Tecnipublicaciones, S.A. (chapters 1, 2, 3, 4, 5, 6, 7, 8, 20, 21, 22, 23, 24, 25).

International Review of Psychoanalysis (chapter 9).

International Universities Press, Inc. (chapter 10).

The International Journal of Psychoanalysis (chapters 11, 12, 13, 15, 16).

Psychoanalytic Quarterly (chapter 14).

Caesura Press (chapter 17).

Bulletin of the European Psycho-Analytical Federation (chapter 18).

Ediciones Paidós (chapter 19).

Chapters 1–8 were published in León Grinberg, *Teoria de la Identificación,* third edition (Madrid: Tecnipublicaciones, S.A., 1985).

Chapter 9 was published under the title, 'The problem of identity and the psychoanalytical process', by León Grinberg & Rebeca Grinberg, in *International Review of Psychoanalysis, I,* part 4 (1974).

Chapter 10 was published in *The Identity of the Psychoanalyst,* edited by Edward D. Joseph and Daniel Widlocher (New York: International Universities Press, Inc., 1983).

Chapter 11 was published under the title, 'Relations between psychoanalysts', *International Journal of Psycho-Analysis, 44* (1963).

Chapter 12 was published under the title, 'New ideas: Conflict and evolution', *International Journal of Psycho-Analysis, 50* (1969).

Chapter 13 was published under the title, 'The razor's edge in depression and mourning', *International Journal of Psycho-Analysis, 59* (1978).

Chapter 14 was published under the title, 'Dreams and acting out', *Psychoanalytic Quarterly, 56* (1987).

Chapter 15 was published under the title, 'The closing phase of psychoanalytic treatment of adults, and the goals of psychoanalysis: The search for truth about one's self', *International Journal of Psycho-Analysis, 61* (1980).

Chapter 16 was published under the title, 'The relationship between obsessive mechanisms and a state of self disturbance', *International Journal of Psycho-Analysis, 47* (1966).

Chapter 17 was published under the title, 'The "Oedipus" as a resistance against the "Oedipus" in psychoanalytic practice', in *Do I Dare Disturb the Universe? A Memorial to Wilfred R. Bion,* edited by James S. Grotstein (Beverly Hills, CA: Caesura Press, 1981).

Chapter 18 was published under the title, 'Drives and affects: Models instead of theories', *Bulletin of the European Psycho-Analytical Federation, 26–27* (1986).

Chapter 19 was published under the title, 'Observaciones psicoanalíticas sobre la creatividad', in León Grinberg, *Psicoanalisis. Aspectos Teóricos y Clínicos* (Barcelona/Buenos Aires: Ediciones Paidós, 1981).

Chapters 20–25 were published in León Grinberg, *La Supervisión Psicoanalítica: Teoría y Práctica,* third edition (Madrid: Tecnipublicaciones, S. A., 1986).

CONTENTS

viii   CONTENTS

PREFACE

T his book stems from the integration of chapters from books and articles, written at different times. The decision to carry out this task was not an easy one because of the great variety of subjects. There was, however, one justification for the attempt: the wish to share with English-speaking colleagues problems concerning psychoanalysis and psychoanalysts, which formed an important part of their professional life; problems arising in the analyst's relationship with himself and his own work, in his relationship with his patients and his colleagues, and in the working through of emotions and phantasies involved in the fulfilment of the aims of psychoanalysis.

The four parts into which this work is divided can be read separately, or they can follow each other in continuous sequence. Part one deals with the concept of identification and is intended to bring some light and order into the confused panorama that exists in the psychoanalytical field with regard to its definition, both from the theoretical point of view and from that of its clinical application. I have tried to define its meaning more clearly and to distinguish it from other terms that are mistakenly considered to be synonymous. In addition to relating identification to the mechanisms involved in internalization and externalization, I have paid particular attention to the mechanism of projective identification, because this has now developed into a subject for polemics in certain psychoanalytical circles and a basic theoretical and clinical element in others. I am also concerned with "projective counteridentification", a term that I coined some years ago to describe the specific reactions that the analyst may suffer in consequence of the "intrusive" projective identifications of his patients, but which may also function as an effective technical instrument for detecting the most regressive levels of his analysands.

The chapters that form part two refer to the feeling of identity. In one of them I develop the idea, worked out together with my wife Rebeca Grinberg, that identity is the result of the interrelation between three links of integration: spatial, temporal, and social. Then, more specifically, I consider the identity of the psychoanalyst, as I did in a paper read at a special symposium organized by the International Psychoanalytic Association. We discussed this subject in a small group of psychoanalysts meeting in a little hotel in Haslemere (England) in 1976. On the other hand, I try to analyse the reasons behind the conflicts that sometimes occur between analysts.

Part three comprises various articles on theoretical and clinical aspects. I have chosen those that seem to me of interest not only for their content, but because they contain ideas relating to the aims of psychoanalysis, especially the search for the truth about oneself.

Finally, in part four, I thought it might be useful to include a few chapters of my book, *Psychoanalytic Supervision,* in which I describe the problems that tend to appear in this special experience of teaching and learning in our discipline, in its theoretical and clinical aspects; here we can see difficulties of a different type, in the transmission of knowledge and technical attitudes that would enable us to fulfil one of the most important aims of psychoanalysis: our effort to understand and to help to solve the conflicts in the human mind.

I wish to express special thanks to my wife and to Mr Riccardo Steiner, and to other friends who encouraged me to carry out this project.

León Grinberg

PART ONE

The theory of identification

CHAPTER ONE

The concept
of identification

The concept of 'identification' is usually placed in the category of concepts the use of which has lent itself to various interpretations leading to controversy and confusion. The different authors who have set themselves the task of specifying its nature and functions within psychoanalytical theory could not resist the temptation to give it the meaning most closely related to their own scheme of reference.

The general tendency to replace the concept of 'identification' by others considered equivalent or interchangeable, such as 'introjection', 'internalization', 'incorporation' etc., contributed to the confusion that reigns over its conceptualization and its location in the wide spectrum of mental mechanisms.

Meanwhile the concept of identification is central and basic to the understanding of the development and organization of the personality. It is a fundamental process in the formation of the ego, the superego and the ego-ideal, character and identity, since it is at the same time a constant in the continual interplay of relations between subject and objects. As Freud maintained (1921c), it was the most primitive form of affective bond with another person. The first approach of a baby to a desired object is to try to swallow it, that is to say, 'consume it and recreate it in the ego'. This is the basis of identification.

In other words, identification plays a part in every human relationship, establishing the current of empathy between the individual and the object, since it not only tends to assimilate attitudes, expressions, and emotions but also enables us to put ourselves in another's place, in order better to understand his thought and behaviour. But this process must not be confused with imitation. We could identify with the sadness or joy of a friend or with the brave or frightened attitude of a character in a film without recording it in our consciousness, were it not for the feeling that overpowers us as we witness some episode or other. On the other hand we try to imitate or reproduce actively and deliberately determined acts that arouse our admiration. Identification is not a category of behaviour; it is an unconscious mechanism that produces lasting changes in the subject. However, both processes may lead to integration. The act of imitating is a normal phenomenon in the child's development, forms part of its apprenticeship, and has a share in the nature of the bonds established with objects in the environment. In the measure in which this activity tends to resemble or possess characteristics of these objects, it becomes one of the elements favouring identification.

The development of the ego consequently takes place thanks to the successive identifications of different types that appear from the first moments of life, starting with the earliest relations of the baby with its mother.

The process of identification is closely related to learning. But here arises another important problem from the conceptual point of view. For the moment it will be useful to point out here too the analogies and differences between the two processes, since they are not synonymous and cannot be substituted for each other. Both phenomena have in common the tendency to change the structure and functioning of the psychic organism as a result of experience. The theories of identification and learning have different origins and different starting-points. The first is a part of the psychoanalytical theory that, basically, is a theory derived from clinical experience, dealing with the motives and meanings of such an experience and with the relations between these motives and meanings, the functions of personality, object-relations, and their influence on the integration and organization of the personality. In contrast, the theory of learning has no clinical basis and is more concerned with examining extrinsic factors and their interrelation. It operates primarily on the basis of the model of stimulus and response (Meissner, 1971).

In a wide sense, it could nevertheless be said that the learning process also tends to contribute to a certain structuralization of the intrapsychic processes, but in a different way from the structuralization determined by the process of identification. In the first case, as Meissner (1972) maintains, learning produces structural modifications in the representational order and in the functional capacities of psychic demands, while identification processes produce deeper internal structural changes, which affect the internal reality of the self and the internal organization of the ego and superego. The boundary line between the two types of process is defined by the nature and degree of internalization in the two cases. The stress is placed on different levels of internalization and structuralization, which have different implications for the organization and function of the personality. The processes of learning have a representational and functional form of structure and internalization, with a level of internalization corresponding to the most peripheral aspect of the inner world, while the identification processes are aimed at psychic structure, and their level of internalization is at the central point of the inner world. I shall come back to this scheme because in my opinion levels and degrees of learning should also be planned. I think there are processes of learning that are internalized through introjective identifications the products of which enrich and amplify the 'nuclear' part of the self, while other experiences of learning take place mainly through projective identification and are included in the 'orbital' part of the self [the terms 'nuclear' and 'orbital' are used here in accordance with Wisdom's (1961, 1963) scheme]. In this latter case there appears another class of phenomenon, which I would include in the category of 'learning by imitation'.

Imitation is a normal step in the process of development and may be a part of identification or an important component of the baby's first identifications. It is very often conscious, but it may also be preconscious or unconscious. In general it implies acquiring a model of behaviour without a deep-seated bond with the object. It does not imply deep internalization, because it does not go to the 'nucleus' of the self; but it may be a precursor of identification.

The lasting and stable establishment of representations of the self and the object is achieved through learning based on maturity and experience. It is this type of learning that consolidates the development of the secondary process and strengthens its connection with reality.

I do not propose for now to formulate a definition of the term 'identification'. My intention is rather to make a more precise delimitation of its concept and to define its relations with other similar mechanisms close to its functions. It is possible that we are calling different processes by the same name, or that we are giving the name identification to both the process and the product of the process. There are those who insist that the term identification should be applied only to the process, while the product would be 'introjection'. Other authors think the opposite. They maintain that it is impossible to separate process and product as they complete and complement each other, so that to consider identification as a process and its correlative product as introjection might cause ambiguity. I think identification refers to both at once. The product includes individual differences in behaviour, motives, attitudes, and values that the subject acquires by virtue of the identification process, which is essentially an ego-process; important ego-functions participate in its different phases. The product implies a change in the psychic structure and brings modifications into the relationship of subject with object.

In so far as identifications are specifically structural modifications of the ego, they form the basic structure of the personality.

I think this is a suitable moment to summarize some of the aspects included in the process of identification as they were developed by Schafer (1968), who maintained that 'the process of identifying with an object is unconscious, though it may have significant preconscious and conscious components. In this process the subject modifies his motives and behaviour patterns, and the self-representations corresponding to them, in such a way as to experience being like, the same as, and merged with one or more representations of that object. Through identification, the subject represents as his own one or more regulatory influences or characteristics of the object that have become important to him, and continues his tie with the object. . . . An identification can acquire relative autonomy from its origins in the subject's relations with dynamically significant objects.'

Identification takes place, not with a person but with one or more representations of that person. The form in which the subject conceives the other person is only one possible version of him. This version will be determined by the pressing needs or intentions of the subject, his state of mind, his projections, the nature and limitations of his objective estimation of that person, and other selective and distorting factors such as those that may correspond to the level of development and organization of the subject at that moment. We must also take into account the concepts of total and partial identification with a partial and a total object. The total or partial character of the object is defined from the point of view of the subject or of an objective observer. In this latter case, partial means an isolated aspect of the object (the breast, the penis, the authority, etc.). But this single aspect, in so far as it exercises an intense attraction over the subject's feelings, may be considered as a 'total object'. On the other hand, the identification may be total or partial, with an object considered as partial or total. The following possibilities may appear:

1. Attempt at total identification (a) with the object considered as total, or (b) with part of the object.
2. Attempt at partial identification (a) with the object considered as total, or (b) with part of the object.

Categories 1a, 1b, and 2a correspond to more primitive functional levels, and 2b to a more highly developed level. Identification with partial objects generally takes place in early infancy and in periods of regression. The Kleinian theory is the one that has worked more with theories of partial and total objects, as we see further on (Klein, 1952).

Identifications imply a selective reorganization of desires, behaviour patterns, capacities, and also previous identifications. Thus, for example, identification does not create the capacity to think, walk, speak, fix objectives, but these capacities appear with particular accents and nuances taken from the representations of the object.

The attempt to be like another person is an effort basically defined by the mode of functioning of the secondary process. The subject clearly recognizes his separation from that object. The effort to be like the object is objective and syntonic with the ego. On the other hand the attempt to be the same as another person implies significant characeristics of the primary process, which can only be illusory and magical by nature. This type of identification, where the subject is confused with the object, presupposes a large decrease in the reality-test. These identifications are the type of 'psychotic identifications' described by Jacobson (1954), in which fusion and sameness predominate, or the type of pathological projective identifications described by the Kleinian school; they are poor in organizing factors and impoverish the already limited relations with real objects.

The object of the identification is something emotionally significant for the subject.

Identification concerns modifications of the self expressed in the behaviour of the subject; these sometimes tend to increase the similarity to an object taken as a model.

Identification, moreover, is one of the most primitive methods of ensuring the satisfaction of bodily and psychic needs, provided by the object.

For my part I consider that the term 'identification' in its widest accepted meaning includes the combination of mechanisms and functions that determine as their result the active structural process that occurs within the ego, on the basis of selection, inclusion, and elimination of elements deriving from external and/or internal objects that are to form the components that amplify the rudimentary structure of the ego in the first moments of life. I do not consider it a single phenomenon, but the result of a process in which different phenomena take part, divided into two large categories—that of internalization and that of externalization.

CHAPTER TWO

The theory of identification in the work of Freud

F reud (1892–1899) used the term 'identification' for the first time in a letter to Fliess, when he described the agoraphobic symptom in women as the product of an identification with the prostitute walking through the street in search of clients. A year later, in another letter to Fliess, he refers again to the identification with a dead person or with the rigidity of a corpse, which underlies the tonic spasm of the hysteric. In manuscript L. (1897), he again treats the theme of identification with the maidservant as a form of devaluation of feminine attributes and as self-punishment for incestuous desires.

Shortly afterwards, Freud developed the concept of *hysterical identification* when he was studying the mechanisms of dreams (1900a) and in his work on hysteria (1905e). This type of identification implies an unconscious process by which a subject identifies himself with an object on the basis of a repressed common desire, generally sexual.

But in his 'Project for a scientific psychology' (1950a [1887–1902]) I discovered that Freud is referring indirectly to projective

identification when, to explain the 'experience of satisfaction', he
points out that the child, incapable of carrying out a 'specific
action', does it 'by means of extraneous help' (the mother who
identifies herself with him) to attract the attention of an 'experienced person to the child's longing and distressful state'. 'This path
of discharge', continues Freud, 'thus acquires a secondary function
of the highest importance, that of communication' (comprehension, empathy) '. . . . and the initial helplessness of human beings
is the primal source of all moral motives'. I consider this paragraph
of fundamental significance because in it Freud is already making
clear the importance of object-relations with the mother from the
beginning of life, on the basis of the mechanism of identification,
for the later acquisition of thought, symbols, and communication.
This concept, bringing out this type of object-relations, was
developed years afterwards by M. Klein (1946) and by Bion (1963)
in their studies on projective identification and the theory of
thought.

His works 'On narcissism: An introduction' (1914c) and 'Mourning and melancholia' (1917e [1915]) examine the problem of the
nature of identification from another angle. In his essay 'On narcissism: An introduction' the theme of identification is treated to
the full, although implicitly. In this article Freud introduces his
theory of the ego-ideal and of conscience, the precursors of what he
later termed 'superego'. Here he develops the importance of a link
with another person based on something different from the sexual
impulse and desire. He alludes to this type of link as an 'anaclitic
object-choice', giving it an essentially pre-sexual character. This
anaclitic relationship will later be transformed into the basis of a
mode of identification (called by some authors 'anaclitic identification'), which appears in response to a loss of love. It is in 'Mourning
and melancholia' (1917e [1915]) that Freud describes this identification process in the greatest detail. From the point of view of its
development, he takes it through three phases: the first takes
place in early infancy, in which the ego and the object blend into an
undifferentiated structure; after that, in the second phase, begins
choice, or the binding of the libido to one person; finally, in the
third phase, faced with the loss of the object (either real loss,

injury, or disillusionment), the cathexis of the object remains abandoned, but an identification with the abandoned object is established (1916–1917 [1915–1917]).

Freud appears to have been inclined at the beginning to consider identification as being structurally associated with the oral or cannibalistic phase of the development of the libido. Thus identification would correspond to a preliminary stage in object-choice; it would be the first route by which the ego chose an object and wished to incorporate it according to the cannibalistic phantasy— that is, by devouring it. In other words, in melancholia object-choice is replaced by identification. [H. Etchegoyen (1985) insists that the critical ego formed in this identification corresponds to the subject and not to the incorporated object, an aspect that is not usually taken into account.] It is a *narcissistic-type identification* in which object-cathexis is abandoned and replaced by a regression to a more primitive form of object-relation. At another point, Freud brings out the fact that 'the difference . . . between narcissistic and hysteric identification is manifest in that in the former object-cathexis is abandoned, while in the latter its influence is maintained and continued, although in general it is limited to certain isolated actions'. In this way hysteric identification implies the desire to preserve the sexual bond of the libido with the object, assimilating some of its characteristics. In contrast, narcissistic identification implies that the self replaces the object and becomes the target for the hate that the subject has originally directed against the object (Weiss, 1947/48).

In his clinical study on 'The wolf-man' or 'From the history of an infantile neurosis' (1918b) Freud returns to identification on the basis of the dream of the 'primal scene' about which the patient told him. In his phantasy, his mother had taken on the role of the castrated wolf that allowed the other wolf to climb on top of it. He had then identified himself with his castrated mother (without a penis), threatened by the wolves of his dream. The anus was the organ through which he identified himself passively with the woman in his homosexual phantasies. This identification with the mother in the primal scene was an important cause of his illness. To obtain sexual satisfaction from his father, he must be castrated like his mother. [But he also identifies with the father in his active position. He identifies with both parents, as Freud described later in *The Ego and the Id* (1923b).]

It is in *Group Psychology and the Analysis of the Ego* (1921c) that Freud refers most extensively to the concept of identification. He defines it there as 'the earliest expression of an emotional tie with another person', adding that it plays an important part in the early history of the Oedipus complex. He gives three sources of identification: (1) identification is the original form of affective bond with an object; (2) in the regressive form it becomes a substitute for a libidinal object-bond by means of introjection of the object into the ego (as in the case of Dora, whose cough was a symptom of identification); and (3) it may appear with a new perception of a common quality shared with another person who is not an object of the sexual instinct. The common bond between the members of a group is in the nature of an identification based on an important common emotional quality.

In this article, Freud compares identification with being in love and tackles the problem of the constitution of groups. In the first case, the ego is enriched by acquiring the properties admired in the object; in the second case, the ego is impoverished by its submission to the object, which is given the place of the ego-ideal. From being in love to hypnosis is only a step. A primary group is a union of individuals who have put the same object in the place of their ego-ideal and have consequently identified one with the other in their ego.

Each individual is a component part of numerous groups; he is pulled by bonds of identification in many directions and has constituted his ego-ideal according to the most varied models. The distinction between the identification of the ego with an object and the replacement of the ego-ideal by an object can be illustrated by two artificial groups: the army and the church. The soldier treats his superior as his ideal, while he himself identifies with his equals. Incidentally, when Freud describes the identification of each soldier with his leader by projection of the ego-ideal, he is implicitly establishing the mechanism of projective identification later developed by M. Klein.

As we see, Freud (1921c, 1923b) explains the evolution and the future of primary identification by defining it as the earliest form of affective link with another person before any object is involved (Fenichel, 1926). According to Freud, 'the child shows a special interest in his father, he makes of him his ideal, which does not mean that he adopts a passive-feminine attitude, but that it is strictly masculine and can very well be reconciled with the Oedipus complex, to the preparation of which it contributes' (1923b). Simultaneously, or a little later, 'the child begins to take his mother as the object of his libidinal impulses'. From this confluence the normal Oedipus complex is born. The Oedipus complex can be inverted, in which case 'identification with the father is the preliminary phase of his conversion into a sexual object. . . . In the first case the father is what he would like to *be,* in the second, what he would like to *have.* For this reason, identification is always possible before any object-choice' (1923b).

Freud apparently does not consider identification only as a mechanism to prepare the way for an emotional link, but as the link itself. On the other hand, identification for him is not now a part of psychopathology, but a general process of development.

Identification is by nature ambivalent from the beginning. It can be appreciated that for Freud identification with a loved object is inextricably bound up with identification with a hated object. He clearly brings out the distinction between identification with the father and the choice of the father as an object; in the first case, one would want to be the father, and in the second case one would want to possess him. In subsequent articles he accords ever-increasing importance to the fear of the primal father as a primary force leading to the resolution of the Oedipus complex and the development of identification.

In *The Ego and the Id* (1923b) Freud shows how identification transforms object-libido into narcissistic libido. And this is a method by which the ego can obtain control over the id. Behind the ego-ideal is hiding the first and most important identification of the individual, identification with the father and one's own personal pre-history. [J. Chasseguet-Smirgel (1975) distinguishes between the ego-ideal, the heir of primary narcissism, and the superego, which is derived from the Oedipus complex. She adds that primary identification remains bound up with the ego-ideal and secondary identification with the Oedipus complex and the formation of the superego.]

The character of the ego can then be considered as a precipitate of the abandoned object-cathexes. The formation of the character through such modifications of the ego gives the ego control over the impulses of the id, since it presents itself before the id as a substitute for the object. The object-libido is changed to narcissistic libido, with the consequent abandonment of sexual objectives. The result of this desexualization is sublimation. Freud suggests that all sublimation may take place through the change from sexual object-libido to narcissistic libido with the modification of the ego as intermediary. If these identifications are too numerous, too intense and incompatible, they may be isolated one from the other, resulting in disruption of the ego and pathological consequences.

To sum up: in the first oral cannibalistic phase 'object-cathexis and identification are no doubt indistinguishable from each other' (primary identification). 'We can only suppose that later on object-cathexes proceed from the id (1923b).

He then adds that 'the effects of the first identifications carried out at the earliest age are always general and lasting. Behind the ego-ideal is hidden the first and most important identification with the father, which takes place in the prehistory of each individual.' Primary identification is, as we have said, 'direct, immediate and previous to any object-cathexis' (1923b).

In the normal Oedipus complex, the boy identifies with his father and takes the mother as object. But as the father is an obstacle to reaching the mother, identification with him becomes increasingly ambivalent, 'as if ambivalence, existing from the beginning in identification, externalized itself at that moment'. As the Oedipus complex dissolves, it may happen that identification with the father is reinforced, keeping an internal bond with the mother and affirming the child's masculinity, or that he identifies himself with the mother. The latter event forms the negative Oedipus complex. The male–female balance of the bisexual position—says Freud—channels identifications. The complex is generally complete: positive and negative. A similar process takes place in the girl.

In *The Ego and the Id* (1923b) he again took up what he had observed in melancholia, in which identification appeared as a substitute for the lost object, but added the concept that identification intervened in the form taken by the ego and contributed essentially to the building of character.

Freud was preoccupied by the origins of the superego through the resolution of the Oedipus complex (1924d); he took identification into account but had to base his opinions on bisexuality and on the strength inherent in the masculinity or femininity of the boy as the factor deciding the course of identification. The superego is not only the residue of the earliest object-choices of the id; it also represents an energetic reaction formation against such choices. In relation to the ego, the precept 'you must be like your father' also involves the prohibition 'in some aspects you will not be like him', since these correspond to his prerogatives (1923b). His concept of identification allows a variety of meanings: (1) in melancholia it appears as a regression in the face of object-loss; (2) as a primitive type of object-relation in the small child who admires his father; (3) as the internalization of the parents' values during the resolution of the Oedipus complex; (4) in the relationship between brothers, where it develops as a reaction-formation against envy and rivalry; (5) as the bond between the members of an adult group that has replaced the leader by their ego-ideal.

In his 1933 lectures Freud (1933a) introduces the concept of identification as a process by which the relationship with the parents is internalized, and the result of which does not entirely depend on the parents' behaviour, but also on the transformation of instincts in the formation of the superego. He says: 'The basis of the process is what we call identification, that is to say the assimilation of one ego to another one . . . as a result of which the first ego behaves like the second in certain respects, imitates it and in a sense takes it up into itself.' 'The superego . . . normally departs more and more from the original parental figures; it becomes, so to say, more impersonal.' Later identifications, including those with the parents, facilitate 'important contributions to character-formation, but then refer only to the ego, not influencing the superego, which is determined by earlier images.'

In the opinions I have expressed up to now I have mentioned on various occasions the concept of primary identification. I should like to go on to specify its nature and difference from secondary identification.

As Laplanche and Pontalis (1967) point out, the notion of primary identification has different meanings according to the theories about the early stages of individual existence. It is characterized not only by being the first, but by the fact that it is not established as a result of an object-relation properly speaking, but is 'the most primitive form of affective link with an object'. This type of link of the suckling has been described as the first relationship with the mother, before there exists a clear distinction between one ego and another. But it is difficult to link primary identification with an absolutely undifferentiated state.

Primary identification was described by Freud as an identification taking place in the prehistory of the individual, which is 'direct, immediate and previous to any object-cathexis' (1923b). The object is the model of what one would like to be. It is closely bound up with oral incorporation. This type of identification, which is established when there is still no distinction between the ego and the external world, would be connected with primary narcissism. But that primary identification which is previous to any content of libido in the object leads to a narcissistic stage that is nevertheless marked by the existence of the incorporated object, which is not cathected and is still undifferentiated from the subject. (Secondary identification is aimed at the reconstruction of the lost object in the ego, which seeks not to 'be' but to 'possess' the object. [For Meissner, 1971, primary identification refers to 'the symbiotic union previous to all identification between subject and object'. Sandler, 1960, affirms that primary identification in a fusion or confusion between the self and the non-self, when, however, there is no distinction between the two.])

It is possible that what Freud called primary identification can be understood as a very early object-relation, symbiotic and immature, in which primitive projective identification acts as an executive mechanism; the self is not distinct from its object; the relationship with oneself is massive and total. Secondary identification, on the other hand, allows a movement towards more mature identifications that require a clear differentiation between the images of the self and the object.

O. L. Belmonte, E. del Valle, A. Kargieman and D. Saludjian (1976) bring forward their own hypothesis with regard to the concept of primary identification. They point out that for Freud there were two classes of object: (1) the object of the instincts or partly libidinal tendencies, and (2) the sexual object of the ego, which corresponds to the moment of object-choice. Taking this differentiation into account, the argument as to whether primary identification is objectal or not would be resolved. Thus when Freud then maintains that primary identification constitutes the first affective bond with an object and is at the same time anterior to any object-choice, we must understand that it comes before the ego has chosen its first love-object (generally the mother), which represents the *total libido-cathexis of the already unified instincts* on to a total external object; this does not contradict the continued existence of an object-bond represented by partial tendencies towards the object.

According to the concepts developed in his work, we see that Freud considered identification as taking part in the building of the psychic apparatus, the ego and the superego, in the later evolution of the individual and in the historical development of humanity, in the formation of groups, in sublimations, in learning, in creativity, in control of aggression, in object-choice, in the development of the Oedipus complex, in empathy and understanding, in the mechanism of dream-construction, in phantasies and daydreams, in parapraxes and symptom-formation.

CHAPTER THREE

The concept
of identification
in psychoanalytical literature

T he term *identification* is the one generally used to define and represent the active structural process that takes place within the ego, and for which it metabolizes certain internalized components, producing an identificatory matrix. It thus becomes significant to note that from Freud onwards, authors committed to different schemes of reference—such as M. Klein (1955), Meissner (1971, 1972), Widlöcher (1969–1970), White (1962), Brody and Mahoney (1964)—have agreed in pointing out the very important part played by identification in forming and consolidating the basic structure of the personality.

As I said in chapter one, I propose to use the term *identification* for the combination of operations that determine the process of structuring that takes place within the self on the basis of selection, inclusion, and elimination of elements deriving from external objects, internal objects, and parts of the self. Identification thus considered would be the result of a series of processes that include different phenomena comprising two large categories: internalization and externalization. On the other hand, I suggest that the term *introjective identification* should be reserved specifi-

cally for processes characterized by a deeper level of internalization, or, in other words, for the product of internalizations that
affect the nuclear part of the self and that will form and develop the
rudimentary structure of the ego starting from the first moments
of life.

But before developing these concepts, I would like to refer to
some of the definitions and uses of the term 'identification' in the
psychoanalytical literature.

For Freud, at the time when he was writing *Group Psychology
and the Analysis of the Ego* (1921c), identification was: (1) the
original form of the affective bond with an object; (2) a regressive
way of making oneself a substitute for the object's charge of libido;
and (3) the result of each new perception of the common attribute
shared with another person who is not the object of the sexual
instinct. Thanks to identification, one ego is converted to another;
the first behaves in certain aspects in the same way as the second;
it imitates it as though it were incorporated within it. Identification must not be confused with object-choice. The difference can be
expressed in the following way: when a child identifies with his
father, *he wants to be like his father*; when he makes him the object
of his choice, *he desires to possess his father*. The two processes are
independent of each other. On occasion object-choice can regress to
identification; in such a case, to compensate for the loss of a loved
object, the subject identifies regressively with it.

From his second theory of the psychical apparatus, Freud brings
out the growing importance of the concept of identification, as
Laplanche and Pontalis show (1967). The effects of the Oedipus
complex in the structuring of the subject are described in terms of
identifications. The father and mother are at the same time the
objects of love and of rivalry. It is probable that this ambivalence is
essential to the construction of any identification. In passing, I
mentioned that Laplanche and Pontalis also refer to the differentiation between a 'heteropathic and centripetal' identification (in
which it is the subject who identifies his own person with another)
and an 'idiopathic and centrifugal' identification (in which the
subject identifies the other person with himself). They add
'reciprocal identification' (of individuals among themselves, as can
be seen between the members of the group).

Edith Jacobson (1964) maintains that the first identifications are magical by nature and lead to phantasies or temporary beliefs that the subject is fused *with* or converted *to* the loved object without taking reality into account. On the other hand, the later identifications of the ego promote and may well achieve real changes in the ego which justify the feeling that one is, at least partially, similar to the object of identification. In regressive conditions, especially in psychotic states, there is disintegration or replacement of the normal identifications of the ego and superego by identifications of a magical type, which are more primitive. Thus E. Jacobson establishes the difference between the three stages of identification according to the various grades of participation in the primary process: feeling fused with the object; seeing oneself as the same as the object; or feeling similar to the object, in cases where the secondary process has more influence.

For Lampl de Groot (1965), identification is a normal mental process that leads a person to be like another person. Identification thus achieves three main objectives:

1. It is one of the means of ensuring the satisfaction of physical and psychological needs provided by the object.
2. It promotes the process of learning. The child learns through identification with its parents, siblings and other people.
3. It forms the basis of the ego ideal. In the magical pre-oedipal phase of development, the child identifies with the images of the omnipotent parents in order to be as powerful as he imagines them. In normal development the ego-ideal is amplified and evolves with new identifications.

Among pathological identifications she describes hysterical and narcissistic identifications.

Rycroft (1968) defines identification as the process by which a person (1) extends his identity within another; (2) takes upon himself the identity of another; (3) merges or confuses his identity with another's.

He distinguishes four types of identification: primary, secondary, projective, and introjective.

1. *Primary identification* is the state of things as it is assumed to exist in childhood, when the individual must, however, distinguish his identity from that of his objects, when the distinction between 'me' and 'you' still has no sense.

2. *Secondary identification* is the process of identification with an object the separate identity of which has already been discovered. Unlike the previous type, secondary identification is a defence, reducing the hostility between the self and the object and enabling experiences of separation to be denied. Nevertheless, secondary identification with parental figures is considered as a part of the process of normal development.

3. *Projective identification* is the process by which a person imagines that he is within objects external to himself. It is a defence, as it creates the illusion of control over the object and enables the subject to deny his impotence and to obtain satisfaction from his activities.

4. *Introjective identification* is the process of identification with an introject, or the process by which a person imagines that another is inside him, forming part of himself. Sometimes it is indistinguishable from secondary identification and introjection.

For Moore and Fine (1968), identification is an unconscious and automatic mental process by which an individual can assimilate to another person in one of several ways. It is a natural accompaniment to mental development and maturation and is of great help in the learning process (especially learning speech and language) and also in the acquisition of interests, ideals, and so forth. At the same time, it is considered as a pattern of defensive reaction.

Fuchs (1937) considers identification as a process that takes place in the ego and represents the *factor* of inclusion in the ego-system, unlike introjection, which is the *act* of inclusion in the ego by means of an instinctive model.

Koff (1961) suggests the following metapsychological definition of identification: (1) from the *economic* point of view, it represents a change of direction of the libido from an external to an internal object; (2) *structurally* it represents changes in the self tending to assimilate to the object; (3) from the *dynamic* point of view, it is accompanied by a regression to the early stage of primary identification, in which a portion of the self is offered as a substitute for the external object; it occurs when there is an object-loss. For Koff the term 'identification' implies the recognition of one person or thing in particular, to which one can assimilate, putting oneself in another's place, or making various persons or things form part of a whole, or specifying the uniqueness of an individual.

For Brody and Mahoney (1964), identification refers to assimilative processes that take place when the ego has formed and object-cathexes have been established. It arises mainly from perceptions of the ego and is essential to the transition from the primary to the secondary process of thought.

Widlöcher (1969–1970) suggests the existence of two instinctive sources of identification: narcissistic libido, which cathects the mirror-image of itself and its doubles, and object-libido, which cathects the loved object but through a pathological incorporation as in melancholia and, in a certain way, in hysteria. He also considers the interplay of identifications in psychological situations, id, ego, and superego, forming in addition conclusions about its nature and functioning. Among these conclusions is the idea that identification is a mechanism by which the subject takes upon himself features perceived in others. It may correspond to a phantasy by which the subject assumes a particular role in the primal scene, using the image of the other; that may take place in the ego-system and contribute to the formation of the character and the integration of the instrumental functions that are at its service; or it may occur in the defensive system, which is a substitute for external prohibitions, that is, the system of the superego.

For Schafer (1968), in its widest sense, 'the process of identifying with an object is unconscious, though it may also have prominent and significant preconscious and conscious components. In this process the subject modifies his motives and behaviour patterns, and the self-representations corresponding to them, in such a way as to experience being like, the same as, and merged with one or more representations of that object. Through identification,

the subject represents as his own one or more regulatory influences or characteristics of the object that have become important
to him, and continues his tie with the object.' The subject may
desire to produce this change for various reasons: an identification
may acquire relative autonomy, from its origins, in the subject's
relations with dynamically signicant objects.

Schafer divides the representations of the self, in accordance
with his experimental components, into representations such as
'I', or 'mine', or as occupying a place or space in the self. He
considers internalizations of external objects, which change the
representations of the self into aspects of 'I' and 'mine', as identifications. But he notes the existence of internalizations of another
type, which do not transform themselves into 'I' and 'mine' but are
experienced as occupying an uncertain place in the self. He calls
the latter type 'presences of the primary process'; he takes them as
concrete entities, emotionally significant, with the thought-
characteristics of the primary process, especially with regard to its
atemporality. They are generally found outside the limits of the
self, but in close contact with it. He calls internalizations located in
the body 'introjects'.

To sum up: the external object may be represented in three
different ways in the internal life of the individual:

1. as an object-representation in the thought of the secondary
   process, firmly placed in time and space according to its
   reality;
2. as a 'presence of the primary process' with an uncertain
   location in time and space, or located in the body (introjected);
3. as identifications resulting from the transformation of the
   representations into 'I' or 'mine'.

Robert Fliess (1956) suggests that the objects of primary and
secondary identifications correspond to what has been known as
'early' and 'late' parents. The distinction between the two, he says,
is as follows: 'early' parents correspond to an ontogenetic elaboration of a philogenetic object; 'late' parents correspond to something
purely ontogenetic, for example to persons as educators, masters,
and so on. Primary repression, primary identification, and 'early'

parents have one characteristic in common, which is that they are early.

Fliess also maintains that identification follows the model of cannibalistic incorporation. The result is that the image of a parent can be deposited in some part of the ego, and in analysis we must be prepared to recognize this image in the adult patient, as a constituent part of his morbid ego, and also as the nucleus of his morbid superego. But the deposit is not complete; it is a continuous process. That is to say that incorporation, even though it occurred a long time previously, remains clinically in existence through constant reincorporations. This occurs especially in cases of patients who have living psychotic parents with whom they still have permanent introjective contact.

Marjorie Brierley (1951) says that the term identification, like many others, is an 'omnibus' term containing a variety of different situations. Apart from the three types described by Freud, it is obvious that there are considerable differences in agreement with the personality and social behaviour of people. Some are more orientated towards an introjective type of identification and others towards a projective type. In the introjective type, the object is identified with the operative self and with the ego-ideal. In the projective type, some aspect of the personality is identified with the object, and it is the object that the person seeks to serve, sometimes to his own detriment. Michael Balint (1952) also suggested a genital identification as being characteristic of genital love; this identification is obviously projective or centrifugal by nature. Freud's (1921c) formula of the blind devotion of the one who loves (the object has taken the place of the ego-ideal) implies a projective identification of the ego-ideal on to this object, etc. He also points out that the concept of primary identification (oceanic experience) continues to have very great importance, especially in the first moments of life.

M. Klein (1952), describing the child's mind in the first years of life, with the creation of an inner world peopled with phantastic beings characterized by their intensely persecutory or extremely idealized nature, brought out the importance of a psychic reality built on the foundations of internal object-relations established through the mechanisms of projection, introjection, and identification. She particularly stressed that the development of the ego depends to a high degree on internalized good objects. In other words, introjective identification with the good breast, through a series of gratifying experiences, will contribute to the building and consolidation of the budding ego. [M. Klein (1952) attached special importance to mourning for the loss of the breast; her theory of the depressive position, with the elaboration and internalization of the loss, is bound up with the early Oedipus complex.] But the greatest contribution made by Kleinian theory to the identification process was its original concept of projective identification, with which I deal in greater detail in subsequent chapters.

Fairbairn (1952) referred to the child's dependence characterized by the persistence of primary identification (an emotional state comparable to that of the baby in the womb) and distinguished it from mature dependence, characterized by secondary identification, in which there is complete distinction between the ego and the object. Fairbairn contrasted primary with secondary identification. He pointed out that the breaking point of primary identification is the birth process, as from this moment the baby becomes an entity in itself, seeking to relate to a separate object.

He asserts at the same time that primary identification is not a process 'lacking an object', but the most primitive form of object-relation. At certain points in the development of his ideas, Fairbairn appears to oppose the concepts of identification to those of object-relations. He maintains that the baby struggles intensely between keeping the distinction in the quest for object-relations and falling back on identification. The two essential characteristics of infantile dependence are, according to him, secondary identification (regressive re-activation of the primary emotional identification of the baby before birth) and oral incorporation. This tendency to identification, he says, leads to the personality being 'swallowed' or absorbed by the object.

It is known, on the other hand, that Fairbairn differs from Melanie Klein with regard to the criterion of the objectives of internalization. Whereas M. Klein (1952) considers that the child internalizes from the beginning both good and bad objects, Fairbairn maintained at first that only bad objects were internalized, with the intention of dominating them. He saw no reason for internalizing good, gratifying objects with which the subjects's ego could keep good object-relations in the real world. Years later he modified this criterion, saying that in the first pre-ambivalent oral stage good and bad objects were not separated in the child's mind; thus at this stage the pre-ambivalent object is internalized, and it is only after internalization that good and bad objects are dissociated in phantasy, and so ambivalence arises. The bad object is then dissociated into two separate images, one with an excitant and the other with a repellent image, whereas the good object is kept in its idealized form. This tripartite dissociation of the internalized object corresonds to a similar tripartite dissociation of the ego.

For Nunberg (1950), identification lies essentially in the displacement of an object to the ego where it'is incorporated, consumed and recreated by the ego. It is also the most primitive method of repelling certain intense stimuli that, passing over the protective apparatus, act traumatically. He distinguishes a *partial identification* from a *total identification*. *Through the former all that disappears is a fixed relationship with the object, as observed in hysteria, for example; through total identification all relationships disappear, forming neuroses of the narcissistic type.*

O. Fenichel (1926) stresses instinctive behaviour and oral incorporation in primary identification. He also emphasizes that identifications play an important part in the process of building the ego.

Lacan has given special importance in his writings to the concept of identification. In his description of the 'mirror phase' through which the baby passes during its development towards consciousness of itself as an entity, Lacan brings out 'the drama of the dialectic between alienation and subjectivation'. The recognition of the self takes place through two progressive phases. In the first place, a baby between six and eight months, looking into a mirror with an adult, confuses the reflection with reality and tries to take hold of the image. In a second phase the baby grasps the notion of the image and understands that the reflection is not a real being. Finally, it realizes not only that the reflection is an image, but also that this image is its own, distinct from that of the other person. In the mirror phase, he says, there is also an initial process of identification with an image—that of the child's own body. In this sense the ego is built in the direction of alienation, before symbolism has given back to the child its subjectivity. The whole entity of the body is perceived, enabling the previous phantasies of fragmentation or mutilation to be resisted; but it is the mirror image of a body exterior to oneself, and inverted, an image with which the subject is confused. It is a narcissistic identification with the image of oneself and then with that of others. The mirror phase is a true 'structural crossroads' and determines, as Rifflet-Lemaire (1971) maintains in his book on Lacan, 'the formalism of the ego, which is that of an erotic relationship of the individual with an image which alienates him and that of an identificatory transitivism directed against the other'. Depending on this transitivism, the child who has hit another says he has been hit; there is confusion with the other. 'It is in the other, above all, that the subject lives and is identified with himself.'

W. W. Meissner (1972), who has studied this theme exhaustively, asserts that identification is an active process in the construction of the ego, through which it builds its internal elements of regulation and control on the basis of selective elements derived from an identificatory model. This model is composed of introjects, aspects of real objects, and components of group structures and cultures.

In the 1980s, three works were published, anticipating the main theme of the Thirty-Fourth Psycho-analytical Congress in Hamburg, 'Identification and Its Vicissitudes'. In the first of these, H. Etchegoyen (1985) stresses the structural importance of theories of projective and introjective identification and maintains that envy and libido are the factors of a dialectic from which proceed at the same time both object-relations and the earlier processes of identification, antedating the Oedipus complex. Widlöcher (1983) points out that identification results from a process in which one representation is identified with another and converted into wish-fulfilment; but identification in itself becomes a pulsional objective: the desire for identification. In this respect he stresses the importance of the dualistic impulse: primary identification–object-relations. M. Kanzer (1985) divides the theme of 'identification' into three periods: (1) the *pioneers* (1915–1945), who present the concepts and terminology in an imprecise way; (2) the *synthesizers* (1945–1975), for whom the differentiation of the ego and the importance given to reciprocal ego-object relations contribute towards a better conceptualization of identification; and (3) the *commentators* (1975–1985), who select themes like individual and group identification, the correlation between direct observation and analytical reconstruction, and the personal and professional functioning of the analyst himself.

CHAPTER FOUR

The relationship of identification with the processes of internalization: incorporation, assimilation, imitation, introjection, introjective identification

I n the preceding chapters I developed the concept of identification as it was studied in the various approaches to psychoanalytical theory. [All the modes of identification may without a doubt be observed in analysis. The question is to know to what level of psychological function the mechanisms of identification observable in the course of the analytical process correspond.]

I brought out the fact that we were dealing with a fundamental mechanism in the evolution and organization of the personality, at the root of the formation of the ego, superego, ego-ideal, character, and identity. I also described, using Freud as a basis, how the process of identification was essential in every type of bond or human relationship. In addition, I summed up the different passages in Freud's work in which this concept appears with different meanings, establishing its relationship with, and also its difference from, similar concepts that have, from time to time, been wrongly used as substitutes for the concept of identification. In this chapter I wish to study in detail the distinction between identification and the processes of internalization, introjection, and incorporation.

I shall begin by mentioning the hypothesis that internalization may be considered a comprehensive process, including practically all other processes and mechanisms that constitute the psychological inner world; among these we may mention incorporation, introjection, and identification. For Freud, the concept of identification refers to the process by which 'a portion of the external world which has been abandoned (at least partially) as object and (by identification) remained included in the ego, becoming an integral part of the internal world' (1933a). Some authors, like Schafer (1968), following Hartmann, point out that 'internalization includes those processes by means of which the subject himself transforms the regulating interactions, whether real or imaginary, into internal regulations and characteristics' (Sanford, 1955). Internalization thus conceived refers to the movement of all structural elements coming from outside the purpose of which is to integrate the basic psychical structure for the inner identity of the individual. In order better to understand this definition, we need to make clear that the term 'regulation' is used to refer to those elements that play a part in behaviour patterns and mental images, as well as in the motives underlying these images and this behaviour.

I therefore propose first to attempt a classification of the identificatory mental processes that take part in the transfer of the characteristics and elements of the external world to the internal world, and all those that, conversely, situate in the 'outside' certain aspects of the self or of internal objects. The first belong to the categories of internalizations, the second to externalizations. In accordance with this classification we have the synoptic picture shown in Figure 1.

(A) Internalizations

If we take the first approach mentioned above, which considers internalization as a more general and comprehensive process, we have to include under this term all mental mechanisms, with their corresponding phantasies, the ultimate purpose of which is to

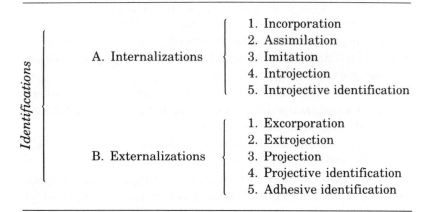

FIGURE 1

transform an *external* experience, either as a whole or taking some of its partial constitutent elements, into an *internal* experience. In more simplified terms, internalization refers to the transfer of an object ('portion of the external world') into the interior of the subject ('integral part of the internal world').

Melanie Klein (1952) studied at length the quality of the internalizations that occur in the first periods of the child's life, especially the internalizations corresponding to the different characteristics contained in the link with the breast, which thus functions as the first internalized object.

It must be explained that when an object is internalized, it does not necessarily mean that it disappears from the external world in the unconscious phantasy of the subject. In any case, it will depend on the quality of the internalized objects and the nature of the respective links with them.

If we consider in general terms the process of internalization of objects, we must take into account the fact that there are two qualities or modes of internalization, as shown by Meltzer (1968). Some are based on love and co-operation, others are sadistic (mainly oral–cannibalistic) and destructive.

When the bond of love predominates, a good object is internalized, which constitutes one of the essential foundations for an integrated and stable ego, which feels rich and capable of project-ing and re-introjecting love into and from the external world. Reciprocally, when hate and sadism predominate, the internalized breast is felt as persecuting and becomes the prototype of all bad internal objects.

The internalization of an object involves giving it space within the mental apparatus. In the unconscious phantasy the object is felt as coming in and going out freely, doing what it likes. It functions, if the simile may be permitted, like a foreign guest who has full liberty to move within the country that shelters him. On the other hand, there are internalizations that by nature respond mainly to phantasies of sadistic aggression and attack, in which the internalized object is then imprisoned and kept shut in and forced to be whatever the subject wishes. This happens, for example, when possessive jealousies prevail and there is absolute and tyrannical domination over the object. But by projection the subject can experience the situation as though he has been invaded and attacked by the object, which then comes to be considered as about to take possession of one part of the mental apparatus and of the personality of the subject. Sometimes this type of internaliza-tion corresponds to a relationship with objects that really are aggressive and harmful.

When the object is internalized with love, in the unconscious phantasy of the individual the internalized object can have direct access to the tissues and organs of the body, giving expression to the life-processes of the individual. But if greed, hate, envy, or possessiveness have predominated in the internalization, then the quality of the object will be mainly persecutory, and the organ that harbours it is felt as a damaged organ, which, in its turn, becomes very persecutory for the subject. This is one of the foundations of the hypochondriacal stage, in which it is felt that the dangerous objects may attack the tissues and organs, causing damage that may on occasion become the starting-point for somatic illnesses. Internalization, on the other hand, might be considered in a more restricted way.

I think that it might contribute to the elucidation of the con-ceptual differences of the terms 'internalization', 'introjection', 'identification', and 'incorporation' if we keep the general and comprehensive character of the first but give the name of 'introjections' to those internalizations that are included in the more peripheral, 'orbital' part of the self and towards which the ego maintains an object-relation, reserving the term 'introjective identifications' for internalizations directed more specifically at the central, 'nuclear' section of the self, with which they fuse and function actively as forming a constituent part of the ego.

I believe that the graphic diagram suggested by Wisdom (1961, 1963), showing a peripheral zone of the self, which he calls 'orbital', and another, more central, which he calls 'nuclear', adequately expresses the pattern of differentiation that I propose. In this case the graphic representation would be as shown in Figure 2.

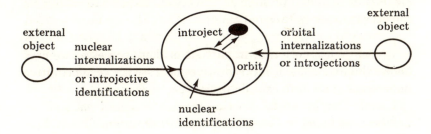

FIGURE 2

Orbital internalizations or *introjections* correspond to the formation of introjects which, though they may modify or influence the dynamics of the internal psychic structure in a significant way, keep a certain autonomy that distinguishes them from the nuclear components of the ego with which they maintain an object-type relationship: they may gratify and be gratified by them or attack and be attacked by them. The majority of internal objects (both persecutory and idealized) are constituted from these products of introjections. They may remain permanently established in the orbit, be projected anew on the external world or, in a second step, be assimilated by the nuclear zone and transformed into introjective identifications. Sometimes they are the result of nuclear internalizations that lose that condition: these would be detached or dissociated aspects of the nuclear ego, which then go on to function as orbital objects with which the nucleus forms an objectal bond.

Nuclear internalizations or *introjective identifications* are those that are directed mainly at the nucleus of the self, coming from outside, or they may be the result of the assimilation of certain characteristics of internal objects that first function as orbital introjections and then go on to form part of the nucleus of the self and the central structure of the ego. The reverse process may also occur, and certain nuclear aspects of the self may pass into the orbital zone in a transitory or permanent form, for example for reasons of defence. In that case we would speak of projective identifications into internal objects.

I repeat once more that in any one of these processes we may detect the existence of incorporative modes with very primitive phantasies of an oral–cannibalistic type.

I shall now go on to describe in greater detail each of the processes included in Category A of internalizations.

(A.1) *Incorporation* is a primal pattern equivalent to a physico-biological act of oral ingestion, including sadistic oral and cannibalistic desires and phantasies. For Hartmann and Loewenstein (1962), incorporation is the genetic precursor of identification. Many authors agree that incorporation is at the root of the later mechanisms of introjection and identification. For some, incorporation is the specific mechanism of the processes of mourning and melancholia that underlie introjection. Abraham described it as the equivalent of the ingestion of food, assimilating to the object within the self in a physical, almost corporeal way.

For Fenichel (1926), incorporation could be the explanation of the problem related to primary identification, expressing the wish to recreate the symbiotic union undifferentiated from the object.

This primary identification is described by Freud as the identification that occurs before every object-cathexis. According to Fenichel, there is a double incorporation, or an incorporation of the object by the self, and another incorporation of the self by the object. Each absorbs the other, and the result is the indifferentiation or fusion of the subject with the object.

This is an early, primal mechanism, specifically based on oral ingestion; it is a psychic act equivalent to a physico-biological act with oral–sadistic and cannibalistic connotations, which is found underlying introjection.

Incorporation is related to a particular content of the conception of the primary process. It corresponds to the phantasy of having put part or all of another person inside the self in a corporeal form. This act is the basis of new sensations, impulses, feelings, and actions, and of changes relating in experience to the environment. Incorporation is represented in general as taking place through the mouth and is therefore cannibalistic in character. The anus and other body orifices may be thought of as a means of entry, as well as the surface of the body. The subject may sometimes think of incorporation as a hostile form of destruction or control of the object; at other times it is thought of as a way of preserving it and loving it—and, typically, as a combination of the two. In certain pathological states, such as those characterizing mourning and melancholia especially, we may find elements of the primary process relating to incorporation. There are also reasons for believing that the primitive identifications of childhood, those in which the representations of the self and the object are directly fused, are experienced as the incorporation of the object by the self or of the self by the object. The same thing does not happen with later identifications—those, for example, that go to form the superego. It has nevertheless been pointed out that the identification with the father that constitutes the superego is based on oral incorporation.

Freud's (1926 [1925]) first ideas with regard to incorporation are linked with a scheme of development in which the sexual objective of the primitive oral phase was the incorporation of the object. This implied both primitive desires for union with the object and primitive oral-sadistic desires to destroy the object in a cannibalistic way. It was then suggested that incorporation was the prototype of later introjections.

There have been other attempts to specify the meaning of incorporation. Meissner (1970) argues against Fenichel's (1926) affirmation that incorporation tends specifically towards primary union with the object, through primary identification. In his view it is more exact to say that the phantasy of incorporation expresses the wish to recreate the union implicit in primary identification, instead of saying that it creates or produces the primary union as such. In this sense, incorporation would mean a regression to primary identification.

In their study on incorporation, Brody and Mahoney (1964) follow Freud's formulations on melancholia and propose that the term 'incorporation' should be used only with reference to the modification of the ego in melancholia, thus distinguishing it from introjection and identification. Incorporation is then seen as a regressive reaction to the loss of an object, by means of which that object is introduced into the ego. It has, therefore, defensive and adaptative functions and is associated with the discharge of inadequate amounts of unneutralized aggressions.

Thus incorporation is the primary and most primitive form of internalization linked with primitive oral phantasies that reflect the action of the primary process. These phantasies are unconscious or, when they are conscious, are repudiated by the non-psychotic subject. They may be associated with more evolved forms of internalization (which does not mean that incorporation is the mechanism for more organized and elaborated forms of internalization) such as introjection and identification. It is the biological prototype of the psychological model of introjection.

(A.2) *Assimilation* is also defined as the product of an instinctive activity of the oral type. At the physical level it is equivalent to digesting a substance from the external world. Psychologically it responds to the phantasy of fusion of the characteristics of the external surface with one's own. It is the biological prototype of the psychological model of introjective identification.

(A.3) *Imitation.* It is obvious that imitation is not synonymous with identification, but it is very closely linked and involved in the processes of identification. Often it is conceptualized as a form of learning.

What is the difference between one process and another? A first answer could be expressed as 'to want to be like the other' or 'to do something to appear to be the other'. The former corresponds to identification, the latter to imitation. To want to be like another person implies that the model has for the subject a transcendent importance and emotional significance. In the view of some authors, we can speak of identification only when a certain level of development of the ego has been reached, and it would derive from the imitative behaviour that is prominent at around six months of age. Language (speech and gesture) is one of the first things that the child acquires through imitation. Piaget (1969) has also pointed out that the child has formed, through his own actions, a sensory-motor scheme into which he can insert the stimulus he wants to copy.

The child increases his possibilities of action and behaviour by imitating the adult and making a pattern of conduct his own. In this way the child becomes more like the adult, and the foundations for the development of identification are laid. The primitive forms of imitative behaviour serve to initiate processes of identification that contribute to the development of the first partial functions of the ego.

To imitate means to acquire a model of behaviour without a deep emotional bond with the object. It may be a precursor of identification or function in a form independent of it. To imitate means to act (think or feel), in one or various aspects, in the same way as another person with whom the subject has been in contact. It takes part as a constant element in every learning process. It does not necessarily produce significant internalizations; they may be superficial and transitory or deeper and more lasting. Though this is often conscious, it can also be pre-conscious or unconscious. It may be impersonal or emotionally detached from the object, or extremely personal, as in the case of the child who copies his father's gestures. Imitative behaviour can be the start of identification processes. Imitation implies the acquisition of a specific form of behaviour of a (social) object without any other link with this object apart from the process of acquisition.

The product of imitation generally arises in the orbital part of the self, while (introjective) identification goes to the nucleus of the self.

Both Gaddini (1969) and Meissner (1974) showed that the development processes of imitation are distinct from the processes of identification, but that they take place simultaneously and gradually become integrated with each other. Imitative activity is placed at the service of the functions of the ego in the course of normal development.

At more primitive levels imitative behaviour may reflect the organization of the child's primary process, or else a psychotic organization expressing a lack of differentiation between the behaviour of the object and the reflective activity of the self.

The child's imitative efforts are gradually directed towards resembling the admired and powerful parents. They are part of the incipient need to control the external environment and also the internal flow of instincts.

Imitation provides the channel through which the child can begin to do actively what he has previously experienced in a passive form (Blos, 1962).

The processes of identification fail in the 'as if' personality—as described by H. Deutsch (1942)—and are replaced by imitative or mimetic behaviour patterns that take place without deep internalization and make those individuals act according to a primary model of reflected activity. They lack originality in their day-to-day activity and in their object-bonds; they lack subjectivity and initiative of their own; there is a void in their emotional life. The same type of failure of the processes of identification and internalization can be found in autistic personalities, in which imitation takes the place of significant internalizations (Mahler, 1952, 1967). Other authors (Meltzer et al., 1975), as we shall see later, suggest that in this type of 'as if' and autistic personalities the mechanisms of adhesive identification play a part.

(A.4) *Introjection.* this term was postulated by Ferenczi (1948/49). Freud took it up initially in his work 'Mourning and melancholia' (1917e [1915]), in which he described the reaction of the ego faced with the loss of the object, through which the latter remains within the ego as an introjected object. That means that Freud first applied the term introjection to the analysis of depressive states and later extended it to the process of formation of the superego. The first introjections have a more rudimentary and disorganized form; they are linked with the most primitive levels of the development of the libido and of aggression. Thus, for example, when the first frustrations are experienced with primitive objects, the latter may be internalized in the orbit of the self, that is to say, be introjected as bad objects; in the same way gratifying objects are introjected as good internal objects. These first introjected objects gradually fuse with introjected objects that are more organized and differentiated, so that the introjections are orbital internalizations that influence the internal psychic constitution in a significant way. The introjected material corresponds to functional aspects of the internal organization of the self, without taking on characteristics similar to those of external objects.

Introjection would correspond to the inclusion of objects or parts of objects in the self; this is a psychological process based on the tendency to incorporate objects with an oral modality, mainly at the service of the instincts. Introjections also differ from identifications in that the latter, well established (in the nucleus), are characterized by their intentional, voluntary, and active nature. All introjection does not necessarily lead to identification, but to the establishment of an intrapsychic relationship.

According to Fuchs (1937) introjection is simply a form of incorporation based on an oral impulse that, at a later stage of development, is transformed into a mode of inclusion of the object-representation in the ego and the superego, respectively.

Knight (1940) remarks that the term 'introjection' seems to be used in general as an equivalent and a synonym for incorporation and may be defined as the unconscious inclusion of an object or part of an object in the subject's ego. It is a psychological process based on the tendency of the id to incorporate objects with an oral modality.

Introjection, like the subsequent identification, serves really to preserve and develop the individual's object-relations.

In regressive states, the most complex and developed introjected objects may be broken down afresh into their most primitive
elements.

Introjection is a specific type of internalization by which transitional object-relations are replaced by an internal modification of
the self in the form of an introjection. Introjections are then results
of a primary process, enjoying quasi-autonomy within the self,
which enables them to replace the transitional object as sources of
activity linked with the instincts and depending on the impulses.

Introjection also leads to the formation of the superego through
the incorporation of certain selected aspects of the parents.

Kleinian theory considers two types of introjection: in the
first the process occurs as described by Freud: that the subject
introjects an object by assimilating it gradually, as happens in
mourning. In the second type of introjection, it is produced simultaneously with a splitting of the ego, where a part of the ego comes
to contain the introjected object, maintaining an intrapsychic relationship with the rest of the ego. Moreover, not every introjection
leads necessarily to identification, but to the establishment of an
intrapsychic object-relation. It is important that this difference
should be taken into account because it implies, in the first place,
that introjection does not lead automatically to identification and,
in the second place, because it enables us to discriminate between
identification and other mental processes that, as a consequence of
introjection, occur within the psyche at the level of internalized
objects. The mechanisms of introjection and projection appear as a
defence against anguish and frustration and protect the child from
being overwhelmed by aggression, anguish, and rage, allowing
him a transient substitute pleasure that will make it easier for
him to accept the real external breast when it re-appears.

(A.5) *Introjective identifications* are the result of internalizations that are directed to the nucleus of the self and assimilated by
it. They are identifications that come to form part of the constitution of the ego and of the personality and are the basis of the
identity of the individual. The experience of identity is built up
through a continuous sequence of introjective identifications,

which lead to the integration of successive states of mind and object-relations.

Introjective identification is a part of normal development. The mother, and, in the first place, the breast, is the first object of introjective processes. The good breast, internalized in the nucleus, and its corresponding introjective identification, act as a focal point in the formation of the ego and in its stabilization. [According to J. Begoin (1984), the giving-up of narcissistic identification in favour of introjective identification constitutes the principal economic problem of analysis. The change from narcissistic identification to introjective identification is conditioned by the working-out of the depressive position, as M. Klein develops it (1955).]

The concept that the development and strengthening of the feeling of identity are based on assimilated introjective identifications is implicit, in one way or another, in almost all definitions of identity. But in order that this may happen, it is necessary that in the course of development introjective identifications should come to predominate over projective identifications. The capacity to continue feeling oneself the same person over a succession of changes forms the basis of the emotional experience of identity. In a book written with Rebeca Grinberg (1971) we maintained that the acquisition of the feeling of identity resulted from a process of continuous interrelation between three links, which we call links of spatial, temporal, and social integration, respectively.

[I have described introjective identifications as resulting from predominantly nuclear internalizations, which contribute to the development and enrichment of the ego. They occur especially in the first periods of life. But I wish now to make clear that introjective identifications are also found in the orbit, as the product of orbital internalizations of objects considered as good, with which the nuclear ego maintains a positive, discriminated, and mature relationship, and which persists for the rest of life. I prefer to reserve the name *introjective identifications* for positive or normal nuclear or orbital internalizations that occur when the depressive position has been reached and sufficient advance made into it. On the other hand, I apply the term *introjections* to predominantly orbital internalizations of objects with which a conflict-relationship is established, whether persecutory or idealized, and which correspond to failures to reach the depressive position, or regressions to the schizoid-paranoid position. A good example of introjection that is at once nuclear ('the shadow of the object falls upon the ego') and orbital is that described by Freud in 'Mourning and melancholia' (1917e [1915]).]

CHAPTER FIVE

The relationship of identification with the processes of externalization: excorporation, adhesive identification, projective identification

I n a form analogical to that which we used in considering internalization, we can also use the concept of externalization in a more comprehensive form, including under this heading different processes such as excorporation, extrojection, projection, adhesive identification, and projective identification. I shall follow the classification described in Group B of the synoptic picture given in chapter four.

(B) Externalization

Externalization is the reverse process to internalization, tending to situate in the outside world one's own impulses, ideas, conflicts, states of mind, or any aspect corresponding to the self or to internal objects, by means of different mechanisms. It consists of the transformation of all internal regulatory interactions to external regulatory interactions.

(B.1) *Excorporation,* ejection, or primary expulsion is a primitive, early process, limited to externalizing different types of elements of the internal world, without situating them in any special place. Unlike projection and projective identification, it

47

establishes itself *between* objects and not *into* objects—that is to say, it does not seek for appropriate receptacles or containers. It would appear that the specific underlying phantasy is to cast out—no matter where—any sensation or stimulus that is particularly unpleasing or painful. This phantasy is supported by a physical substrate, as though the expulsion were to take place through an orifice of the body; it would be the equivalent of spitting, vomiting, or getting rid in urine or faeces of something unpleasant to the ego. It is the biological prototype of psychological projection.

(B.2) *Extrajection* is a term suggested by Weiss (1947/48) to indicate the opposite process to introjection. The latter consists, according to him, of the 'transformation of a part of the self into the representation of an object'; thus the extrajectory is 'the withdrawal of the cathexis of the ego from part of the personality, so that the representation of this aspect remains outside the limits of the ego' (or, I would add, of the self), and he calls it the 'extraject'. Projection, on the other hand, is in his view any hallucination that falsifies the facts of the external world, or an incorrect imputation of the traits corresponding to external objects. He calls this aspect of projection 'true projection'; it implies an incorrect externalization of mental contents. When the subject finds the present traits of an extraject in a real object, the process must be called 'objectivation'.

(B.3) *Projection.* This is one of the most primitive psychical functions, existing in the first phases of the evolution of the ego. It is a defensive activity tending to move the growing internal excitation away from the ego. In order to avert the danger, it is moved a certain distance outside the self. Projection is at the service of the pleasure principle and is used against all those instinctive impulses, painful ideas, and manifestations of anxiety that threaten the stimuli-mitigating system. It is a defence mechanism used by the unconscious part of the ego, by which internal impulses and feelings unacceptable to the ego are attributed to an external object and then enter consciousness disguised as a perception coming from the outside world.

Projection is often preceded by denial. Projection was described by Freud (1911c [1910]) in relation to persecution mania in the paranoid patient who denies his homosexuality, projecting it on to the outside world, through transformation, inversion, and concealment of the homosexual impulse, which is then converted into the delusion that he is hated. The patient denies that he loves X, maintaining, on the contrary, that he is hated by X.

Melanie Klein (1946) considers projection (together with introjection) as basic processes in the development of the child's psyche. Although the projection of what is bad and dangerous was discovered early in psychoanalysis, it could also be proved that the ego projects what is good and useful. The combined action of introjection and projection and their dynamic interplay is what contributes to the building of the mind, strengthening the ego in its first stages. Projection has an equal part to play in the formation of the superego.

Projection, in short, is a primary defence mechanism whose essential characteristic is an expulsive action consisting of the rejection of something internal that is intolerable to the individual. By placing in the external world what has been considered undesirable, a dangerous situation is externalized, bringing into relief the defensive aim that is one of its main functions.

Projection treats impulse, which is internal excitation, as though it were a perception coming from outside.

Although it may seem obvious, perhaps it would be as well to explain that when we speak of the projections of the baby on to the object, we are not referring to conscious intentions on the baby's part. Such projections may be considered as being based on the model of physical actions such as spitting, defaecating, vomiting, coughing, sneezing, and so on. It is natural for the suckling to 'throw' out anything it considers unpleasant, painful or intolerable, as Freud pointed out. The mother can, as a rule, see it as a signal that the baby needs special attention, and she accepts its 'projections'; sometimes they will appear as a 'tantrum' or as a fit of crying, where the tears are part of the contents thrown out.

In a previous or initial period of early infancy, the mother and child co-operate to create the 'illusion of unity' of the baby in its relations with the object-breast. Both Winnicott (1958b) and Marion Milner (1952) emphasize the importance of this 'illusion of unity' and the danger implied in premature separation. Such separation is experienced as a 'break' in continuity, as the actual loss of a part of the body. The change of state from 'nipple-in-the-mouth' to 'nipple-out-of-the-mouth' can cause severe tension, sometimes felt as explosive, which may lead to the feeling of vanishing into a 'black hole', according to the expression used by F. Tustin (1972); this expression can be compared with Bion's 'nameless terror' (1962). Such feelings appear or increase when there is a mother who is insecure or has serious conflicts that make her incapable of acting with *reverie* towards her child's untolerated projections. In seriously disturbed children, with congenital intolerance of frustration and strong destructive and envious tendencies, their psychosis will be reduced but not eliminated even when their mothers are understanding and well-balanced. The psychotic child cannot help but attack his bond with such a mother, through hate and envy of her capacity. This relationship can be observed in clinical practice with psychotic or borderline patients who attack their relations with the analyst and have 'negative reactions to treatment' when he shows greater understanding and power to contain.

Green (1971) maintains that projection, through the displacement of the subject's cathexis to the exterior, leads to a knowledge of the object that, although it may largely depend on what the subject introduces into the object and thus be converted into a distorted perception of the reality of the object, allows real knowledge of the object's unconscious. This knowledge is acquired at the expense of radical ignorance of the subject's unconscious; but deviation through knowledge of the object constitutes, by retroaction, a hidden but implicit knowledge of the subject. That is to say, the projection involves the problem of relations between the subject and the other. The other is simultaneously the object of a certain knowledge and the object of ignorance but appears only in the distorting mirror of the image in the subject's mind; nevertheless, this has a certain reality. Freud asserts that every delusion is built upon a certain nucleus of truth. This linking of knowledge and ignorance is established through construction. It is a construction *in* the space of the other and *of* the space of the other as the externalization of the inner space of the subject.

Projection, then, originates when the object is offered as a surface for projection. Projection is contemporaneous with splitting. External projection onto an object constitutes the division between an inside—the ego—and an outside—the object—separated by the metaphorical frontier of the space between them, on which their distinction is partly based. But this separation is denied at the same time through a fusion taking place by means of the identification of the subject with the parts projected into the object. This is projective identification—which implies an omnipotent narcissistic position—seeking a receptacle (the mother's or the analyst's body) and leading to an objectal and narcissistic fusion, which impoverishes the ego and is expressed in a feeling of fragmentation that reflects the empty spaces left by the projected and ejected parts of the ego.

Freud (1911 [1910) gave two definitions of projection, which appear to contradict each other.

1. 'An internal perception is suppressed, and instead its content, after undergoing a certain kind of distortion, enters consciousness in the form of an external perception.'

We observe that here it is a question of the effect of a 'suppression', followed by a distortion, which enables it to reach consciousness, but after a displacement of such a nature that internal perception is transformed into external perception. It can then be said that projection transforms impulse into perception. This operation is not specific to paranoia, as it may occur in phobias and even in dreams.

2. 'It was incorrect to say that the perception which was suppressed internally is projected outwards; the truth is rather, as we now see, that what was abolished internally returns from without.'

The modification implicit in this last definition centres on the difference between 'suppression' and 'abolition' on the one hand, and on the other on the distinction between projection from inside to outside and the return of eliminated material from outside to inside. It is an inversion of the sense—centrifugal in the first case and centripetal in the second. Freud notes here the specificity of psychotic projection; according to Rifflet-Lemaire (1971), it is a question of the repudiation, which Lacan has called 'forclusion', which leads to the radical concealment of the time of centrifugal projection in order to consider that projection as the return of something projected in which there are no traits to suggest that this return was preceded by an exit. A synthetic definition would make it possible to conceive projection as a permanent to-and-fro movement the first occasion of which is excluded in the paranoiac.

(B.4) *Adhesive identification.* This concept was suggested by E. Bick (1968) to describe the type of identification used by certain regressive patients who have no well-constituted inner space, nor objects with adequate space for a stable projection. They appear to move in a two-dimensional world. Their identificatory projections, therefore, do not penetrate within the object (as happens in projective identification), but remain on its surface, with the phantasy of being stuck to this surface like a 'stamp' or a 'bit of skin', becoming in this way a part of the object. They imitate its external appearance and behaviour and have an 'as if' relationship with its personality; they have nothing of their own and are very fragile. Meltzer et al. (1975) studied these adhesive identifications in autistic children.

I also observed that there are patients who do not appear to have a real inner space and whose constructions and phantasies are situated externally or in a more superficial place in their personality. I have noticed, similarly, that these patients, who live exclusively in the external world, with little inner life, base their conduct on external values, not having their own ethical nucleus; they are very fragile and can tear themselves to pieces at any moment and, in an attention-seeking way, can as easily recover.

Years ago, working with colleagues who were treating autistic children and exchanging information with E. Bick who was observing sucklings, Meltzer came to the conclusion that there was a series of identification phenomena with different qualities from those that characterized what up to then had been called projective identification. That which Bick observed in certain children had to do with the child's and the mother's skin, but as containing not only the body but the structure of the personality. Such individuals develop a sort of 'second skin', not in the concrete form of clothes, but in a muscular form, or by developing a talent for wrapping themselves in their own words, talking constantly. That defective skin originates in these patients' identification with a primitive object, which was a defective container. So they do not possess a well-constituted inner space into which objects could be safely introjected, nor do their objects have an adequate space for stable and secure projection. Instead of projective identifications, they use adhesive identifications, which show what might be called object-imitating identifications. They imitate the external appearance and the behaviour of the object, and they do it through the phantasy of being stuck on the outside like a piece of skin, like a poster or a stamp, thus becoming part of the object.

The characteristic of this form of identification is what could be called 'dementalization': they are not identified with the mind of the object but with its appearance and behaviour. This would correspond with 'as if' personalities and throws some light on the character of people who have nothing of their own and let themselves be led by fashions, by what other people do, and so on; they change like chameleons.

At the same time, while treating autistic children, he discovered in them very similar phenomena, but with different motives. He discovered that children who were beginning to emerge from severe autism were also incompetent to form an inner world and use projective and introjective mechanisms; this was expressed in marked difficulties in learning. It was not that they had no phantasy, nor impulse to put themselves into the object; on the contrary, that desire was very intense, but it was as though they were trying to enter a house without doors or windows and with holes; as though it made no difference whether they were inside or outside. Their object is so full of holes that it cannot contain them, and by identification with that object they, too, are so full of holes that they cannot contain introjections. For that reason, this type of identification or adhesive identification leads to learning by imitation or mimicry (Meltzer et al., 1975). [In the opinion of J. Begoin (1984), adhesive identification is the only form of identification that could correspond with Freud's definition of primary identification, previous to all object-cathexis, which introduces the notion of a two-dimensional world.]

(B.5) *Projective identification.* This mechanism, which is studied in detail in chapter six, is characterized by dissociation and later projection of parts of the self and of internal objects within external objects. It differs from projection, as we shall see later, in that the contents of the latter are mainly ideas, affects or abstract qualities, while the contents of projective identification refer to more concrete aspects, dissociated parts of the self, and so forth. Projective identification, on the other hand, tends to free the mind from those evacuated aspects that are felt as existing within the external object.

The diagram in Figure 3 illustrates the relationship of these different mechanisms with external objects.

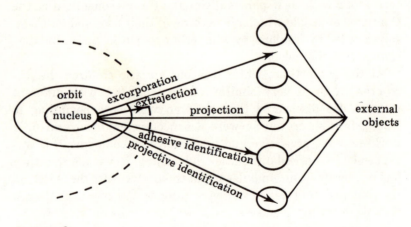

FIGURE 3

CHAPTER SIX

Projective identification according to M. Klein, Bion, Rosenfeld, and Meltzer

Melanie Klein's contribution

The mechanism of projective identification, described by Melanie Klein in 'Notes on some schizoid mechanisms' (1946), is included in her hypotheses regarding emotional development in the first months of the life of the child. It consists of the phantasy of omnipotence by which unwanted parts of the personality and of internal objects can be dissociated, projected, and controlled in the object into which they have been projected.

This identification mechanism is very primitive and functions with its maximum expression at the beginning of life, when the differentiation of ego and objects is not yet completely defined; that is to say, it is used at the most regressive moments.

M. Klein describes attacks directed against the mother's breast and body, based on anal and urethral impulses. The underlying unconscious phantasy is that the excreta and the bad parts of the self are projected into the mother, not only to hurt her, but also to control her and take possession of her contents. As a consequence, the mother is not felt as a separate individual but as a bad part of the self, or the bad self, against whom all hate is directed. It is the prototype of an aggressive object-relation.

The result of the extreme action of projective identification leads on the other hand to a weakening or impoverishment of the ego, through the aspects that are felt to be lost or trapped in the object. One of the consequences may be a state of mental confusion with the incapacity to discriminate between the subject and the object. The phantasy of being imprisoned inside the mother's body may be transformed into an important factor in some clinical pictures such as claustrophobia, impotence, and so forth.

Paranoid anxieties resulting from projective identification may disturb the mechanisms of introjection, and these may then be felt as violent reintrojections forced in from outside as reprisals for previous violent projections. M. Klein gives the name 'projective identification' both to processes of the splitting of the ego and to 'narcissistic' object-relations created by the projection of bad parts into the object.

If projective identification functions particularly intensely, it may cause serious disturbances of the sense of identity, giving rise to psychotic symptoms and states of depersonalization, confusion, and so on. Despite the fact that this mechanism is generally used as one of the essential defences of the ego against anxiety, it is converted—paradoxically—into an attack on its integrity, thus weakening it. In this way, when splitting and projective identification operate with particular violence, the subject is afraid that the fragmented and detached parts of his self, once they are projected into the object, will never come back; they will be lost forever. In addition to the persecution anxiety thus caused, feelings appear which take the form of a depressive reaction, with the consequent sorrow for the state in which the self remains.

In the 1946 article already mentioned, M. Klein especially emphasizes the child's earliest anxieties and the defences against them as mechanisms of dissociation, denial, and omnipotence. She adds that these mechanisms play, in the early phase of development, a role similar to that played by repression during a more advanced period in the development of the ego. She describes the child's early instinctive impulses and maintains that while oral libido predominates, impulses and phantasies from other sources may come together with oral, anal, and urethral desires, both aggressive and libidinal. She also brings out the fact that the forced intrusion of projective processes into the object may arouse paranoid anxieties and disturb the function of the processes of introjection. These may be felt in phantasy as an intrusive penetration from the exterior to the interior, as revenge for the previous violent projection.

It is clear that M. Klein is giving the name of 'projective identification' both to the processes of dissociation of the ego and projection and to 'narcissistic' object-relations created by the projection of parts of the self into the object. But she also describes the projection of good parts of the ego into external objects that are identified with the parts projected. She considers this identification to be essential for the ability of the child to develop good object-relations (1955).

In her work 'On identification' (1955), M. Klein returned to the subject of projective identification, but now not only with the pathological connotations with which she had endowed it in previous articles, but as a normal process of psychological life involved in the bond of empathy with the object. In this work, M. Klein interprets psychoanalytically Julian Green's novel, *If I Were You*. The essence of the story is the magic power to transform oneself into other people, which is conferred upon the protagonist Fabian through a pact with the devil. These transformations are clear examples of projective identifications determined, as M. Klein shows, by the intense greed and bitterness of the protagonist, indicating the privation and frustration of his early infancy. The impulse, among others, to compensate for the early death of his father, contributes to the overwhelming wish to put himself in the place of others and take over their lives. In the course of his transformations he takes on different identities. But when he wants to be the same again and is reconciled with the original Fabian, he longs for love and feels happy a moment before his death. He had also projected good parts on to the objects with whom he had identified himself. Describing the projection of these good parts of the self, M. Klein considered that projective identification was also essential for the development of good object-relations. This is the basis of empathy and normal communication.

To sum up, the Kleinian concept of projective identification, as explained by Hanna Segal (1964), is that from the original projection of the death instinct there develops another defence mechanism of fundamental importance (in the paranoid–schizoid position)—projective identification. In this mechanism, parts of the self and of internal objects are split off and projected into the external object, which is then possessed and controlled by the projected parts and identified with them. Projective identification has many aims: it may be directed towards the ideal object in order to avoid separation, or it may be directed towards the bad object in order to take control of the source of danger. Different parts of the self may be projected for different purposes: one's own bad parts may be projected so as to get free of them, or to attack and destroy the object; similarly, good parts may be projected to avoid separation or to safeguard them from the internal bad parts, or to perfect the external object thanks to a kind of primitive projective reparation. Projective identification begins when the paranoid–schizoid position is consolidated for the first time in relation to the breast, but it persists and is very often intensified when the mother appears as a total object and the whole of her body is penetrated by projective identification.

Bion's contribution

Bion attached particular importance to the concept of projective identification as postulated by M. Klein. He was one of the first to consider not only its pathological but its normal function, which is increased in the change from the paranoid–schizoid to the depressive position. It is the type of realistic projective identification that takes into account the real existence of the external object and constitutes one of the main factors in symbol-formation and in human communication.

Bion formed a concept that he called 'the container–contained relationship' (1962) starting from an aspect of the function of projective identification, which enabled an advance to be made in the knowledge of this mechanism. According to this concept, the suckling projects a part of its psyche, especially its uncontrollable emotions, which act as 'content', into the 'container', the good breast, so as to receive them back detoxicated and be able to tolerate them. This happens especially with anxiety or the fear of death that the baby sometimes experiences and which must be put into its mother through projective identification, to receive it back in the form of attenuated fear. In this case the mother has been able to 'detoxicate' this fear thanks to her capacity for 'reverie'. If the mother reacts with anxiety and incomprehension, she returns the fear to the child without modifying it. If the mother is very disturbed, instead of detoxifying the child's fear of death, she acts as a bad object, robbing the baby's projection of its specific meaning and turning it into 'a nameless terror' (Bion 1963).

Bion particularly stressed the role of projective identification in primitive pre-verbal communication (1967). He pointed out that this mechanism was the precursor of the act of thinking when the 'apparatus for thinking thoughts' was not yet formed. This activity consisted originally of a procedure intended to free the psyche from the excesses of stimuli that overwhelm it; this procedure takes place through projective identification. He postulated, similarly, a theory of the 'alpha function', which acts on sensory impressions and emotional experiences, transforming them into 'alpha elements', which can be stored as visual images, dream-thoughts, and waking thoughts. Untransformed sensory impressions and primitive emotions are called 'beta elements'; they are not suitable for thinking, dreaming, remembering, or carrying out intellectual functions generally attributed to the psychological apparatus. They are considered as 'things-in-themselves' and can be evacuated by means of projective identification.

Projective identification later takes part in the formation of the 'apparatus for thinking thoughts' through the interaction of two mechanisms: the first is that of the dynamic 'container–contained relationship' ($\female \Leftrightarrow \male$); the second is represented by the dynamic relationship between the paranoid–schizoid and depressive positions (P-s $\Leftrightarrow$ D). These mechanisms, together with the mother's capacity for 'reverie', bring about the formation of the first outlines of thinking and symbol-formation. This process is favoured if the baby has sufficient inborn capacity for tolerating frustration. If, on the other hand, it is very intolerant of frustration, the equipment for thinking thoughts will not form in its personality. In its place it will use continuous discharge evacuation through a hypertrophic projective identification characterized by omnipotence and omniscience.

This type of pathological projective identification may appear among the symptoms of psychosis, or in cases in which the psychotic personality predominates, together with envy and voracity. It is then that we find a pathological split of the parts of the ego, resulting in a multitude of fragments that are violently expelled by pathological projective identification. There is thus created, for the patient, a reality peopled by 'bizarre objects', a reality that becomes increasingly painful and persecutory. The violently evacuated fragments penetrate and encapsulate real objects or are embodied in them. The possessed object, in its turn, attacks the projected part of the personality, robbing it of vitality. The 'bizarre objects' are formed by a part of the personality, beta elements plus remains of the ego, superego, and external objects. The patient's attempt to use these elements for thinking leads him to confuse real objects with primitive thoughts and to treat real objects in accordance with the laws of mental function, becoming confused when they obey the laws of nature. The psychotic personality lacks the essential means for the development of verbal thought. If the patient wishes to recover part of the projected aspects in an attempt to reconstruct his ego, he will try to bring them back by the same route by which they had been expelled. He will then use 'reversed' projective identification. This was expressed by a patient who said that to be able to think he had to use his intestines and not his brain.

According to Bion, the Kleinian formulation of projective identification is based on the common idea of the three-dimensional space of the individual. But his experience with more disturbed patients convinced him of the need for a more rigorous formulation. When the regressive psychotic patient faces an experience against which the neurotic would have recourse to normal projective identification, he will feel prevented from projecting parts of his personality because he has no conception of a container in which the projection can take place. There will then be an 'explosive' projection in a mental space that is felt as so immense that it cannot be represented in any way. This generates intense panic, experienced as a 'psychotic catastrophe'. Bion differentiates projective identification from another set of realizations that acquire a fixed shape, and which he calls 'hyperbole'. This term corresponds with the system of theories of observation and represents a set of statements in which we find projection, rivalry, ambition, violence, and the distance to which an object, or aspects of it, is projected.

Rosenfeld's contribution

In Rosenfeld's view, the concept of projective identification is especially fertile for the understanding of the transference relationship in the treatment of patients with severe psychological disturbances.

He considers that projective identification is essentially a defence mechanism of the primitive self. It implies, nevertheless, that some separation between the self and the object must exist. But it is obvious that certain patients live in a permanent state of projective identification, and for that reason he thinks that they should be treated by a more primitive process. The primal forms of projective identification could be considered as precursors of the primitive states of fusion between mother and baby. In addition, he thinks that some processes of projective identification begin in the womb. The foetus might be sensitive to certain disturbances in the mother's mental processes or to very primitive forms of communication. He quotes certain authors, such as Bion, Steiner, and Felton, who maintain a similar hypothesis. The two last are convinced that the most primitive forms of projective identification are the residues of an 'osmotic system' of communication in the womb.

Rosenfeld affirms that psychotic patients have a very special relationship with objects, narcissistic in purpose and completely omnipotent. For this type of relationship he suggests the name 'narcissistic–omnipotent object-relations'. Projective identification is an integral part of such relations, giving rise to phantasies of 'uniqueness' in order to deny separation, love, aggression, envy, and dependence. On the other hand, he brings out the need to differentiate the libidinal from the destructive aspects of narcissism.

He distinguishes two qualities of projective identification: (1) projective identification used for communication; and (2) projective identification used to free the self from untolerated parts. If the analyst is capable of containing these aspects projected into him and analysing them, he can then give them back in his interpretation, but with a more easily tolerated quality, in the sense described by Bion. We can extract from his work the following classification (Rosenfeld, 1969).

(1)   Use of projective identification as a method of communication

This may be found not only in neurotic patients but also in psychotics, who may use this process in transference, either consciously or unconsciously. The psychotic patient hopes that the analyst will understand his experiences and contain them until they lose their threatening element and will then be able to turn them into words through his interpretations. This situation is of essential importance for the development of introjective processes and for the development of the ego and helps the patient to tolerate his own impulses. The interpretations make the most regressive responses and feelings accessible to the healthiest part of the self, which can then begin to think through the experiences that it had previously considered dangerous and meaningless. As this type of communication reflects a receptive aspect of the patient, it must be recognized and interpreted by the analyst each time it appears.

(2)   Use of projective identification for the denial of psychical reality

The patient dissociates parts of his self together with the corresponding impulses and anxieties and projects them into the analyst, with the aim of throwing out his disturbing mental contents; this leads him to a denial of psychical reality. But as he wants to hide at the same time the evacuation and denial of his problems, he will react to interpretations with violent recriminations; in his phantasy, these interpretations constitute the analyst's violent return of the untolerated mental contents.

(3) Use of projective identification as an omnipotent control of the analyst's body and mind

This is based on a very early type of object-relations. The psychotic patient believes he has penetrated omnipotently into the analyst, achieving fusion or confusion with him. At other times the analyst is perceived as having 'driven him mad', threatening him with retaliation and 'forcing' madness anew into the patient. This type of projective identification interferes with the capacity for verbal and abstract thought; it leads to concrete thought and to confusion between reality and phantasy.

(4) Use of projective identification to deal with envy

While the patient is experiencing a state of fusion with the analyst (by projective identification), he attributes to himself everything valuable that the analyst possesses; it corresponds to a state of omnipotent narcissism. But when he begins to feel separate from the analyst, there appears an aggressive and violent reaction against any interpretation that shows the analyst's capacity. He feels humiliated and tries to destroy the interpretations by envy. But he may come to feel alarmed by his reaction; then he may begin to use dissociation and projection of envy into an external object as a defence. Another form of defence is to use an omnipotent phantasy of penetrating into the admired and envied object in order to transform himself into it and take on its role. When this happens, envy disappears because it is denied.

(5)   Use of projective identification as a parasitic object-relation

The psychotic patient has the phantasy of living entirely within the object—the analyst—and behaves like a parasite depending on the capacities of the analyst. It is a combination of defence and the acting-out of aggression, which gives rise to the parasitic state and creates a particular therapeutic problem. Such patients have an attitude of extreme passivity and inertia, protecting themselves in this way from any painful emotion.

(6)   Use of projective identification as a form of hallucination or delusion

In this case the patients are disconnected, wrapped up in their hallucinations, which they project into the analyst. Living within the object of the delusion, they seek to oppose it to the real external world and to avoid dependence on a real object. This world or object of the delusion appears to be dominated by an omnipotent or omniscient part of the self. They try in addition to exert influence on the healthy parts of the personality to make them retreat from reality and take part in the world of the delusion.

Meltzer's contribution

In Meltzer's view the concept of projective identification is essential to the work of M. Klein and very different from the earlier Freudian concept of a projection referring primordially to ideas, impulses, affects and attitudes. Projective identification also plays a part in verbal communication, when it transcends the syntactic mechanisms for transmitting information.

Massive projective identification is the sovereign defence against separation anxiety.

In his article, 'The relation of anal masturbation to projective identification' (1966), Meltzer examines a specific characterological constellation, 'pseudomaturity', in intelligent persons in whose clinical material a close relationship between erotism, anal masturbation, and projective identification emerges. Such patients have a tendency to idealize the rectum and its anal contents. Such idealization appears to be the consequence of an identity confusion due to the particular use of projective identification: at the critical moment of separation from the mother, the child who sees his mother going away with her back to him identifies the breast with his mother's buttocks, and the latter with his own buttocks. He then feels compelled to anal masturbation, the essential object of which is the 'delusive' projective identification with the internal mother, so as to wipe out the difference between the child and the adult in the matter of capacities and prerogatives. Anal masturbation is usually accompanied by simultaneous genital masturbation, with perverse sado-masochistic phantasies. This type of delusive projective identification with the mother, with confusion between the anus and the vagina, would cause frigidity in women and the feeling that their femininity is false; in men it leads to homosexual phantasies and activities.

Meltzer attaches particular importance to the function of projective identification in the link between patient and analyst during the analytical process. To carry out his function successfully, the analyst must receive projective identification and its pain, without letting himself be dominated or led to action by it.

The various motives underlying the tendency to use massive projective identification are as follows: intolerance of separation, omnipotent control, envy, jealousy, mistrust, and excessive persecution anxiety.

1. Intolerance of separation appears when there is absolute dependence on an external object in order to maintain integration. It is observed in autistic children and in psychotics. They need an external object to keep together the parts of the self and to fix the bounds for an area of vital space within the self that might contain the objects of psychic reality.

2. When the difference between good and evil is poorly defined, the use of projective identification serves to promote omnipotent control and works as a precondition for object-relations, preferably with a narcissistic organization.

3. The use of projective identification as a defence against envy is very well known.

4. Jealous delusions are based on an omnipotent relationship with the mother's body, and possessive jealousy appears as a form of primitive love, oral and applied to a partial object; it plays an important part in perpetuating massive projective identification.

5. When projective identification is consumed in phantasy through deception or cunning rather than by violence, mistrust of the object and the consequent claustrophobia are intense, since it is suspected that the object may deceive with its apparent vulnerability.

6. With regard to excessive persecution anxiety, we must distinguish between various types of paranoid anxieties that need the use of massive projective identification.

It is a premise of the psychoanalytical theory of the personality that sexual behaviour does not need to be taught because it derives from instinctive impulses modified by identification processes. The terms 'male' and 'female' for the parts of the child's self can be understood instinctively; they take shape together with the processes of introjective and projective identification that go with them. The concept of projective identification and its relationship with the destructive forces of the personality, and particularly envy, with the consequent production of confusional states, enables us to make a clear distinction between polymorphism and perversion, linking them unmistakeably with the concepts of good and bad sexuality.

The foundations of sexual life in a mature person must be sought in the sexual relations of the internal parents in all their complexity; the individual identifies projectively with them in both roles, male and female. Well-integrated bisexuality makes possible an intense intimacy with the sexual partner through projective identification and through a modulated projective identification, which takes its place in the other's mind without controlling or dominating him. This is similar to the use of projective identification as a primary mode of identification, as Bion tells us.

CHAPTER SEVEN

Contributions
to the concept
of projective identification
and its classification

I propose to study the possibility of considering the evolution of the mechanism of projective identification with a dynamic approach, starting with the most primitive levels and working up to the most organized. I shall, moreover, bring out its qualitative aspect and make an attempt to classify its functional modalities. Finally, as illustration, I shall study the functioning of projective identification in psychopathy and in manic states (Grinberg, 1956, 1957a, 1958, 1962, 1963a, 1965).

In normal conditions projective identification determines the empathic relationship with the object, not only because it makes it possible to put oneself in the place of the other and understand his feelings better, but by what it evokes in him. The subject always produces some emotional echo in the object, by the attitude with which he presents himself to him, the way he looks at him or speaks to him, the content of what he says, his gestures, and so forth. I mean that projective identifications are always in action; they come from the different sources that originate them and arouse the corresponding emotional responses: sympathy, anger, pain, hostility, boredom, and so on. This happens, within certain limits, in all human relationships and forms the basis of communication. The object, in his turn, also functions with his respective identifications, thus producing an interchange in both directions.

The concepts of the normal and the pathological are closely bound up with the greater or lesser predominance of the aggressive impulses, the degree of tolerance or intolerance of frustration, the type of contact with external and psychical realities, the state of the functions of the ego, the quality of defensive mechanisms, and the deep-rooted dynamics of object-relations. According to the predominance of one psychological state or the other, normal or pathological, different modes of projective identification come into play. Another factor that must be taken into account is the use (at a more organized level) of 'realistic' obsessional mechanisms that allow control of the parts that are dissociated or projected outwards, as the failure of these mechanisms could cause disturbances, to varying degrees, in the functioning of the ego with respect to the object. [I have given the name, 'realistic control' to the obsessive control that functions at a more mature and developed level, in contrast to the 'omnipotent control' that functions at more regressive levels (Grinberg, 1966).]

Without a doubt the quality of the relationship with the primary objects, mainly the mother, will determine the quality of the functioning of projective identification in later object-relations. If the first objects show serious disturbances in the personality, they will inhibit the normal functioning of projective identification and promote the tendency to use pathological projective identification. This happens when the objects refuse, or are not able, to receive the parts of the self with anxiogenic contents that the child is trying to project into them. The situation becomes even worse when these objects fling back at the child his own projective identifications charged with sadism.

When M. Klein (1946) refers to 'massiveness' or to 'excessive' projective identification, these terms should not be considered from the quantitative, but from the qualitative point of view. It is not a question of the frequency or intensity with which this mechanism is used, but of its omnipotent nature and its mainly sadistic and destructive ends.

The relationship between projection and projective identification has been stated on various occasions. For some authors they are the same thing; others have brought out the difference between the two concepts. For Wollheim (1969), projective identification is different from the Freudian concept of projection in that the latter refers to the projection of ideas, impulses, emotions, and attitudes, whereas projective identification concerns, more specifically, concrete parts of the ego and of the internal objects containing emotions and anxieties.

The contents of projection are usually properties or qualities, as for instance rage or curiosity. The contents of projective identification, on the contrary, are substances, things or fragments of things, split-off parts of the self or of internal objects, and so forth. Another difference lies in the objective: in projection we transport a property from ourselves to others: we are not ridding ourselves of anything, not even of the projected property that remains in our minds. In projective identification we are freeing our minds; thought or substance has been evacuated, and 'it is now within an external object'. This is a phantasy that is followed by another phantasy of introjection: the person attacked or controlled may be incorporated together with what has been projected.

In Kernberg's opinion (1934), projective identification is an early form of defence, with an ego structure centred on a primitive dissociation, while projection is more mature. He then defines projective identification as a primitive mechanism that consists of projecting intolerable aspects of intrapsychic experience on to an object, maintaining empathy with what is projected, and controlling its contents so as to continue the defensive effort. Projection, on the other hand, consists of the repression of an unacceptable intrapsychic experience, a lack of empathy with what is projected, and a distancing of the object in order to complement the defensive effort. He adds that projective identification has the capacity to discriminate between the self and the non-self, between psychic reality and external reality, thus giving it a certain function in evolutionary development.

Betty Joseph (1984) sees projective identification as a phantasy that, in one way or another, has a powerful effect on the object. She brings out the considerable clinial value of projective identification with its "concrete" character and its different types, from the primitive and massive to the mature and empathetic. There is always an object relationship in the use of projective identification. It can be used either as a *method of communication, when there are difficulties in verbalization,* or as an attack on the object. Projective identification of envious parts may be an attempt to maintain a complex equilibrium of narcissistic omnipotence. It may also be used as an attempt to enter again into the object so as not to be differentiated from it and thus to avoid all pain. She sees the idea of projective identification in terms of what the patient makes the analyst feel.

Sandler (1988) distinguishes three stages in the development of the concept of projective identification. In the first stage, starting from Melanie Klein's description, projective identification occurs only in phantasy and does not affect the real object. In the second, the analyst is identified with the object representation existing in the patient's transference phantasy. In the third stage, projective identification is described as the externalization of parts of the self and of internal objects occurring *directly* in the external object. Bion's conception of the "container" clearly illustrates this last assertion.

Though Freud did not refer explicitly to projective identification, he nevertheless described, in various passages of his work, certain processes that correspond—without doubt—with the main characteristics contained in that mechanism. And in 'Project . . .' (1950a [1887–1902]) he shows one of the critical situations the small child must face, which leads him to demand urgently outside help to stop the painful stimulus that is making him suffer. He adds that this way of relief used by the child (for example by crying) acquires 'the most important secondary function of communication'.

The passage to which I refer is to be found in Part II of 'Project . . .', under the heading, 'The experience of satisfaction'. It says: 'At first the human organism is incapable of bringing about the specific action. It takes place by *extraneous help, when the attention of an experienced person is drawn to the child's state by discharge along the path of internal change* [for example by the child crying].

In this way this path of discharge acquires a secondary function of the highest importance, that of *communication,* and the initial helplessness of human beings is the primal source of all moral motives. The total event then constitutes an experience of satisfaction which has the most radical results on the development of the individual's functions' [italics are mine].

It is perhaps in *Group Psychology and the Analysis of the Ego* (1921c) that Freud comes closest to the description of the process of projective identification, although he does not call it that. In developing the dynamics of two important groups, the Church and the Army, Freud shows that both groups have a leader (Christ and the Commandant, respectively) who loves all members of the group equally. In the first example, that of the Church, there is identification of the members with each other, due to the introjection of a common object: Christ. In the second case, that of the Army, identification is generated by projection, as each soldier projects his ego-ideal on to the Commandant, and the group is built around this common object. Freud quotes the example of what happened in the Assyrian army when its leader, Holofernes, was beheaded. The soldiers fled in terror because each one of them, in his phantasy, felt that he had lost his own head, by projection. Freud amplifies his remarks on this type of projection, calling it 'sympathetic projection'.

Other authors have referred to the mechanism of projective identification, without naming it specifically. For example, E. Jacobson, in his book *Psychotic Conflict and Reality* (1967), speaks of a 'psychotic regression to a narcissistic level in which the weakness of the frontiers between the images of the self and the object gives rise to phantasies and experiences of fusion between the two images. These projective and introjective identifications are based on infantile phantasies of incorporation, of invading, devouring, or being devoured by the object.' She adds that such phantasies are characteristic of the early narcissistic stages of development, and that in the adult patient there may be a narcissistic regression to these early stages.

M. Mahler (1952) described 'infantile psychotic symbiosis', suggesting that the mechanisms used were introjection and projection with a psychotic elaboration. The child phantasizes that he and his mother form an omnipotent system (a dual unity with a common limit or frontier, like a symbiotic membrane). 'Symbiosis' is used by Mahler to denote a state of indifferentiation or fusion with the mother, in which, however, the 'ego' is not differentiated from the 'non-ego'. This could only be explained by the functioning of the omnipotent modality of projective identification.

Etchegoyen (1985) observes that the decisive element of projective identification is that the subject maintains a bond of identity with the projected parts. This means that there is an object-relation and an identification at the same time; the ego fulfils the two ambitions indicated by Freud: to be the object and to hold it. Later (1986), he maintains that the idea of projective identification also introduces a revolutionary concept of narcissism, considering that these are parts of the self that enter into the object. The self maintains a relationship with this object, in that in some obscure way it recognizes these parts as its own. This defines an object-relation in which there is a strong narcissistic component.

We should also consider intrapsychic projective identification, directed towards internal objects, as can be seen in manic defences, melancholic states, introjections that occur in schizoid states in which dissociation predominates, paranoid reactions, dreams, and many other phenomena, both normal and psychopathological. The fundamental basis of the process consists of the bond established between the ego-nucleus of the self and an orbital internalization situated in the peripheral zone of the self. Sometimes this bond is formed between the nucleus and a detached or dissociated aspect of it, which then begins to function with orbital characteristics, thus losing its attachment to the ego and its state of introjective identification. Projective identification then occurs, through which certain dissociated aspects of the nucleus of the ego are projected into the internal object, giving it some of their characteristics or taking those of the object. Thus, for example, certain manic states come into being mainly through the projective identification of the nucleus of the individual's ego with an internal (orbital) object, idealized and omnipotent. The subject's 'ego' is 'introduced', through projective identification, 'into' the internal object, which is phantasized as omnipotent; it takes on its qualities, and from the 'interior' of the object it treats external objects in a denigrating way (Grinberg, 1966).

The tendencies and phantasies corresponding to each of the phases of the libido will condition the emergence of projective identifications with oral, anal, urethral, and genital contents, which will also give rise to modalities specific to the respective object-relations. The predominance of any of these phases (by either fixation or regression) will naturally affect the content of the phantasies included in the projective identifications. We can mention as an example those phantasies that are projected into the object to devour, suck, or bite it at an oral level, poison it or destroy it with excrement or flatus at an anal level, or burn or destroy it with urine or its equivalents at a urethral level, and so forth. We can also consider regression from the depressive position to the paranoid–schizoid position, which will bring into play primitive projective identification, with its phantasies of omnipotence, and so on. It may happen that on certain occasions projective identification acts with particular violence; this occurs especially in psychotic states, some forms of psychopathy, and so forth.

At the polymorphic–perverse stage of the development of the impulses, in which the child tries out, in an uncoordinated way, excitation of all parts of the body and vehemently desires immediate gratification, as Freud (1905) and P. Heimann (1952) have pointed out, projective identifications are also violent. On the one hand, there is potentiation of the sadistic aspects of all zones as they function simultaneously; and, on the other hand, there is confusion caused by different phantasies coming into play, also simultaneously. As P. Heimann places this stage between the oral and the anal-expulsive stages, she adds that the following process of development, or the anal-expulsive tendency, is a defensive reaction, which relieves the ego of confusion and allows it to evacuate internalized persecutory objects, together with its conflicts and its overwhelming tensions, which are likened to its own excrements. This means that the anal organization is the one the most used by the mechanism of projective identification, bearing contents corresponding to the other organizations. Projective identification determined by the anal tendency may express an oral content, since it may consist of the evacuation into the object of a breast destroyed by biting, or of biting what is good within the object.

The most regressive projective identification would very probably be that which takes place through the eyes.

M. Klein (1955) has maintained that one of the most important motive forces for the functioning of projective identification from the earliest periods of life is envy; it had already been pointed out that the etymology of this term of Latin origin contains the idea of the 'evil eye'. The eyes act not only in a receptive, introjective way, but also projectively. [Rebeca Grinberg (1960, 1961) has developed the various aspects related to vision, in both its introjective and projective connotations; the latter is considered as a vehicle of the particular function of projective identification.]

A classification of types of projective identification, intended only to explain the different characteristics of their function, taking different approaches into account (Grinberg, 1965), is shown in Figure 4.

As illustration I should like to use the concepts I have listed as a help to understanding the mode of action of projective identification in psychopathy and in mania.

(1)   Projective identification and psychopathy

Psychopathy is characterized essentially by disturbance of thought, intolerance of frustration, and tendency to action.

We can make the hypothesis that the psychopath is an individual who has not been able sufficiently to metabolize the different narcissistic bonds with sadistic contents—his own, and those received by projection from his first relationship with the breast.

It is of interest to know not only how the subject's projective identifications work in his first object-relations, but also the working of the projective identifications of his primitive objects and the type of repercussion they cause in the subject (Grinberg, 1965).

We should consider the following aspects of every psychopath:

(1)   The existence of a narcissistic link formed by a part of the self and another part, which contains an object-breast mutilated by greed and envy.

This link could not be metabolized by the ego and remains isolated like an encapsulated body which keeps hidden its violence, danger, and persecution.

(2) To this situation has to be added the reaction caused by violent projective identifications received from parents, containing in their turn links with damaged objects. It seems probable that the mother of the psychopath has not been able to take upon herself her infantile projective identifications (she had no capacity for *reverie*), making him the victim of the projection of her own conflicting relationships.

The massive irruption of these projective identifications potentiates the danger of the encapsulated primitive narcissistic link, forcing the ego to carry its defensive recourses to extremes, with the use of regressive mechanisms to change and encapsulate them.

(3) Among the mechanisms used we find a combination of manic mechanisms and a particular type of dissociation to keep the 'encapsulated bodies' separated from the rest of the self. Manic defence is organized mainly through projective identification within another internal object, which represents the image of an idealized, omnipotent and inexhaustible breast, from within which omnipotent and devaluating projective identifications are directed against external objects. These manic defences often co-exist with the psychopathic symptoms or even precede them, since their failure implies the appearance or the intensification of the psychopathic symptoms.

The particular form of dissociation to which I have referred recalls that described by Bion (1967) in those patients with strong feelings of envy of the breast, who have recourse to a type of splitting that separates material from psychical satisfaction. This means that these patients, throughout their lives, are avidly seeking material well-being without admitting the existence of a living object upon which they depend. They are incapable of showing gratitude or interest towards others or towards themselves. They can maintain relationships with others only by treating them like inanimate objects or things; they cannot form a bond with them as human beings.

(4) The 'encapsulated bodies' (which contain the narcissistic links and the invading projective identifications) do not always

By quality	normal or realistic P.I. (projected parts unchanged—normal dissociation).
	pathological P.I. (omnipotent, hypertrophic, with multiple fragmentation, with 'bizarre' objects, explosive, hyperbolic type).
By orientation	directed into the interior of an external object.
	directed to the surface of the external object*.
	directed to an internal object.
	directed to the body.
By aim or objective	communicative
	preservative
	reparative
	evacuating
	controlling
	destructive

*At the present time I would consider this type as equivalent to adhesive identification.

retain their passivity and innocuousness. On the contrary, they react to any circumstance and then appear as a sadistic nucleus of the superego which ill-treats the rest of the ego, even when hidden by the manic façade of the internal object. Then the tyrannical intrapsychic relationship between a dominating and a dominated part comes to the fore and brings to pass many of the masochistic acts that occur during this manic period of the psychopath.

(5)   When the frustration is already intolerable for the psychopath's ego, because it is weakened by the working of regressive

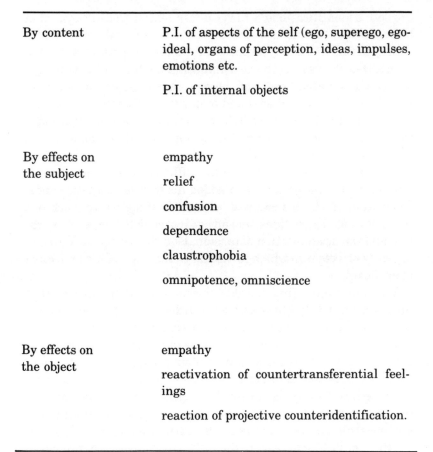

By content	P.I. of aspects of the self (ego, superego, ego-ideal, organs of perception, ideas, impulses, emotions etc.
	P.I. of internal objects
By effects on the subject	empathy
	relief
	confusion
	dependence
	claustrophobia
	omnipotence, omniscience
By effects on the object	empathy
	reactivation of countertransferential feelings
	reaction of projective counteridentification.

FIGURE 4.   *Classification of types of projective identification*

defences, there is a sudden break in the precarious balance that has been maintained up to this point. The immediate consequence is the building-up of tension within the psychic apparatus and an increase in the danger and violence of the encapsulated bodies. Another source of tension is the failure to maintain the dissociation described earlier, and this causes confusion, which recharges the already increased tension.

It is then that the psychopath's ego, to free itself from this unbearable tension, resorts in desperation to the use of violent projective identifications (which contain reactivated encapsulated bodies) which break into the external object and force it into action. In this way the tyrannical relationship is projected into the object, that is to say both the dominating nucleus of the superego and the dominated aspect of the ego. Or the identification may remain with the dictatorial and omnipotent superego, projecting only the dominated part, with the result that the action takes place this time in a new scenario: the interior of the dominated object.

The quality and the particular violence of projective identifications received in childhood, with the difficulty of their metabolization, to which there have been added his own narcissistic bonds, which remained encapsulated with their inability to work out thoughts and abstractions, and an ego too weak to tolerate frustration and the accumulation of tension, lead the psychopath to seek urgently objects into which to discharge the mass of his projective identifications.

When he cannot find suitable objects, it is often observed that the psychopath takes his own body as a depository for those identifications, causing hypochondriacal or somatic reactions.

If we can understand what happens in the object that becomes the depository of the psychopath's violent projective identification, we shall understand what happens in the psychopath himself when he has the impulse to act. This leads us to the question why the object, which is empty of the projective identifications of the psychopathic subject, is obliged in his turn to act instead of absorbing them or failing to react to them. The first answer that comes to mind is that these may be people who in their turn have latent psychopathies, which may be reactivated by the influence of the projective identification they receive.

But this cannot be the only explanation. We can understand better what happens if we concentrate on the inductive aspect of projective identifications, which, in such cases, have specific psychopathogenic properties. For the present, as we have seen, they are the result of an increased charge of tension, which produces a violent intrusion of projective identification into the object. This appears to paralyse the normal ego-functions in the object, preventing the cushioning and synthesizing functions of the ego from adopting adequate measures against falling under its influence. In Bion's terms, we could say that the 'alpha function' of the object is temporarily inhibited by the intensity of the impact, and the experience is then converted into 'beta elements' with a similar quality to 'beta invaders', and with the same pressing need to discharge themselves through action.

From the point of view of the dynamics of the process, and to express it in terms of instances, it could be said that material projected through the psychopathic modality of projective identification, once within the object, acts as a parasitic psychopathic superego, which omnipotently induces the object's ego to act or feel as the subject needs it to act or feel. I believe it can in a way be compared with what happens in hypnotism, as Freud points out (1921c). The hypnotist has put himself in the place of the ego-ideal, and the docility that occurs under hypnosis must be understood as being masochistic by nature.

Freud adds that in the hypnotic relationship there is a kind of paralysis resulting from the influence exerted by an omnipotent person over a subject who is powerless and defenceless (1921c). The same happens in the psychopathic relationship in which object B, induced to act because he is not aware of the whole of this process, can later rationalize his actions in the same way as a hypnotized person does after carrying out the hypnotic orders he has received. Subject A, who does the inducing, goes on controlling, through his mechanisms of obsessive control, what has been projected into object B, who has been induced, and this gives consistency to his omnipotent phantasies, as he feels them confirmed in reality by the object's response. There may then be established a type of reaction, tyrannical by nature, by the submission of object B. It is a narcissistic relationship, since what is projected into the object consists of parts of the subject's self.

Another of the important factors in this process is the deep-rooted need to project the guilt that these patients feel, as they cannot tolerate it, nor deal with it on the mental plane; they feel their ego too weak. That is why such people appear to have a marked lack of responsibility and ethical sense; sometimes they are cruel and unscrupulous. But the incapacity to feel depressive guilt determines their regression to persecutory guilt that is implicit in this same psychopathic conduct, since the impulsive action is usually masochistic in tendency (Grinberg, 1968).

In view of the characteristics of the psychopathic personality— the lability of its ego, its inability to tolerate frustration, its thought disturbances and the need to use the language of action, its strong narcissistic components and belief in omnipotence, the use of massive splitting and excessive projective identification— one of the questions that have to be asked is this: why are such people not psychotic? Despite the seriousness of their symptoms, especially in some cases, they remain in contact with reality and have considerable capacity for understanding what is happening in other people and grasping their specific needs and weaknesses, and their behaviour is syntonic with their ego. I think that one of the explanations lies in the use of obsessional mechanisms of realistic control which keep control over material projected into the object and give the ego a feeling of cohesion and security, despite the intensity with which projective identification functions in such cases. This leads me to formulate the hypothesis that there exists, between psychopathy and obsessional neurosis (or at least certain obsessional mechanisms), a much closer relationship than has been admitted up to now. Among elements in common we can discern the apparent lack of emotion, the incapacity to love, and, in the last instance, thought disturbances, although they take different forms in obsessional patients.

I also pointed out that this hidden and subtle obsessional control which the psychopath maintains over his emotions and links projected into the object give him reinforcement for his omnipotent phantasies.

I also believe that, on the basis of the functioning of these obsessional mechanisms of realistic control and the use of a special form of projective identification with an obsessional content (obsessional mode), there exist latent psychopathic personalities who, in their outward behaviour, show no signs of psychopathy but have a subtle, specific ability to convert the objects to whom they are linked into psychopaths. Their ego is usually made up of obsessional traits and an obsessional character, but their 'psychopathy' is projected into, and controlled in, their objects.

The failure of these obsessional mechanisms to function, or the psychopath's loss of contact and control over the parts of himself projected into the object, may mean that the precarious balance of his ego crashes, and then he falls into psychosis or into a state of depersonalization.

(2) Projective identification and manic states

Manic personalities are characterized by the intensive use of mechanisms of denial and omnipotence with which they attempt to protect themselves from their persecutory and depressive anxieties and from their persecutory guilt. They have a precarious and unstable relationship with objects. They cannot make deep-rooted links with them, and when they do, it is on the basis of devaluation of the objects; they need always to feel successful (Grinberg, 1965).

Kleinian theory has shown a triad of sentiments that is typical of these personalities: control, triumph, and contempt. Control serves to deny dependence; triumph, which includes omnipotence, is at the service of the denial of depression; and contempt is a defence against the feelings of envy, loss, and guilt (Klein, 1952).

Some of these typical characteristics of the manic patient arise from the form, nature, content, and objective of his projective identifications, which are directed for preference towards an internal object idealized and endowed with absolute omnipotence; parts of the ego (self) are invested with these qualities, which then pervade subsequent projective identifications and give the link that they maintain with the external object its special qualities. In other words, the ego of the manic patient is projected into an idealized and omnipotent internal object with which it is projectively identified, and from within this object it treats the external object with contempt and a feeling of triumph.

As I showed in the case of the psychopath, the control of the manic patient is also exerted through obsessional elements contained in projective identification, which enable him to keep a certain contact with reality; that is to say, they make it easier for him to deal with external objects.

To sum up, the projective identifications of the psychopath are of oral–sadistic and anal–sadistic origin; they control and induce. They are omnipotent, but with more contact with reality. They are directed towards external objects; they are more permanent and more violent; they make the object act by causing projective counteridentifications.

The projective identifications of the manic patient are of primitive origin; they are more omnipotent, less intense; they are directed towards the internal object. They are more transitory and unstable; they are simultaneous; they seek to charge themselves with the energy and omnipotence attributed to the internal object and do not tend to provoke responses in the external object, as the psychopath does.

CHAPTER EIGHT

Projective counteridentification

I have made a fairly thorough study of the disturbances caused in analytical technique by the excessive intervention of projective identification on the part of the analysand, which gives rise in the analyst to a specific reaction for which I suggested the term 'projective counteridentification', and these have been published in various articles (Grinberg, 1956, 1957a, 1958, 1962, 1979).

It is known that the psychoanalytical process is conditioned by a series of factors of different types. Among them it is important to single out the continual interplay of projections and introjections which develops during the analysis, on the part of both the analysand and the analyst. Starting from the approach of the latter, we can consider two co-existing processes: in one, the analyst is the active subject of those mechanisms of introjection and projection; in the other, he becomes the passive object of the projections and introjections of the analysand.

In the first, process A, we can describe schematically three important phases or moments: (1) when the analyst introjects, actively and selectively, the different aspects of the verbalized and non-verbalized material, with its corresponding emotional charges, presented by the patient; (2) when he works out and metabolizes the identifications resulting from these introjections that arise from the patient's inner world; (3) when he (re)-projects the results of metabolization by means of interpretations (Fliess, 1942).

In each of these phases dangerous situations may occur, mainly determined by neurotic residues that will give a special tinge to his countertransference reactions, and the inevitable consequence of which will be a disturbance in interpretation, unless the analyst becomes aware of it in time and succeeds in avoiding it. On the other hand, if the countertransference is successfully sublimated, it will be the most useful instrument for detecting, building up, and formulating whatever is capable of interpretation.

The second, process B, is of special interest for the problem I am posing in this chapter. In one of its phases it is the analysand who, actively though unconsciously, projects his internal situations into the analyst, who acts as a passive receptacle. But in this case two situations may occur: (1) the emotional echo that arises in the analyst may be due to his own conflicts or anxieties, intensified or reactivated by the patient's conflicting material; (2) the affective response may be largely independent of his own emotions and mainly or exclusively a response to what the analysand projects into him.

What happens then? The analyst reacts to these identifications as though he had taken in and assimilated *really and concretely* the aspects that were being projected.

It is as though he ceases to be himself and turns unavoidably into what the patient unconsciously wants him to be. For this special state I propose the term 'projective counteridentification' as a specific response to the patient's projective identification, which is not consciously perceived by the analyst, who is consequently 'led' passively to carry out the role that, actively though unconsciously, the analysand has forced upon him. When this happens—although it may only be for a short space of time, but sometimes dangerously prolonged—the analyst will resort to every kind of rationalization to justify his attitude or his disturbance.

Sometimes the analyst cannot tolerate this situation and reacts in various different ways: (1) with an immediate recoil, as violent as the material the patient is trying to project into him; (2) by ignoring or denying this recoil through strict control or some other defensive mechanism; nevertheless, at any moment the reaction may become obvious in some way; (3) by postponing or displacing his reaction, which will then become manifest with some other patient; (4) by suffering the effects of this intense projective identification and 'counteridentifying' in his turn.

Actually, the analyst's response will depend on his level of tolerance.

Once this counteridentification has taken place, it is obvious that normal communication between the analysand's unconscious and that of the analyst will be interrupted. [A number of different analysts in the last few years have incorporated these ideas about 'projective counteridentification' into their work; we may mention Langs (1979), Segal (1977), Kernberg (1984) and Sandler (1960).]

I should like to point out in passing that it was a moment of particular satisfaction for me to find confirmation of my ideas on projective counteridentification in Bion's *Learning from Experience,* in which he says explicitly that: '. . . the theory of counter-transference offers only a partially satisfactory explanation because it deals with manifestation only as a symptom of the unconscious motives of the analyst and therefore *it leaves the patient's contribution without explanation* . . . thanks to the beta-screen *the psychotic patient is able to provoke emotions in the analyst'* [Bion, 1962; the italics are mine].

Bion also accepts the emergence in the object-analyst of emotions provoked by the patient (through his projective identifications) which are independent, up to a point, of the analyst's countertransference. He adds that . . . 'the use these patients make of words is more an action directed towards freeing the psyche from an increase of stimuli than a language'. To understand this last statement it would be as well to say a few words first about the theory of the alpha function, as Bion calls the function that allows the transformation of sensorial experiences into alpha elements that can be stored and used to form dreams, memories, and so on. They are those that enable us to dream, think, and keep the distinction between the conscious and the unconscious. On the other hand, if the alpha function fails, beta-elements then arise, which cannot be used to form thoughts but contain undigested facts, which can only be evacuated through projective identification and appear in the process of acting out. These theories offer a new contribution to the understanding of thought processes.

When, for various reasons, the thinking function fails, we can accept that it is replaced by projective identification as a means of freeing the psychic apparatus from increasing tension.

Racker (1960) is one of the authors who have paid most attention to the problem of countertransference; he has succeeded in explaining the complexities arising from the different meanings attached to the term.

On the basis of Freud's complementary series, he accurately describes a countertransferential disposition on the one hand and current analytical experiences on the other, with counter-transference as a result. He adds that this fusion of the present and the past, of reality and phantasy, of external and internal, and so forth, gives rise to the need for a concept embracing the whole of the analyst's psychological response, and he recommends that the term 'countertransference' should be kept for this concept. He explains, however, that it is sometimes possible to speak of 'total countertransference' and differentiate between, or separate, one aspect or another within that term.

On the other hand, Racker emphasizes the existence of a 'countertransference neurosis' in which 'oedipal and pre-oedipal conflicts, along with pathological processes (paranoid, depressive, manic, masochistic, etc.) interfere with the analyst's understanding, interpretation and conduct'.

At this point Racker, who has had the great merit of exhaustively studying the dynamics of countertransference in its various aspects, refers with particular emphasis to two types of identification of the analyst with parts of the analysand. On the basis of some ideas of H. Deutsch, he points out that the analyst, with his empathic tendency to understand everything that is going on in the analysand, can reach the point of identifying 'each aspect of his personality with the corresponding psychological part of his analysand; his id with the id, his ego with the ego, his superego with the superego of the analysand, *consciously accepting these identifications'* (my italics). These are *concordant or homologous identifications* based, according to Racker, on introjection and projection, on the echo of the external in the internal, on the recognition of what is alien as one's own—'this (you) is I'—and the association of one's own with what is alien—'that (I) is you'. Concordant identifications would be a reproduction of the analyst's own past processes that are being relived in response to the stimulus from the patient, giving rise to a sublimated positive countertransference that determines a higher degree of empathy.

The second type of identification, called *complementary identification,* results from the analyst's identification with internal objects of the patient; he feels treated like these internal objects and experiences them as his own.

Racker also describes a *concordant countertransference* in which there is an approximate identity between parts of the subject and parts of the object (experiences, impulses, defences) and a *complementary countertransference* in which there may exist 'an object-relation' very similar to others, a true transference in which the analyst 'repeats' earlier experiences, the analysand representing internal objects of the analyst.

Here I should like to outline the difference between these countertransferential terms and my concept of 'projective counteridentification'.

To begin with, confusion arises only with regard to the distinction between 'projective counteridentification' and 'complementary countertransference', as 'concordant countertransference' is related to the empathic link towards the analysand, the longing to understand him; and these are identifications *that are accepted by the analyst's conscience,* as Racker describes. This means that they depend almost completely on an active attitude towards them on the part of the analyst.

We then see what the essential difference is between complementary countertransference and projective counteridentification. As I explained above, it follows that complementary countertransference arises when the analyst identifies with internal objects of the patient and experiences them as his own internal objects. In another paragraph, Racker stresses that the analyst *'repeats' earlier experiences in which the analysand represents the analyst's internal objects*; the combination of these latter experiences (which always and continuously exist) can be called 'complementary countertransference'.

In my opinion, this countertransference reaction is based on an emotional attitude due to the analyst's neurotic residues *reactivated by the conflicts introduced by the patient*. This means that it takes shape within the first situation of process B, which I have described above, in which the analyst is a passive object of the analysand's projections, for example his internal objects, but he reacts with countertransference because of *his own anxieties and the reactivation of his own conflicts with his internal objects*.

'Projective counteridentification', on the other hand, corresponds to the second situation of process B—that is, the analyst's reaction is largely *independent of his own conflicts and corresponds predominantly or exclusively with the intensity and quality of the analysand's projective identification*. In this case the accent of the process is placed on *the patient* and not on the analyst. It is the patient who, in one particular moment of regression, and because of the functional modality of his projective identification, will actively provoke in the analyst a fixed emotional response, which he will experience in a passive way (Grinberg, 1963b).

In 'complementary countertransference' a reaction always arises which corresponds to the analyst's own conflicts. In 'projective counteridentification' the analyst *takes upon himself* a reaction or mechanism which *comes from* the patient.

To clarify this point we can take one of the examples quoted by Racker. This is the case of the analysand who threatens the analyst with suicide. The anxiety which such a threat sparks off in the analyst can lead to various reactions or defence mechanisms within him, for example a dislike of the patient. This anxiety and loathing would be the contents of the 'complementary countertransference'. His awareness of dislike may give rise in its turn to guilt-feelings in the analyst which may lead to desires for reparation and to the intensification of concordant identification and countertransference (Racker, 1960).

Now if we analyse this extract, we may find both processes superimposed on each other or co-existing simultaneously. (This usually happens). The analyst experiences anxiety in the face of the threat of suicide. But this anxiety has two components; one corresponds to the analyst's own anxiety due to his feelings of responsibility when faced with the possible risk of the death of his patient, who, at the same time, represents one of his internal objects. (It may also be an internal object of his analysand which is felt as an internal object of his own). This type of anxiety corresponds to a 'complementary countertransference'. On the other hand, the analyst takes upon himself the specific anxiety of the analysand who, by projective identification, has placed this in him with the idea of the analyst controlling and resolving it. This anxiety response now forms part of 'projective counteridentification'. The analyst then reacts with dislike (a mechanism actually belonging to 'complementary countertransference') and guilt. If we go more deeply into the analysis of this guilt, we find that part of it has a persecutory characteristic, which determined the feeling of annoyance at having incorporated, even though only partially, the impotence and desperation of the analysand and his fear of not being able to make reparation. Another part corresponds to the 'depressive guilt' (Grinberg, 1963b) which the patient cannot yet perceive nor manage, and which, projected into the analyst as depository, makes him feel capable of making reparation. These latter considerations with regard to projection on the patient's part of the two types of guilt and the analyst's response demonstrate how projective counteridentification works. It does not exclude the two types of guilt, which the analyst may experience through his own conflicts, reactivated or unleashed by the patient's material (complementary countertransference).

Naturally these processes are never pure nor isolated but generally co-exist in different proportions.

When, mentioning other examples, Racker maintains that a 'depressive–paranoid' transference situation of the analysand has its counterpart—from the point of view of complementary identification—in a 'manic' countertransference situation of the analyst, he is implying, in my opinion, the co-existence of the two mechanisms. Since the analyst can react manically through his own conflicts, which make him feel strong or dominant towards a depressed object, or because he has taken on the manic and triumphant attitude of the analysand, he has been 'placed' in this situation due to the special use of projective identification.

In other words, through *complementary countertransference* each analyst identifying himself with his patient's internal objects will react in a personal way, according to the type and nature of his own conflicts. Different analysts will react *in a different way* faced with the same patient material. On the other hand the same patient, using his projective identification in a particularly intense and specific way, could evoke the *same countertransferential response* (projective counteridentification) in different analysts. I had the opportunity to confirm this through the supervision of material of a patient who had been in analysis successively with various analysts.

This is one of the important reasons that explain why I prefer to keep the name 'projective counteridentification' to refer to the process that takes place in the analyst in response to the analysand's projective identification. Just as a transferential attitude calls forth a countertransferential response, so projective identification will be responded to by a certain projective *counteridentification*. Although from this point the analyst introjects, albeit passively, this projective identification, the important thing is to make clear that the analyst's specific reaction is due to the form in which the analysand projects, places, or 'forces' his projective identification into him.

Here I should like to add that projective counteridentification will have, in its turn, different modalities, according to what the respective modalities of projective identification have been. This mechanism will be coloured by qualitative nuances, which will give it a functional specificity. Normally, in all extraverbal communication, the type of function (degree and quality) of the projective identification of the transmitter (analysand) does not go over the critical threshold of the receptor (analyst), and the extraverbal message produces countertransferential resonance. It stimulates the response that can be grasped, controlled, and verbalized with relative ease by the analyst. But on certain occasions, when the degree and quality of the projective identification impregnate its functional modality in a special way, the result is that the extraverbal communication will pass over the critical threshold, producing projective counteridentification. This threshold will depend in every case on the analyst's personality, on his previous analysis, and on the degree of knowledge or awareness he has of this phenomenon (Grinberg, 1976a).

I also think that on some occasions the analyst, because of his fear of an excessive projective identification on the part of the patient, may respond with a paranoid attitude, thus determining a counterresistance, which will indubitably affect his work. Although he understands and justifies rationally the analysand's wish to project his parts into him, using him as a dynamic reservoir for his conflicts, another, unconscious part of him will be afraid of feeling invaded and annihilated and of losing, even temporarily, his personal aspects, which have been expropriated— magically—as a consequence of projective identification.

A clinical example will illustrate this last point: a woman patient arrived for her first session fifteen minutes late, lay down on the couch and remained motionless, without saying a word. After a few minutes, she said the session felt like her oral examination, to which she reacted with considerable nervousness and anxiety, and which, on the other hand, she related to her wedding night, when she also felt very afraid but managed to hide this in such a way that her father-in-law said she was like a statue. I told her then that she was reproducing with me the experience of the oral examination and the wedding night, and that she was afraid I would deflower her so as to put myself inside her and search her out. I said that here, too, she had behaved like a statue with her initial rigidity and immobility, with the aim not only of hiding her anxiety, but of defending herself from the material possibility of being penetrated.

Although I saw that the interpretation of her paranoid anxiety was correct, I felt that there was something wrong, without being able to say exactly why. It occurred to me then that what I had pointed out to her was very close to her consciousness, and that I should go more deeply into the reasons for her exaggerated fear of letting me into herself. On the other hand her initial rigid attitude had caught my attention, and I surprised myself with the phantasy of analysing a corpse. After that something happened that found expression in a humorous form: 'she surely wants to force a corpse into me'. This showed me my own paranoid reaction to her wish to project her objects into me. Guided by this countertransferential experience, I then pointed out that her initial silence and immobility might mean something more than the simple representation of a statue, and that she might perhaps be expressing in this way some feeling of hers in relation to death.

Her immediate reaction was to burst into tears and tell me that when she was small, her older sister had committed suicide because of a disappointment in love, and that she felt responsible for her death because the failure to stop it was due to her delay. She had seen the preparations for suicide (her sister had already attempted it on other occasions), and, deeply affected by them, had gone out and watched from outside for a long time, perhaps fifteen minutes, until it occurred to her to run and seek her father. By the time he arrived, it was too late.

I had felt that the patient, with her 'corpse-like attitude' was not only attempting to show me one of her more serious conflicts in relation to the dead internal object that she still had inside her, but was also trying to free herself from it by means of projective identification. From this initial moment of her analysis, I was the one who was to bear the burden. This motivated my defensive reaction, as I must have unconsciously perceived in her a certain ritual attempt to imitate the attitude of a corpse, which would automatically determine, by a kind of 'imitative magic', the projection of this object into me. [Ph. Greenacre, in *Trauma, Growth and Personality* (1953), considers that one of the determinant factors of acting out is the tendency to dramatize, based on imitative magic, which predominates in the first years of life. These patients unconsciously suppose that to do something in an imitative or dramatic form—to make it appear true—is really equivalent to making it come true. This is related to the wish to avoid or produce something by means of magical activity.] I think this was the essential reason for my interpretation with regard to her paranoid anxiety, because in this way I was concealing or denying my own unconscious fear of feeling invaded by a dead object. On becoming aware of my reaction I could then better understand the deepest roots of the patient's paranoia and realize that her immobility was in itself a magical gesture or action with which she intended not only to immobilize the persecuting object that she had within herself, but also to identify with it in its dead state, while she projected into me her fear of persecution.

Let us look at another example. A young analyst came to his session after having, in his turn, analysed a 'difficult' patient, who made him feel 'utterly beaten' because he had been very active in his interpretations without achieving any appreciable result. Depressed by the feeling that this session had been a failure, he told his training analyst what had happened and described his state of mind, after which he remained silent. Hearing his analyst's interpretations, which for the moment did not alter his state of mind, the young analyst had the impression that the situation he had been complaining of not long before was being repeated, but with the roles reversed; he realized that it was his analyst who was 'beating his brains out' trying to achieve some change in him, while he was reacting in the same way as his patient had. When he told his analyst, with a certain surprise, what his impression had been, his analyst told him that his (the young analyst's) behaviour had 'obliged' him (textual expression) to identify with him. He then completed the interpretation by saying that the young analyst envied him because he had better patients than he had. An intense identification had then taken place, through which the young analyst unconsciously wished his analyst to experience the same difficulties, dissociating himself and projecting into him the disappointed and dissatisfied professional part of himself, while he was left with the part identified with the patient 'who gives him work and no gratification'. The training analyst, in his turn, 'succumbs' (if that is the right expression) to this projection and is unconsciously 'obliged' to counteridentify with the part he has received. When this happens—and it happens more often than is usually supposed—the analysand feels unconsciously that he has achieved by magic the fulfilment of his wish, thanks to the 'placing' of his parts in the object; and the analyst feels that he has not been able to oppose with the 'countermagic' of his work the 'magic', this time more effective, of his analysand.

The student may make the supervisor feel the same type of emotional reaction as the patient made him feel. If the supervisor can become aware of the genesis of his affective repercussions, then he can, having more capability, objectivity, and experience, show the candidate the origin of the emotional reaction that he had experienced in the session with his patient.

Other authors have referred to similar problems, though starting from different schemes of reference and therefore using different terminology for the conceptualization and description of the phenomenon. [From this paragraph to the end of the chapter is an addition based on my work 'Beyond projective counteridentification' (Grinberg, 1982).]

The dynamic interaction that develops constantly between the two members of the analytical couple is a fact to which more and more importance is attached. A happy phrase of E. Balint eloquently expresses the quality and scope of this interaction: '... now we have a more three-dimensional vision of transference'. The analyst is not only a 'mirror' in which the internal objects of the analysand are reflected; the latter often projects his phantasies and feelings not only *on to* the analyst, but also *into* him. I suggest that this conception of a third dimension can also be applied to countertransference.

At present I think that projective counteridentification does not necessarily have to be the final link in the chain of complex events that occur in the exchange of unconscious communication by non-verbal means with patients who, in moments of regression, function with pathological projective identifications. I believe, on the contrary, that it may also be the starting-point of the possibility of experiencing a spectrum of emotions that, well understood and sublimated, may be turned into very useful technical instruments for entering into contact with the deepest levels of analysands' material, in a way analogous to that described by Racker and by P. Heimann for countertransference. But in order to achieve this, it would be necessary to be more *disposed* to receive and contain the patient's projections for as long as necessary. We do not always succeed in this. Very often we are afraid of feeling invaded by the psychotic contents of such projections, because they may threaten our own psychic balance. We then try to defend ourselves by rejecting them in different ways.

We know that the special nature of our work exposes us to running such risks, since we are seeking to communicate with the unconscious of the analysand who, in his turn, often attempts this communication by non-verbal means. Although the situation varies from patient to patient, some of them—with the psychotic patient predominating—use pathological projective identifications so as to evacuate their painful and persecutory phantasies and emotions into the analyst's mind. Such moments especially test our degree of tolerance and our capacity for receiving and containing such phantasies and emotions.

Taken to its most extreme expression, such an attitude shows itself in *consenting* to be invaded by the projections of the analysand's psychotic anxieties and phantasies, and to contain them until their ultimate consequences are fulfilled, so as to be able to *share, feel, and think* with him, to be *consubstantial* with the emotions contained in such projections, whatever their nature may be (murderous hate, fear of death, catastrophic terror, etc.) as though they were part of his own self. It is to offer all the time and mental space one has at one's disposal, to provide all the mental space and time that the patient, with his different affective contents, is going to need. In this way the analyst will arrive successfully at 'at-one-ment' with the patient's 'O'.

In other words, I would say that the analyst experiences, in his own personality, a transformation, which enables him to reach the state of *convergence* with the anxiety, pain, delirium, or hallucination experienced by the analysand. The term 'convergence' was suggested to me by a seriously melancholic patient whose case I followed as supervisor; she used it to express her desperation when she felt that she was not understood by her family, nor her friends, nor, at times, by her analyst. She said that the 'convergence' between them, which she needed and hoped for so much, was not coming to pass. At other times, referring to the same type of problems of lack of communication, she expressed her wish that the analyst might belong to the sort of people who 'when they're with you, they *really* are'. Both the term 'convergence' and the phrase 'being really with somebody' are close to the concept of 'at-one-ment' with the psychic reality 'O' of the analysand.

Another borderline patient insisted on his need for the analyst to 'come down' to him so as to understand him, although he recognized that this involved the risk of 'becoming infected' (I would call it 'counteridentifying'), and that in that case he would not be able to help him.

Joyce McDougall (1979) suggests that communication (from the Latin *communicare*, which means, etymologically, 'keep contact with', 'have a relationship with', or 'be a part of'), in its primitive form is nearer to crying, screaming, and groaning. She adds that such communication would be a means not only of remaining in intimate contact with someone, but 'to discharge emotions in a direct form with the intention of *affecting* the other and making affective reactions emerge'. Fusion and communion are then the most primitive means of binding oneself to other people.

I should like to recall here Freud's phrase that 'there is much more continuity between intrauterine life and early infancy than the impressive "caesura" of the act of birth would lead us to believe' (1926d [1925]).

Projective counteridentification is a caesura. But it is so in the sense of a link in continuous transit (as transference and countertransference are), since what characterizes the analytic process is the constantly changing situations that take place in the interaction between the analyst and the analysand.

Elsewhere (Grinberg, 1981) I have referred to a characteristic that I have been able to observe in regressive and borderline patients: the rapid and unexpected change from one emotional state (pain, for example) to another (persecution and hostility), giving rise to disturbance, irritation, and so forth in the analyst's countertransference. I was also able to show the sudden volte-face that usually takes place in such patients from the 'neurotic part' of their personality to the 'psychotic part' and vice versa. The lability of the limitrophic zone between the different types of emotion and between the two parts of the personality and the frequency and rapidity with which these kaleidoscopic reactions occur in clinical practice suggest to me the name of 'razor's edge' for these situations. I would say *now* that these 'razor's edge' phenomena are also caesuras in so far as they imply changes or transitions from one emotional or mental state to another, sometimes completely opposed, also causing reactions of 'projective counteridentification' in the analyst. The transition to the 'catastrophic change', which leads to 'convergence', understanding, and mental growth, must perhaps pass *inevitably* through projective counteridentification, but this transition must somehow lead *beyond* projective counteridentification, avoiding the danger of remaining blocked in it with the implication of a *mini-castastrophe*.

To sum up: I would include in the 'psychoanalytic function of the personality' of the analyst the ability to regress, to let himself be invaded, and to 'place himself' *within* the patient's productions, even psychotic, experiencing together with him the emotions contained in them, and being able to return to external reality in the same way as the poet who travels into the world of phantasy but finds the way back into reality, as Freud has shown us.

PART TWO

The sense of identity

CHAPTER NINE

The problem of identity
and the psychoanalytical process

The concept of identity has provoked great controversy, both in philosophy and in psychoanalysis. In psychoanalytical literature, the term 'identity' was introduced by Victor Tausk in his classic paper 'On the origin of the "influencing machine"' (1933). In this paper Tausk studied the way in which the infant discovers objects and his own self and stated that man, in his struggle for self-preservation, must constantly repeat the experience of finding himself and feeling himself.

Freud used the term 'identity' only once throughout his work and then in an incidental way and with a psychosocial connotation. The reference occurred when, in his address to the Society of B'nai B'rith, he tried to explain his link with Judaism and spoke of 'many obscure emotional forces which were the more powerful the less they could be expressed in words', as well as a 'clear consciousness of *inner identity* which was not based on race or religion, but on a common readiness to live in opposition, and a common freedom from prejudices which narrow the use of intellect' (1941e [1926]; my italics). It refers then to the core of the individual related to an essential aspect of the internal coherence of a group.

In his commentary on Freud's statement, Erikson (1956) concludes that the term 'identity' expresses 'a relationship between an individual and his group' in the sense of a persistent sameness and the persistent sharing of a certain essential character with others. We shall return to this concept because we consider it essential to the conceptualization of identity as a system in which it is most important to establish a solidarity of relationship among its components.

The formation of identity is a process that stems from the mutual and successful assimilation of all the fragmentary identifications of childhood; in turn, it presupposes a successful containing of early introjections. Whereas this success depends on a satisfactory relationship with the mother and later on with the family as a whole, the formation of a more mature identity, according to Erikson, depends upon the development of the ego, which is supported by the resources of a wider community for its functions. It is the ego that affects the gradual choice of significant identifications, the anticipation of identity, and the resynthesis at the end of adolescence, and this is a part of the ego's work that Erikson calls 'ego identity' (1956) in order to differentiate it from the 'illusory identity' that does not respond to an individual's sense of reality within his social environment.

Other authors connect the appearance of the sense of identity with psychosexual development (Greenacre, 1958). They particularly underline two aspects; one stresses the similarities with oneself, the other the specific differences between the self and the others, which clearly emerge from comparison and contrast. That is to say, an individual is said to be endowed with identity when his components are sufficiently integrated into the organization of a whole to produce the impression of unity and when, at the same time, he features those unique characteristics that make possible his differentiation from all others. Greenacre (1958) maintains that the nucleus of the incipient ego, and later on the image of the self, is the body image; she considers the infant's relationship with objects to be established through the skin and mouth, with the aid of eyes and hands, and points to the fact that the face and genitals constitute the most significant areas in the recognition of one's own body and that of others. She states that after six months of age and extending into the second half of the second year, the gradual increase in genital feelings gives endogenous sensations from within a kind of sensory peg, which combines locally with the body imagery produced by visual and tactile appreciation of the child's own genitals and those of others. However, when the infant is prematurely and frequently exposed to seeing the genitals of others, the incorporation of these perceptions and the accompanying identifications and phantasies may lead to problems of identity.

The face and genitals are the most significant areas for the individual's recognition of his body self and that of others, through comparison and contrast (Greenacre, 1958). Those who have studied identity disturbances in cases of autism and symbiosis hold that the sense of identity is determined by our bodily sensations, the body image being the basis of the above-mentioned identity (Mahler, 1958).

The sense of identity is the personal recognition of being a distinct entity, separate from all others (Kramer, 1958). Whatever man feels to be 'his own' is included in the 'fluctuating limits of the self'; that is, it corresponds to the self, with its belongings (Federn, 1952). For some authors, identity is the oneness of the individual throughout time, in a comparison with himself, constituting his continuity and sameness (Lichtenstein, 1961), and they consider the achievement of individuation–differentiation to be prerequisites of this identity.

I have studied the sense of identity (Grinberg, 1971), relating it to those mourning situations brought about by the loss of objects and of part of the self. My definition is: 'this feeling implies the idea of a self which bears essentially upon the continuity and likeness of unconscious phantasies referring to bodily sensations, anxieties and emotions experienced by the ego'.

At present we consider the sense of identity to be the outcome of a process of continuous interaction between three links of integration, namely the spatial, temporal, and social ones.

We have been able to study these links to our specific field of work, that is, the patient–analyst relationship in psychoanalytical treatment. We shall therefore synthesize the complex vicissitudes that underlie the acquisition of the sense of identity in the analytic process and thereby extract clues as to the configuration of identity and the way in which disturbances in the development of the individual and his relationship with society are produced.

We assume that patients who come to analysis have their identity variously impaired by their conflicts. Much more so, we believe that one of the conscious or unconscious motives for wanting to start analysis is the need to consolidate the sense of identity.

Obsessive and schizoid cases would mark the extremes of a wide range of identity disturbances, consisting, on the one hand, of a rigid identity, which lacks plasticity, and on the other its opposite: a weak and fragmentary one.

The starting point of the process that leads to the acquisition or maturation of the sense of identity coincides with the very beginning of the analytic process, since the analytical setting itself provides a 'container', which contains and delimits projections conveying 'pieces of identity'. At the same time this container will be the melting pot for the complex operations undergone by those 'pieces', until their integration is made possible.

We are using the phrase 'pieces of identity' as a metaphor to describe unconscious phantasies that underlie the absence of a relationship between different levels of ego regression, split-off parts of the ego, certain roles, or else identifications with different objects that operate independently, somewhat loosely, like 'islands'. Although this image describes the characteristics of a diffuse identity of the schizoid type, we think that the concept of a container also holds good for types of identity disturbance that affect other clinical forms of neurosis.

The initial situation of precarious integration is confirmed by observing infants a few weeks old, who become restless and upset when left unclad. Sometimes their whole body shakes, as if they sensed danger; or they hold on to their mother's clothes or whatever happens to be within their reach. Bick (1968) interprets this as an expression of the phantasy of pouring out or overflowing, as if they were in a liquid state, and the fear of endlessly falling, as if pouring out of themselves. They need to grab when they are afraid of disintegration, because their feeling is that of not yet having a 'skin' of their own to contain them. It is a specific anxiety; it can be likened to the sensation of bleeding to death, for instance, as if blood were to flow out of the body. This can be seen later on in traumatic situations, both in children and in adults, when there is loss of control: there is an incapacity to contain the limits of the body.

The baby fears that nobody can contain his integrated self, and that his weakly held parts may fall apart; observation shows that his fears can only be allayed by the nipple in the mouth, like a cork in a bottle, as well as by arms holding him closely. The infant becomes progressively integrated within the maternal 'holding', which gradually takes the form of a good internal object and a containing 'skin', which provides a separation from the bad object that is expelled. As from that moment there is also greater contact with the external object-mother. Not until the containing functions have been fully introjected can the concept of a space within the self appear, and all the confusions related to identity become manifest. In the unintegrated state the need to find a containing object leads to the frantic search for an object that can be experienced as something that joins together disparate parts of the personality.

I agree with Mahler (1958b) when she emphasizes the importance of experiencing pleasurable bodily contact with the mother. This contact libidinizes the body surface, which is perceived as the limit or borderland between the self and the world. She adds that the mother must act as a buffer to intolerable internal and external stimuli, as a prerequisite for the establishment of a sense of identity.

This concept approaches that of a capacity for 'reverie' (Bion, 1962) or the phantasy of the mother who can take upon herself the infant's intense death anxiety. We may say that the mother–analyst contains—and is the depository of—the seed of the patient's rudimentary identity, memory, and synthetic functions; the analyst contains the seed and the material with which the patient's identity will be built.

We think that, reassured by a 'container–skin analysis', the analysand can more readily accept regression, which, in these circumstances, implies lesser risks.

Regression is another essential factor in the process of acquiring a sense of identity in analysis, since it forces the patient to revive different moments of his evolution that determined the pathology of his identity.

The concepts of Winnicott (1955), Kris (1938) and Erikson (1950), relating to regression which enables creative activity can also be applied to the problem under study here. Winnicott, in particular, has emphasized regression as a phenomenon that forms part of the cure, in so far as it permits one to go back, undo the 'false self', and reinstate the real self.

In certain cases extreme regressions appear, in which the patients attempt to 'touch bottom', as if responding to the unconscious phantasy of being reborn with a different identity.

It is also important to consider the object-relations and the mechanisms of identification that are at work on the scene of the analytical process, through the transference relation. Object-relations are momentous for the formation of identity, since depositories must exist so as to take charge of the persecutory and depressive anxieties that the patient is unable to tolerate and whose intensity hampers the adequate organization and stabilization of the ego.

We have referred to some of the identity disturbances in patients who resort to psychoanalytical treatment, and the 'container' aspects of the analyst and the setting, which play a role in the modification of these disturbances.

This 'container' function, together with the work of interpretation, will pave the way for the process of working through, which contributes to the consolidation of the sense of identity. By means of this process, the loss of infantile parts of the self can be accepted, as well as the detachment of regressive aspects that obstruct the establishment of adult aspects.

On the basis of the foregoing concepts Rebeca Grinberg and I (Grinberg & Grinberg, 1971) wish to postulate the idea that identity is the outcome of a process of interrelation of three integrating links, namely the spatial, temporal, and social ones.

By spatial link we understand the relation with the different parts of the self including the bodily self, maintaining its cohesion and permitting comparison and contrast with objects; it tends to the self–non-self differentiation, i.e. individuation. We call it the *link of spatial integration*.

The temporal link refers to the relation of different representations of the self in time, establishing both a continuity between them and the foundation of a sense of sameness. We call it the *link of temporal integration*.

The third link refers to the social aspect of identity and is given, in my opinion, by the relationship between aspects of the self and aspects of objects by means of the mechanisms of identification. It is the *link of social integration*.

Link of spatial integration

The idea of the body is essential to the consolidation of the individual's identity. One feels inextricably linked to one's own body. So long as an individual is aware of being alive, he feels real and substantial; so long as he is inseparable from his body, he will also feel his personal continuity in time and the continuity of his social and object relations that took place in the course of that time (Laing, 1960).

The perception of the body as a unit is the basis of the concept of 'body image' as a psychosomatic unit postulated by Schilder (1950). The body image is based on Freud's 'body ego' plus the affects and motor attitudes associated with every perception. When Freud pointed out that 'the ego is first and foremost a bodily ego, it is not merely a surface but is itself a projection of a surface' (1923b), he was underlining one of the most important factors that form the basis of identity. Schilder held the image of the human body to be an anthropological structure, both physiological and psychological; he considered it not only a decisive factor in every human action, but also a component of the very human being. The image of the human body is for him our mental representation of our own body. How does this image take shape? We have certain sensations; we see parts of the body surface; we have tactile, painful muscular and visceral impressions. All of this leads to the immediate experience of the existence of a bodily unit. The expression 'body scheme' is due to Head and Holmes (1911), who described the postural pattern of the body. The body image is the tridimensional image that everyone has of himself.

The infant needs the progressive formation of the other person as an object of experience, so that he can progressively become an object as regards himself. In the course of the early periods of life an important differentiation comes about between one's own body and the objects outside the body. As a result of diverse experiences, the infant's body is no longer alien to him, and little by little he begins to individualize it. First, he individualizes the parts of his body, but he cannot integrate them as a whole; this integration comes later. The infant becomes aware of the 'whole' nature of his body at the same moment as 'the other' becomes a 'total' object for him. He becomes aware of his own body just as he becomes aware of the other's body. This first occurs with his mother, the first person the infant is faced with.

The sense of sexual identity is based on bodily sensations ranging from early infancy to maturity (one's own and others' genitals are seen and touched, and sensations, tension, and pleasure are experienced accordingly) and correlative to very complex unconscious phantasies of a libidinal and aggressive nature related to his oedipal and pre-oedipal objects.

The establishment of sexual identity implies giving up the sex other than one's own. In fact, each step in the acceptance of one's own identity and of what one is calls for the working through of the mourning for what one is not.

Undoubtedly, the relationship with the mother is an essential basis for the formation and development of sexual identity. In the 'mirror' of the symbiotic child–mother link, the girl identifies herself with the femininity represented by the maternal image, and the boy becomes inversely identified with his mother's unconscious masculinity or with the masculine object she loves and desires. A normal mother will also be able to return to her son the projective identifications related to his masculine sexual identity deposited in her partner and help him establish and strengthen his identity. If the mother has problems with her own sexual identity, with unsolved conflicts in relation to a possible rejection of masculinity, she will foster her son's assumption of an identity of feminine characteristics.

The father's role is equally important in consolidating the sexual identity of his children; he lends himself as a model of identification for the son in all of his masculine aspects and fosters his daughter's identification with the feminine object he loves and desires. For this reason his presence at home should be regular and constant, and, above all, his roles as husband in the marital couple and as father in the family circle should not be impaired by the intervention of a domineering and castrating wife–mother.

Rivalry towards the parent of the same sex arouses in a boy the fear of losing his genitals in different ways, and in a girl the fear of being emptied, which underlies what may appear as penis envy of a defensive nature.

Nevertheless, the oedipal wishes are repressed not only for fear of castration (feminine and masculine), but also because the child realizes that the death of his father—whom he wishes to replace— would be painful to his mother, and also for the grief and sadness the child feels towards his father and his wish to preserve him.

The Oedipus complex is finally solved by introjective identification with the positive and permissive image of the parent of the same sex and the differentiation of the parent of the opposite sex.

Link of temporal integration

Temporal integrations are based on memories of past experiences, and these in turn make up new memories, which are stored in the unconscious. The incorporation, assimilation, and automation of these memories open up the way for the process of learning and the recognition of one's own identity in the course of time. The capacity to remember oneself in the past and imagine oneself in the future is what convinces the individual that he is the one he was yesterday and still the same as he will be tomorrow.

The physical birth of a new living organism in the world sets off rapidly advancing processes; thanks to them, in a surprisingly short time the infant feels real and alive and has a feeling of being an entity with continuity in time and a position in space.

This is due to many factors. The non-permanent presence of the breast, whose appearance and disappearance do not exactly coincide with the baby's wishes or satisfy the omnipotent phantasy of an unconditional and inexhaustible supply, establishes some sort of discrimination between a wishing subject and a satisfying or frustrating object. This rhythm of appearances and disappearances of the breast, which imposes cycles of satisfaction and need, together with cycles of sleep and wakefulness, contributes to the development of temporal experiences.

At the same time the infant discovers that the gratifying mother and the frustrating mother are one and the same. He has managed to integrate images emerging from different moments of his experience. This integration of the mother figure in time goes together with his own temporal integration.

Separation culminates with the weaning crisis, which shows the inexorable need to work through the end of the infant's idyllic relationship with his mother and admit once and for all the presence of the father as different from the mother and different from himself.

This being different implies being 'separated' but with the possibility of being able to come together and meet the others. In this sense the discovery of the genitals convinces the infant he has an instrument for the meeting.

On the ideational level, the increasing capacity to symbolize allows lost objects to be recovered in the mind and re-created through play and words. Play involving loss and recovery, by symbolically fulfilling phantasies that cannot be carried out with the body, enables the baby to work through the depression caused both by weaning and by finding himself different and 'separated'.

When the infant is able to stand upright, he sees the world from a new angle. From the immediate and concrete point of view, when the child rights himself and defaecates, the faeces fall and separate from him, obliging him to recognize the fact that something that up to that moment was his own can become separated and lost. This phenomenon gives rise to anxiety, because it is experienced as a loss of identity. That is why at times the child reacts by becoming constipated, thus trying to retain parts of himself whose loss is felt as a loss of life.

As the experience is repeated, however, if the child can 'learn from experience' and achieve sphincter control, he is able to tolerate the loss of these substances—urine and faeces—which represent parts of himself and of his objects and mourn for them, since he discovers that he is still able to re-create them.

Confidence in the ego capacity is one of the most important supports of identity, since, as aspects of the self and lost internal objects can be re-created, it ensures permanence and stability in the course of time. This confidence based on past experiences acquires a prospective function, which guarantees integrity in the future.

In this period, the differentiation that the child can establish between himself and the others is clearer, since he progressively gains greater control over his movements; he learns to walk and can approach his objects and move away from them.

At about the age of three, the child shows that he can clearly differentiate between his actions and those of others and between his objects and others', which is shown in his language. He stops using the third person singular to refer to himself and begins to use the first person correctly: I, and mine. This process began long before and evolved through successive crises of losses and recoveries. We can say that every crisis implies a loss and imposes a working through of some mourning; in normal development it would be related to the losses in one stage of development in order to support the next.

When the genital drives return to the fore, a new crisis is triggered off, which leads the child to self-recognition and identification. The child relinquishes the direct gratification of his sexual wishes towards the mother or father, which implies an acceptance by the child that he is 'like'—but 'is not'—his father. In this statement, then, we find two factors of great importance for the establishment and consolidation of the sense of identity: identification and discrimination.

In this interplay of identification, of realistic and magical qualities, the sense of identity continues to grow.

As adolescence begins, everything is in a state of confusion, which gives rise to new and varied dissociations as defences. The road to the acceptance of one's own body involves working through the mourning for the loss of the infantile body and the loss of the image of the childhood parents (Aberastury et al., 1966).

In an attempt to consolidate his identity, the adolescent seeks to form a system of theories, of ethical and intellectual standards, which can be organized into an ideology that transcends and limits his own existence and takes on a character of permanence and immortality.

When this convulsed period of crisis comes to an end, the dissociation of the ego will have given way to a new integration and greater capacity for discrimination.

A further period of crisis involving identity awaits the human being when he is forced to face one of the most distressing truths: his growing old and the inevitability of his own death.

These crises, related not only to the temporal link but also to the spatial and social ones, impose the working through of mournings for past experiences, for the inevitable transformation in the quality of object links, and for those aspects of the self that are lost in each of the developmental stages. An adequate working through of mourning at the corresponding stages will contribute to the consolidation of a feeling of being actually a differentiated entity, with continuity in time and a place in space, and with the capacity to recover in the present what was learnt in the past.

Link of social integration

Object-relations are mainly established by means of mechanisms of identification. Freud referred to identification as the earliest form of relation with an object that is regarded as a model: 'Identification is known to psycho-analysis as the earliest expression of an emotional tie with another person. It plays a part in the early history of the Oedipus complex. . . . Identification, in fact, is ambivalent from the very first; it can turn into an expression of tenderness as easily as into a wish for someone's removal. It behaves like a derivative of the first, *oral* phase of the organisation of the libido, in which the object that we long for and prize is assimilated by eating and is in that way annihilated as such' (Freud, 1921c).

The first wish, then, is to incorporate the object and to be the object; the second step in evolution is to have the object, that is to say object-choice; it may, however, revert to the phase of identification through regression. 'The substitution of the abandoned and lost object by identification with it, that is, the introjection of that object into the ego, are facts observable in the infant' (Freud, 1923b).

The ego finds it easier to differentiate objects than to distinguish between the self and objects. With reference to this we can consider two types of identification:

1. *Primitive identification,* in which the unconscious phantasy of the self and the phantasies of objects have not yet been differentiated or, due to regression, have merged again after differentiation has taken place. This corresponds to total symbiosis and to the type of early object-relation between the infant and its mother. Identification is massive and total: the whole object is within the representation of the self and vice versa.

2. *A mature identification,* which necessarily implies a previous neat differentiation between self-representations and object-representations, associated with an adequate level of ego maturity. This is a selective identification that takes up partial aspects of the objects that are incorporated in a stable manner into the representation of the self in the ego, endowing it with a new ability or quality. This type of identification takes place when there is a true object-relation and not symbiosis. Primitive identifications and mature identifications would correspond in Kleinian terms to projective identification and introjective identification, respectively.

On the basis of his study of identifications, Freud emphasized the influence of the environment upon the development of the individual, as pointed out in his description of the 'complementary series', a concept that throws light on the origin of neuroses. Upon investigating the interaction between a world of external objects and a world of imaginary internal objects, he stressed the theory of a superego as an operative theory that explains how society acts upon the individual. The superego is a system made up of certain specific characteristics of all the internal objects. In this way society—with all the complexity of its institutions—becomes an internal entity assimilated into the intimate structure of the individual. This discovery of psychoanalysis, rather than any other, bridged last century's theoretical contradiction between man and society. They cannot be considered in isolation, since both are equally represented within the intimate nature of the ego and superego.

From the beginning of his life, the infant is in constant contact with the social environment represented by his mother. Although it must be admitted that everyone is born with a given constitutional make-up, his personality will develop according to the quality and intensity of the environmental influence, at first symbolized by his family and, more specifically, primarily by his mother, then by his father and siblings.

A person's 'own' identity can never be completely isolated from his 'identity as seen by others'. His identity depends, to a certain extent, on the identity attributed to him by others, but also on the identities that he, in turn, attributes to others, and therefore on the identity or identities that he presumes the others attribute to him. The sense of identity calls for the existence of the 'other person' who knows it. This can be applied to the aspects of identity that are expressed through the carrying out of certain roles: a mother needs the existence of a child in order to be a mother.

Let us now refer to the development of these links in the analytical process.

As regards the link of spatial integration, in the early stages of the analytical process the patient does not feel integrated and cannot distinguish himself from the analyst (subject–object discrimination); on the contrary, this early period is characterized by extreme dependence, which he tries to neutralize by means of an increase in acting out and an intensification of manic and para-noid–schizoid defences.

We have already mentioned that the link between different parts of the self can be gradually established and consolidated with the help of the setting and the analyst as a container.

With reference to the second link, that of temporal integration, while the patient is in the early stages, time is also a victim of splitting, with a predominance of the primary process; thus the notion of sameness in time is insecure and changeable. The patient usually speaks of his past but keeps his previous ego dissociated from his present ego and lacks the capacity to foresee the future.

In this sense, the continuity and regularity of the sessions are aspects of the setting that strengthen the feeling of continuity of the various self-representations in time. For the same reason, it is useful to effect periodic synthesis interpretations to elucidate the sense or the movement of a whole stage of analysis.

The link of social integration implies a notion of belonging to a group that, in the analytical situation, is formed by the patient–analyst couple, which re-edits the first group link—that of child–mother.

The incorporation of the father, represented in the analytical situation by the analyst's double—mother–father—transference connotation, widens the group.

Although for the sake of clarity these three links have been separately described, it should be understood that they operate simultaneously and interact on one another. The various parts of the self could not become integrated in time without also being integrated in space; on the basis of these spatial and temporal integrations, the individual is able to establish links with objects of the external world (social link) in a realistic and discriminating manner.

On the other hand, pathology also involves all three links at the same time, although one may be more severely impaired than the others. In schizoid conditions—depersonalization and confusion, for instance—the most important disturbance is found in the spatial link; in senile states, certain forms of schizophrenia, and brain injuries, the temporal link shows the greatest disturbances; in symbiosis, acting out, psychopathy, and paranoia, the social link is most affected.

These three links, which at the beginning of analysis are precarious and inconsistent, gradually become consolidated as the analytical process evolves; the ego gains greater strength, cohesion, and insight and increases its capacity to discriminate between internal and external world, subject and object, phantasy and reality; it is also able to work through the mourning for those aspects of the self and objects that change in the course of evolution.

CHAPTER TEN

The identity
of the psychoanalyst

I n chapter nine I spoke of the three integrating links—spatial, temporal, and social. I should now like to apply these concepts to the psychoanalytical identity. I would say that this identity gradually becomes consolidated in each analyst on the basis of the interrelation of these three links. The first, the link of spatial integration, would comprise the assimilated relationship the analyst has succeeded in establishing between the different aspects of his psychoanalytic cognitive equipment and his psychoanalytic experience (both the experience afforded by his own analysis and that obtained from his work with patients), keeping up cohesion and allowing comparison and contrast with other, non-analytic, experiences and areas of knowledge. This link aims at the analyst's differentiation and individuation. The link of temporal integration would correspond to the assimilated relationships among the varied attitudes, insights, and experiences developed through time, establishing a continuity between them and laying the foundation of a sense of sameness. It involves the recognition, through successive changes, of experiences and insights that are essentially psychoanalytic in nature. The link of social integration would comprise the assimilated bond with a given institutional group or community, based on selective identifications with its members, with whom interchanges that do not involve the risk of confusion or the loss of inherent ego-boundaries can be established.

In order to outline more clearly what determines the specific character of a psychoanalytic identity, I think a few more detailed characteristics should be noted.

To E. Joseph's (1983) mind, the analytic identity is defined by a capacity for thinking, feeling, and reacting in such a way as to be able to observe reflexively someone else's unconscious mental functioning, phantasies, resistances, and affects. This identity includes the analyst's ability to recognize the danger of the interference of his own emotions and preconceptions, which may occasionally lead him to 'misuse' his analytic knowledge. Dr Joseph also stressed the need for the analyst to be aware of the limitations of the field and not to extend his own psychoanalytic identity beyond that point.

D. Widlöcher (1983) emphasizes the analyst's ability to observe the mental functioning of other people, his insights into his own attitudes, and the capacity to direct his attention, without much effort, towards latent content. A psychoanalytic attitude throws fresh light on activities of another nature.

Based on conclusions drawn from a discussion of this particular point with a group of colleagues (Ateneo de Psicoanalistas de Buenos Aires, 1975), I would add that, in my opinion, on the basis of this identity, we—psychoanalysts—can be regarded as belonging to a 'natural class', possessing certain definite traits, which are channelled through a given task and give rise to the psychoanalytic attitude, or what is called the 'psychoanalytic function of the personality'. Among these specific traits I should mention the following: a particular kind of curiosity about given aspects of the human being, of the mind and of psychic reality, a curiosity that extends itself to the analyst's own psychic functioning; a capacity for introspection and self-analysis; a creative capacity; an ability to think under adverse circumstances ('in the middle of the storm', so to speak); a capacity for discretion, reserve, and ethical behaviour in the relationship with patients, avoiding acting out and the enticements caused by transference and counter-transference; a tolerance of a certain type of frustration (as those stemming from isolation, the lack of immediate results, the occasional inability to understand, etc.); a capacity for waiting and maintaining floating attention, and, using an expression of the poet Keats, a 'negative capability', that is to say, the ability to cope with uncertainties, mysteries, doubts, and half-truths without feeling compelled to the irritating search for reasons and certainty regarding facts.

The analyst's relationship
with the institution and its members

E. Joseph holds that the existence of formal psychoanalytic organizations contributes to and favours the development and consolidation of the young analyst's psychoanalytic identity. He warns us, however, that these academic structures run the risk of becoming rigid means of control and power. Consecutive identifications with members of the institution can at times become factors liable to contaminate identity, thus hindering the development of objectivity, impartiality, and the acquisition of different points of view.

D. Widlöcher maintains that scientific communication tends to reassure the group and each individual member as to their psychoanalytic identity. He adds that, as a rule, 'we do not forgive those who no longer reflect our image'. Thus communication would aim at keeping up group cohesion on the basis of a narcissistic image. Dr Widlöcher suggests that in order to protect our analytic identity, it is not necessary to eliminate our contradictions. In his opinion, the analyst's identity stems both from the difficulties he encounters and from his activity itself.

Joseph adds that institutional and educational activities, by enabling the analyst to teach and gain prestige, also help reinforce psychoanalytic identity. However, he points out the danger of personal ambition and of the search for narcissistic gratification, which may become a source of conflict and rivalry.

I think that neither Freud nor his collaborators succeeded in ridding themselves of this kind of conflict. This is a sort of latent endemic disease that breaks out periodically in different institutions. These struggles sometimes emerge from generational conflicts, in which certain analysts feel compelled to display or perpetuate the rebelliousness of childhood and seek parental figures to revolt against, whereas others act as 'fathers' who cannot bear to see their 'children' grow up into capable and gifted 'men' who threaten their status and prestige. At other times, these members, whose genealogical line (their descent from the same analyst 'father') will make them maintain the 'family' constellation and form groups of 'totemic' cohesion and loyalty, keep up the rivalry that existed among the pioneer analysts, the founders of their respective societies. They simply 'have to' keep the contentious tradition alive—like Capulets and Montagues, as it were. But, as is to be expected, discrepancies are rationalized and are expressed in terms of scientific or idealogical differences. Situations such as these are not to be mistaken for those in which analysts come together in smaller groups, which enables them to study, do research, or set up a fruitful exchange of ideas. When psychoanalytic institutions become too numerous and heterogeneous, the splitting up of analysts into smaller groups can be beneficial, inasmuch as their members are likely to have more in common, thus reinforcing their analytic identity.

The analyst's relationship with society and with the extra-analytic environment

Widlöcher says that the analyst's identity is also determined by the way in which he organizes his life outside his analytic activities. He wonders whether the analytic identity should be protected against any kind of contamination coming from political or philosophical choices, or whether, on the contrary, the analytic identity should be incorporated into the analyst's political and philosophical identity. Further, he asks himself whether we can have a 'good' science and a 'good' practice without 'good' politics. Can we practise psychoanalysis without taking into account the patient's social context? To what extent does our analytic insight provide us with greater lucidity in our political choices?

In relation to these questions, Joseph maintains that the analyst should take part in the political and social life of his country as a citizen and not as an analyst. In his opinion, an analyst should exclude his psychoanalytic function from his political and social activities, in the same way as he excludes his political, social, and economic views from his work with patients. In this sense, Joseph insists, science is non-political.

As can be seen, there is, as regards this point, an obvious divergence in the authors' views, since, whereas Joseph postulates a sharp separation between psychoanalytic activities and philosophical and political stands, Widlöcher makes us doubt whether such a separation is possible at all, and he suggests that, perhaps inevitably, the psychoanalytic identity and the political and philosophical identity influence one another and even blend with one another.

It is quite true that, for a number of authors, psychoanalysis is just a science and a method of treating neurotic disorders; consequently, political and philosophical ideologies are supposed to be excluded from the analyst's specific activity, for they might become disturbing factors in his field of work. In the opinion of others, however, psychoanalysis is a science and, at the same time, an ideology, insofar as it possesses a system of standards and patterns that are inherent in it. In accordance with the latter perspective, the political and philosophical ideologies an analyst may sustain participate—either directly or indirectly—in his specific activity, from which they cannot possibly be excluded, in that the analyst is invariably present with his whole identity, including his ideological commitments. Similarly, his psychoanalytical identity cannot be absent from his way of thinking, feeling, and acting as regards political and philosophical issues. At any rate, it is beyond doubt that for the patient, in a manifest or a latent way, his analyst does have an ideology, that is to say a specific and personal appraisal—in harmony with his doctrine—of the problems of sex, aggression, economy, politics, education, death, and so on.

It would therefore be of interest to examine whether these ideologies are actually incorporated into the analyst's psychoanalytic identity and, if they are, to determine what these ideologies amount to and what they mean to each analyst, for we are liable to approach them in terms of a personal interpretation or distortion. If this were so, each analyst would also have a specific and personal way of dealing with the aims of analytic work.

To go on now to other factors capable of triggering off a crisis of psychoanalytic identity: such crises sometimes come to a head in certain countries because of the deterioration of the overall economic situation, or of the personal financial situation of the analyst in his professional practice. Certain analysts have placed the economic impairment on a superstructural level, that is, regarding it as a political and ideological matter. Others have considered it in terms of the economic infrastructure itself, as a need to re-orient their professional activities, insofar as psychoanalysis ceases to be sufficiently profitable compared with other therapeutic techniques. The latter reason is not without weight with many of those who have lost interest in psychoanalysis.

Erikson pointed to the need for each analyst to examine himself as to the particular constellation of impulses, defences, abilities, and opportunities that led him to his choice of profession. He added that there seems to exist a certain 'psychoanalytic identity', which becomes the cornerstone of the analyst's whole existence as a man, as a professional, or as a citizen.

The relationship of analytic identity
with change and new ideas

I now wish to dwell on another issue that was mentioned by both authors, although in somewhat greater detail by Dr Joseph: the relationship existing between the psychoanalytic identity and the evolution of psychoanalysis on the one hand and, on the other, the capacity to accept change and new ideas. In my opinion, both an exaggerated dogmatism and an excessive superficiality and willingness to dilute analysis—though occupying opposite ends of a wide spectrum—are among the harmful factors that hinder the evolution of psychoanalysis, endanger the stability of psychoanalytic institutions (in matters concerning analytic teaching and practice), and threaten the cohesion of the sense of identity both of psychoanalysis and of psychoanalysts.

It is the 'container–contained' relationship that, to my way of thinking, is the most useful and illustrative model to explain this kind of phenomenon. A new idea usually exerts a disruptive effect upon the environment; consequently, the establishment or institution may fail in its attempt to adopt it conveniently; among other reactions, it is liable to act as a rigid 'container' that ascribes a potential danger to the 'contained' new ideas, thereby tending to suffocate it and deprive it of life. Or, by contrast, it may work as too weak a 'container', thus favouring the dilution and diffusion of psychoanalytic identity.

A fear of change may occasionally give rise to a tendency to adhere rigidly to what one already knows and is familiar with, in order to avoid the new. We are well aware of the fact that each individual's evolution is an uninterrupted series of minor and major changes, the working through and assimilation of which lead to the establishment of a sense of identity, since lack of growth and change amount to psychic stagnation and to emotional sterility—in other words, to psychic death. The same applies to the psychoanalytic identity. Faced with the anxiety aroused by change, certain analysts resort to conservative and dogmatic attitudes in an effort to defend themselves against what they experience as a threat against their analytic identity. But the capacity to go on feeling oneself as the same throughout successive changes, through the effective working through of mourning, is one of the essential features of a soundly established psychoanalytic identity.

As I have pointed out elsewhere (Grinberg, 1969), living necessarily implies undergoing a series of episodes of mourning; the very fact of growing up, of passing from one stage to another, involves the abandonment of certain attitudes and relationships that, although replaced by more progressive ones, impinge upon the ego as experiences of loss that provoke mourning processes.

The capacity to mourn over these experiences of loss underlies the possibility of facing change successfully.

Evidently, new findings should be encouraged as well as the free interchange between different viewpoints, with due respect for other people's ideas and guarding against prejudice even if, as pointed out by Widlöcher, 'they do not reflect our own image'. I also agree that change, just for its own sake, will lead nowhere, as was opportunely observed by Joseph. In our discussion of these matters in Buenos Aires (Ateneo de Psicoanalistas de Buenos Aires, 1975), it was pointed out that certain psychoanalytic institutions lay so much emphasis on change that the sense of sameness vanishes. Following the pattern of the 'market economy', these institutions accommodate themselves to the customers' tastes and demands, and its members come to acquire what may be called a 'protean' or 'ambiguous' identity, thus failing to abide by some of the fundamental tenets of psychoanalytic identity, namely respect for the clinical fact, the capacity to preserve the setting as a precondition for the successful accomplishment of analytic work, and the uncompromising search for truth. It is precisely the fear of psychoanalysis as a means of searching out the truth that constitutes a threat. According to Bion (1962, 1970), psychoanalysis will have a future, provided that it reaches a point at which people understand that, however fierce their attacks on analysis, they still cannot do without it.

In the meantime, the possibility does exist that fear and hatred of analysis may get the upper hand in certain domains, before psychoanalysis has been able to develop enough to become undeniably essential. Attacks on analysis are launched not only from extra-analytical spheres, but also from the analytical circles themselves, disguised as tendencies towards a so-called broadening of views, or liberation. It goes without saying that these tendencies should not be mistaken for genuine aspirations to achieve productive changes on the basis of new ideas capable of enriching existent theories.

And we are here faced with a particularly difficult problem: Who is to assess this difference, and on what grounds? This in turn leads us to another problem: however important the difference between psychoanalytic identity and the identity of a psychiatrist or psychotherapist, it is even more important, and perhaps more difficult, to decide who, among all those who go by the name, is actually a psychoanalyst. What are the essential features of psychoanalytic identity? Is there also a pathology of this identity? Can one lose it after having acquired it?

When referring to the pathological manifestations of a psychoanalytic identity, we might mention, among other examples, the possibility of pseudo-identity or 'as if' identity, which is false, precarious, and not worked through. It amounts to a failure to assimilate adequately the knowledge derived from analytic training and from the reflective and critical study of the work of various authors; a failure to work through that knowledge in the course of the analyst's own analysis and his subsequent self-analysis; it may also reveal a tendency to adhere to the latest 'fashionable' author, who may, in turn, be replaced by the next author to come into fashion. This 'protean' or 'ambiguous' identity would be present in analysts who find their work meaningless and who fail to integrate it into their personal lives. Taking into account that analyses are usually rather long, it is particularly important for the analyst to feel that the years he has devoted to each patient have been worthwhile; if this is so, his psychoanalytic identity strengthens itself.

I now wish to refer to the difficulties in preserving the psychoanalytic identity during the times of social instability and disruption that not a few countries are going through today. Circumstances of this sort have brought about changes in what patients expect of analysis, and they also weigh upon the analyst's work. Thus, for example, the exaltation of violence per se is bound to throw out of balance those patients with characterological disorders and to increase somewhat the precariousness of balance of certain narcissistic, psychopathic, and borderline personalities. Paradoxically, the most severe disturbances of these personalities are well adapted to the environment, whereas they expect to obtain from analysis a solution to their minor difficulties or, echoing the theory of 'liberation from the superego', a warrant for acting out. Under such environmental pressure the analyst, too, may be induced to work in the same way. But here, again, we may well wonder when the analyst's activity ceases to be analytic work and becomes acting out.

Before bringing this chapter to a close, I would like to sum up some of the important points that have so far been raised: How are we to differentiate between genuine psychoanalytic identity and the formal analytic identity afforded by the mere fact of belonging to an analytic institution? Or, to put it in other words, what does it mean to be a psychoanalyst, and who, of all those who call themselves analysts, should be recognized as such? Is there only one way or several different ways of being a psychoanalyst? Applying the theory of transformations, is it right to say that each analyst, or each analytic group, makes his own transformation of being a psychoanalyst, using invariants other than those of other transformations?

CHAPTER ELEVEN

Relations
between psychoanalysts

I n the first place I want to deal with the differences that exist between the dynamics of the relations within a group of analysts and those within any other scientific, social, or working group.

I shall then explain the specific characteristics of the profession, as the activity of analysts bestows a certain specific content and expression on the conflict situations they have to face.

Then I shall enter upon the analysis of some of the factors bearing on the determination of these specific aspects and their consequences: isolation, lack of communication (necessarily partial and dissociated) and a certain degree of regression. All these, added to the predisposing elements in each personality, may lead, on occasion, to the intensification of persecutory anxieties, with the utilization of paranoid–schizoid mechanisms and increased reactions of rivalry, envy, resentment, or fear towards those who represent re-editions of past persecutory imagos.

These states and mechanisms will also be of influence in the need felt to form part of subgroups with common ideologies and affinities, so as to reinforce our defences and to strengthen and amplify the ego. Nevertheless, it is also as a result of the working-through of the depressive aspects, with a reparatory content, that one acquires feelings of solidarity with others, by receiving or imparting knowledge and by exchanging positive sentiments and emotions and so fostering good relations.

I feel that the best way to begin is to go back, for a brief moment, to the first period in the history of the psychoanalytic movement, not only for the sake of preserving chronological order, but also, and more basically, because of the great significance and the repercussions of the conflicts and disagreements that sprang up between Freud and some of his first disciples. Freud himself (1914d, 1925d [1924], 1937c) frequently refers in his writings to these painful events in his life.

Perhaps it was the influence of these distressing experiences that led him, years later, to postulate (Freud, 1937c) that not all analysts have attained the degree of psychic normality that they would like for their patients. He adds that, unfortunately, training analysis does not ensure that the modifications brought about in the ego will last. He compares the practice of psychoanalysis with the possible effects of X-rays when used without proper precautions. He proposes, as an adequate preventive measure, that every analyst should undergo analysis periodically—say, every five years. Among the authors who have dealt with this problem I may mention Balint (1948), Thompson (1958), Menninger (1942), Rickman (1951), Wälder (1955), and Langer (1963).

I shall now examine some of the factors inherent in the nature of analytic practice that, to my mind, are very important causal agents in many of the tense conflict situations that arise between analysts.

I think that an important step towards understanding relationships between analysts is to tackle the question.

Although we are far from making the ingenuous statement that analysts, from their very condition as such and from their knowledge of the unconscious and of human reactions to problems of competition, rivalry, or envy and so on, must be free from this type of reaction, there is, after all, some truth in this presumption.

Theoretically, the analyst should be able to tolerate conflict situations and cope with them, at least to the same degree as he expects his patients to do with their own conflicts. Yet we all know, to our regret, that this is not the case. My main endeavour will be to try to point out the causes and motivations that underlie this unhappy circumstance, as a first step in our efforts to remove them. It has been argued that at their beginnings the various analytic groups had sharper and more serious conflicts, since they were small, closed family nuclei. But this is only partially true, and the statement loses some of its cogency if we turn our attention to what happens in larger and more developed groups. Here the members are not in such close contact, yet they suffer from difficulties of like quantity and intensity, even though there may be shades of difference.

Do the conflicts that may arise among analysts differ in essence and quality from those arising in any kind of group? Some will maintain that the nature of the relations concerned is exactly the same, and therefore the disturbances that may affect them cannot be very different. It seems to me a mistake to minimize the differences between the dynamics of a psychoanalytic circle and those of any other scientific, social, or working group. *There are certain specific attributes in the activity of analysts that bestow a specific quality on the content and expression of the conflict situations that arise between them.*

The first of these is *the analyst's own analysis.* This involves, from the outset, a differential characteristic of prime importance as compared with what occurs in other groups. Another factor concerns his professional activity. We should recall what Freud (1937c) said about the painful obligations an analyst must comply with in his daily work.

The 'dangers of analysis' mentioned by Freud refer to the possibility of awakening instinctive urges that may have a harmful influence on the analyst's personality because they cannot find an adequate mode of discharge with his patients. At times, in a displaced form—and leading to acting-out—the analyst unconsciously chooses a target for discharge. This target is his colleagues, as he unconsciously feels them to be a legitimate justification for exteriorizing his reaction. But, I think, something further must be added to this mechanism, and that is the weight the analyst feels he must bear in consequence of what his patient deposits in him, by means of multiple and successive projective identifications. This means that it is not only a question of enduring his own conflicts, reactivated by the impact of transference vicissitudes, but also the various conflict situations his patients project into him, which continue to weigh upon him as their depository.

In previous papers (Grinberg, 1958, 1962) I have been concerned with the importance, from a technical point of view, of taking into consideration the effects of *projective counteridentification,* as I have called the specific partial aspect of countertransference determined by the patient's excessive use of projective identification.

Acting-out also arises, on occasion, from the need to 'change' the idealized position in which patients are accustomed to place the analyst on account of the screen quality he possesses for them. We all know that, even though we tend systematically to reject and interpret this idealization, it is sometimes difficult not to submit to it. Thus, for instance, one may hide from the analysand some illness or important happening in one's private life that entails a temporary interruption of the analysis. We cannot afford to fall ill, lest we foster the phantasies or modify the idealized image of us the patient has built up. But the analyst may also feel that he must maintain this ideal of health and perfection even in the face of his colleagues, trying to avoid possible criticisms and the exploitation of these 'flaws'. Some analysts will then seek refuge, pathologically, in the apparent 'humanization' achieved through acting. [Gitelson (1962) touches on this aspect of the analyst's 'humanization'.] Paradoxically, they will try to claim for themselves as well the right to be neurotic and not to be invulnerable embodiments of health. But I feel that the analyst's acting out is also a consequence of his difficulties in working through anxieties increased, as we shall see later, by his isolation and regression. He would therefore tend to dramatize those aspects of his conflict that he feels to be most acute or pressing.

The influence of some specific aspects
of analytical practice

I shall now speak of some of the factors I consider of primary importance in fostering many of the difficult or negative aspects of the relations between analysts. They are those that concern the analyst's *isolation* and *deficiency* of ordinary communication with others.

Owing to the nature of his activity, the analyst spends most of the day isolated in his room. Not only does he feel cut off from the rest of the world during relatively long periods of his daily life, but also, for reasons peculiar to his work, he is reduced to a minimum of opportunities for communication with others.

To this we must add the almost inevitable consequences that follow from the specific features of analytic work and its technique. If we accept that in every analytic situation there arises from the very beginning, and almost automatically, a regression in the patient, largely determined by atmosphere or environmental influence, then we cannot deny that the analyst himself is scarcely able to escape from this *regression*. Furthermore, analytic work requires the analyst to be in 'connection' and 'communication' with the patient in order to apprehend what is deep and latent in his material. But this type of communication, even in the best of cases, is only partial and of a very particular quality. The analyst is fulfilling a role that involves certain features to which he must invariably and rather strictly adhere—that is to say, he must confine himself exclusively to interpreting the material offered by the analysand. He must not converse with him, still less express any thoughts, ideas, or feelings that concern his private or professional life but are foreign to the patient's interest. Even when his reactions happen to be related to the analysand (all that is implicit in the countertransference panorama), only very seldom will he be permitted to transmit them to him. Thus his communication will always be *partial* and *dissociated*; he intervenes actively only with the professional or analytic part of himself, while the rest must remain denied, controlled, suppressed. If this does not happen, if his attention wanders and he withdraws to *communicate* through his thoughts with the *outside,* guilt feelings arise, a technical problem ensues, and there is the need to break or cut off this *communicative fugue* with the exterior.

As a consequence of this *isolation,* the inevitable *regression* that he suffers to a certain extent, his *frustration* and *dissociation,* and other well-known phenomena (reactivation of anxieties, exacerbation of remnants of conflicts never totally overcome, the need to bear tensions projected on to him, insufficient discharge of increased instinctive urges, and erotic and incestuous phantasies) many situations or aspects contained in the paranoid–schizoid position tend to become more acute. Persecutory anxieties are strengthened; reactions of rivalry, envy, and competition are intensified; phantasies appear (reinforced by isolation) of being excluded and the victim of injustice.

The particular conditions and circumstances in which analytic work proceeds undoubtedly determine *great deprivation of informative data and stimuli* (with the single exception of the material the patient supplies). This deprivation contributes considerably to an increase in the autonomy of the ego with regard to the external world, and a reduction of this autonomy with regard to the id, increasing its needs and dependence.

We know that analytical technique demands a reduction in contact with reality to allow the expressions of the id to reach consciousness. But, as Rapaport postulates, we do not know when the lack of stimuli will exceed the 'therapeutic regression necessary in the service of the ego and under its control', and when the situation will lead to a 'pathological regression'. How to obtain therapeutically effective insight, while at the same time keeping a certain control that will prevent a greater pathological regression, is one of the basic problems of psychotherapy.

Isolation, regression, and the *lack of communication* with the outside sometimes provoke a particular greed for the supply of external stimuli, and this explains, in such cases, the great attention the training analyst pays to the candidates during the *supervision sessions,* because for him they signify, on occasion, a real safety-valve, offering him the social contact he desires.

Here, however, I feel it opportune to make some further re-marks, for there are several implications involved in the process of supervision with candidates. As a rule, in view of what has been stated above, the analyst tends to behave in a more active and communicative manner with candidates coming for training than with his own analysands. This is obvious enough, and would not deserve mention, if it were not for the fact that this aspect of the two-person analyst–candidate relationship contains some special elements. I said earlier that through the specific conditions of his work, the analyst suffers a regression, which tends to increase his latent anxieties and his schizoid mechanisms, and consequently the division into good and bad objects. Thus in the analyst's phan-tasy the candidate may stand for another analyst belonging to a rival group. He may feel, for example, as already pointed out, the temptation to interpret the candidate's countertransference or to procure, consciously or unconsciously, a competitive situation with the training analyst through latent or manifest rivalry, fos-tering even more the dissociation that his own candidate some-times brings to the analysis. [This latter aspect of the problem of supervision in the analyst–candidate relationship and its many derivatives is excellently dealt with in the work by Arminda Aberastury, *La enseñanza del psicoanalisis* (1958), and also in Enrique Racker's work on countertransference (1958).]

This and other analogous considerations that may arise during a training session (a regular background for relations between analysts) mean that the analyst, if he wants to avoid being influ-enced by the corresponding affective substrate and falling into 'acting-out' attitudes, remains on the margin of all these situa-tions and, when supervising the candidate, retreats behind a neutrality similar, though not as extreme, to that which he uses when analysing patients. Thus in this activity also he will feel re-stricted in his need for communicative expansion.

This relates to his active participation; but it will sometimes be difficult for him to avoid feeling passively inclined to want to know and inquire into what is going on 'outside', with the other analysts, especially if the events he wants to learn about have some direct or indirect connection with himself.

This can, of course, happen in analyses too; and it cannot be denied that when the training analyst wants to know in detail the information that his candidate can supply about certain experiences he has had in meetings of the Association, seminars, study groups, and so on, this is not always due exclusively to the convenience of having available the greatest possible number of associations or phantasies with a view to interpreting the transference relationship better, but is sometimes the result of his own need for outside stimuli. Depending on the type and content of the anxieties that he has at that moment, he will be interested to know what climate exists 'outside' with regard to him: whether he is appreciated or criticized, and so on. In the classic question to the candidate: 'What did you think of me?' or 'How did you regard me at that meeting?' the latent wish is sometimes to know what the others felt about him, since at that moment the candidate represents the 'outside' and all his colleagues.

Another manifestation of the avidity for stimuli is related to the *genesis of rumours and their psychopathology*—in our circle, at least.

To begin with, both the spreader of the rumour and the one to whom he tells it, who is his counterpart, are reacting to a lack of communication and a feeling of isolation.

Whoever spreads a rumour is seeking to satisfy the part of himself that is eager to learn of current events and, by adding to it some elements from his own phantasy, he strives after a certain omnipotent control of the external situation from which he feels excluded.

In the paranoid content of his reaction there is the feeling of having been left out of certain subgroups, and he has to prove to himself and to others that this does not affect him, but that, on the contrary, he is up-to-date with all that goes on behind the scenes. Just as in the child there is an attempt to supplement with his phantasy and omnipotence his feeling of exclusion from the primal scene, so I consider that a similar process very often occurs in the adult. Moreover, owing to the setting of isolation and regression in which the analyst carries on his work, and through the increase of his paranoid anxieties, he will unconsciously feel that all those whom, as they are not present with him, he cannot control, are automatically and permanently living the primal scene. The one who receives the rumour, although he participates in a passive manner, presents similar mechanisms. He at once forms an alliance with his informant against the common enemy who has excluded them.

Another of the ways in which the analyst defends himself against his feelings of loneliness and deprivation is by resorting to his *phantasies of omnipotence and denial.* According to them he has no need to make an effort to communicate with the outside world in order to find out what has happened. He can feel like God, since, without moving from the throne (his chair), he can be everywhere through his analysands, who, like a sort of pseudopod (or antenna) link him with the 'outside', sharing with him all that has happened.

But these phantasies conceal exactly the opposite experience of isolation and lack of communication and sometimes an intense longing to 'go elsewhere' and join other circles.

It is to combat his feeling of loneliness and his anxieties, among other reasons, that the analyst feels the need to belong to some group. His ego requires to be strengthened and enlarged by other egos that will offer him support, share many of his preoccupations, and give him reassurance, albeit indirect, in moments of anxiety or weakness. Naturally enough, in addition to this need, there are other more authentic and valid reasons. The advantages of being together to study and explore certain problems, to discuss and exchange ideas, to investigate and develop theories, and so on, are grounds so real, solid, and positive that they do not require the support of further argument. I will only refer here to one of the motives for forming groups of which their members are not always fully conscious. Besides, even though within the sub-group conflicts similar to those of the large group may arise at any time or exist in latent form, it will be easier to set them aside or counteract them by the well-known mechanism of the common enemy or persecutor placed outside.

Although I cannot speak at great length on the structure and dynamics of these sub-groups, I should still like to say a few more words about them. Factors of different types may enter into their formation. For example, some groups are based on family connections (parents and siblings)—they maintain their family ties and so remain cohesive and loyal. Others are based on ideological affinities and the like.

I believe that one often requires that a certain ideology should be shared by others as an adequate form of reassurance. At other times, in so far as a certain ideology signifies an aspect of oneself, for example the good inner object that must be preserved, one seeks to contact those who share it so as to make up a strong group able to face those who maintain a different ideology.

It happens at times that the reaction to the reactivation of anxieties for the reasons described may be just the opposite. Instead of seeking the company of others, one tends towards *solitude* and *ostracism*. Without claiming to seek support in analogy with the attitude of 'flight to internal good objects' described by Melitta Schmideberg, this picture can give a fairly adequate idea of the latent meaning of this reaction. There may have been, at first, a feeling of frustration and disappointment that is added to the persecutory experience: the predominant emotions are rage, indignation, a feeling of having been betrayed; then, finally, the defensive response of withdrawal, of uniting with the idealized inner object and cutting off communication with others; one tries to prove that one can get along very well—or even better—without them, and one trusts that the final victory will prove one right. Secretly one hopes for reinstatement and indemnification for the unfair treatment and exclusion. [This should not be confused with the *capacity to be alone,* as set forth by Winnicott (1958b), where he explains the positive aspect of this situation.]

Privation and isolation will bring about an increase in the *feelings of envy and rivalry* that may pre-exist for various reasons. Melanie Klein's (1957) work suggests that the first envied object is the nourishing breast. This primitive envy is, in a sense, revived by the analyst during his seclusion, and unless it is counterbalanced by feelings of another type, it will invade his phantasies, giving them an aggressive content and directing them against his colleagues and their sundry activities; analyses, lectures, seminars, scientific papers, and so forth.

With regard to this, it usually happens that when we receive a work that is to be presented and discussed, almost simultaneously with the title we look at the last page, not so much to check the author's bibliography as to find out whether we are mentioned, whatever the subject of the work may be. It may be thought that this is due to pure narcissism on the part of the analyst, but if we go deeper we see that it is done in order to estimate, by the inclusion or exclusion of the analyst's work, what the author's affective evaluation of him may be. (How often does this fact, with other similar ones, influence the emotional frame of mind in which the work will be read and judged!)

The meagre attendance when scientific works are presented is not always due to lack of interest in them. It is, rather, an expression of the conflict situations mentioned above, since attendance or absence may in themselves be a judgement of the work. Sometimes only the author's friends are present, as a proof of loyalty and solidarity. Of course things do not always happen like this, but as such motives appear at times, it is only right to mention them.

This aggressive tendency may show itself in other circumstances too. But since at the same time the internal objects that are the counterpart of the external objects are also being attacked, the result will be a reduction in the capacity to bear anxiety, because there is no feeling of protection and positive stimuli from the inner world.

Denial and *idealization* will be used as more effective defences against persecution and envy. To these must be added *dissociation* as a means of preserving the good and idealized objects from the persecutory objects on to whom one has projected one's own capacity for aggression and destruction. This may be reflected, for example, in the analyst, in his seeking to relate himself to certain persons or groups with whose technical or theoretical principles he feels affinity, so that they thus become depositories of what he has idealized. Then he will necessarily place all that is evil or persecutory into the rival persons or groups, from whom he will try at all costs to keep separate so as to avoid the danger of the resulting integration and reintrojection of the rejected aspects.

I cannot give an exhaustive list of all the possible defences to which the analyst may have recourse in such circumstances, nor do I intend to do so; he may add, at any rate, the feeling of omnipotence and manic attitudes, to mention the mechanisms most commonly used. My essential purpose is to put special emphasis on all the situations included in the conflicts and defences I have described, and which everyone knows very well. The ultimate objective is to suggest some possible solutions that, even though they will not make the negative aspects of such relationships disappear once and for all, may help to disguise them and even—why not?—modify them and transform them into good relationships.

However, I should like to deal briefly with another important motivation that is of particular significance, closely bound up with some of the feelings mentioned above. *Guilt* felt by the analyst about his work may lead to reactions of various kinds. I refer here to the feeling caused by the experience of having failed in his need to make reparation and finding himself unable to cure his patient as he had hoped. In such circumstances it may happen that the analyst falls into a frank depression, or submits masochistically to the criticism of his superego and assumes attitudes that may well cause him serious difficulties in his relationships. On other occasions there will be a denial of his own guilt and its projection on to others whom he will criticize, at times harshly, for errors of technique that he ascribes to them or for theoretical concepts he deems erroneous. He will tend to underrate the activity and production of others, not only to defend himself against envy, but also to free himself from his own feeling of self-devaluation caused by his guilt feelings.

I must make it clear that I am deliberately leaving aside the whole of the positive and gratifying aspects of our work: all it implies as an expression of life, the capacity for sublimation, and the possibility of satisfying our reparative impulses. I am only concerned here with some of the conditions under which we perform our task, which, when they are present too intensely or too continuously, may produce negative effects. And though I have especially stressed the conflicting aspects of the relations between analysts, with the intention of pointing out some of their motivations and thus contributing to their elimination, this does not in the least mean that I deny the existence of good relations. I consider, on the contrary, without thereby implying any contradiction, that manifestations of solidarity, sympathetic understanding, comradeship, and loyalty are both frequent and profound. In so far as our colleagues are identified as members of the same family—the analytical family—we have positive feelings towards them like those we feel towards the primal imagos (parents and siblings). In this way the longing to make reparation and the libidinal attitudes arising from the depressive position continue in force with regard to our colleagues. I should like to recall here Melanie Klein's (1940) dictum that a good relationship with the world depends on our success in the struggle against inner chaos (the depressive position) and in firmly establishing good internal objects.

I think I should linger over this point for a moment. Freud described the happiness of feeding at the breast is the prototype of sexual gratification. According to M. Klein (1957), this experience is the basis not only of sexual gratification but of all later happiness and makes possible the feeling of unity with someone else: such unity means being fully understood, a fact that is essential in every friendship or happy love relationship. From this standpoint, drawing the corresponding parallel, I would say that it is not enough to know that one's analysis has been sufficiently long, since one is interested in its quality also. If one feels one has been well 'breast-fed' by one's analyst, with ample gratification, there will be firm grounds for feelings of gratitude, and consequently one will achieve better relations with other people.

M. Klein (1957) has particularly insisted on this aspect, pointing out that the experience of possessing a good inner object increases gratitude, which in its turn is closely connected with generosity. There is a feeling of inner wealth, and the subject feels able to share his gifts with others.

I have referred above to the need to suggest possible solutions to improve our relations. Freud has already pointed out that within the therapeutic process one of the first steps in the work of interpretation is to bring into the patient's consciousness what was unconscious in him. I believe this is implicit in our task. Perhaps we shall meet the almost foreseeable reaction in many of us that we knew all this. It is like one of the other results of therapeutic work, which Freud also pointed out, that after the period of resistance the patient ends by admitting that he knew what was interpreted to him . . . but does not add that he had repressed it and that now at last he is able to recognize it again.

As regards the ideas and motives I have dealt with in my work, I think it would be reasonable to act in some positive way against the effects of isolation and the lack of communication. It seems to me that one effective method would be to keep to certain rules of 'mental hygiene' that are of the highest preventive value. Thus, for example, I feel that, in view of the nature of our professional work, we ought to devote fewer hours to work with our patients under present conditions. This would be not only to our own benefit but also to theirs. Furthermore, it would be advantageous up to a certain point to have greater contact and communication with the 'outside' of the analytic and non-analytic environment. A gradual trend in this direction has been visible lately among our members, several of whom have been devoting themselves to courses, lectures, professorial chairs, hospital work, and so on. I do not know far these could be said to be ideal solutions. But without going so far as to consider the different possible motives for such activities, they do appear to respond to the need to establish greater compensatory communication.

It is my belief that in most of us there is a lack of capacity to integrate our work with so many other spheres of interest that are equally necessary and sometimes essential. I refer to the different expressions of culture, science, and art, moments of expansion, and, at the basis of everything, our family life. We feel, at times, that our work absorbs our energies absolutely and inexorably. But we cannot deceive ourselves; we know very well—as we should interpret to any analysand—that we allow ourselves to be absorbed, among other reasons, because it pleases us, because it gratifies many of our unconscious aspirations and impulses. But how often do we lament and complain that we cannot find time for the things we should like to do! Time then becomes our implacable persecutor, to whom we submit with all kinds of rationalization.

I am aware that the problem is far more complex and cannot be rounded off as easily as I am doing. I shall confine myself to enumerating some of the reasons implicit in its genesis: narcissistic satisfaction; the need to build up, maintain, or increase our prestige; rivalry and envy; the search for refuge in hard work so as to escape other conflicts; real or phantasized financial necessity; genuine gratifications, and so forth. The most likely thing is, of course, that several of these motivations appear in combination, in varying proportions.

The important thing would be to find where to draw the line and how to keep everything in proportion at every level of activity. If we claim a better life for our patients, it is only natural that we should allow ourselves to live better too and satisfy our own libidinal needs more fully.

On the other hand I would add that—to a certain degree—we need these other activities or their equivalents, since we cannot tolerate the uninterrupted impact of intense analytical activity. Freud pointed this out when he declared that we had to take temporary refuge in sleep because we could not stand without interruption the impacts and agitations of the outside world.

Another useful positive attitude is to communicate more fully and exchange ideas between the different groups, which would tend to decrease dissociation and foster association in the liberal sense of the word. Obviously we cannot agree on everything; it would be absurd to expect it, and it would not lead to good scientific development. But I do think it is essential to arrive at *a minimum of common elements* in our ideas and principles and in our respective positions, so as to consolidate the bonds that unite us.

PART THREE

Theoretical and clinical aspects of psychoanalysis

CHAPTER TWELVE

New ideas:
conflict and evolution

I n this chapter I hope to make a synthesis of the past, present, and future perspectives of psychoanalysis. I am mainly concerned with the problem of stagnation in the evolution of psychoanalysis, and my words are especially directed towards those analysts who are not fully aware of this stagnation and the reasons for it.

I lay stress essentially on how the prejudiced rejection of new ideas was and continues to be one of the greatest obstacles to the development of psychoanalysis. A dogmatic attitude and parochialism are pernicious factors attacking progress in analytical theory, hindering genuine communication between analysts and suffocating the possibility of bringing to light the still unexplored wealth of psychoanalysis.

This was originally written for the fiftieth anniversary number of the *International Journal,* in response to an invitation to consider the past and present development of psychoanalysis.

I take as a model of this conflict between the dogmatic faction and the innovators what has happened with the Kleinian theory, but it can be applied, without a shadow of doubt, to many other past and present experiences. On the other hand, I am convinced that the essence of the Kleinian theory, like many of Freud's concepts, still has the freshness, value, and vigour of new ideas and also possesses their most specific quality: that of promoting change.

I have based some ideas for the future of psychoanalytic investigation on the achievement of better communication between analysts of different trends of thought through a common denominator: clinical language.

Finally, I postulate that psychoanalysis—and we analysts—cannot remain in our ivory towers when faced with the problems of present-day society. I believe that we can do something: we can use the specific tools of our trade. In this I am optimistic. I believe that analysis can give considerable help, without falling into the omnipotent attitude that it can solve everything. I might say that 'what we do not know exceeds in many ways what we know, and what we know greatly exceeds what we apply'.

Despite its tremendous impact on mankind, paradoxically enough, it has not yet been possible to place and classify psychoanalysis within any of the existing fields of knowledge.

It is usually agreed that the cultural development of our century has been deeply influenced by three outstanding thinkers: Einstein, Marx, and Freud. The transcendence of their discoveries and of the revolution they have brought about in their respective areas is widely acknowledged. Einstein's theories resulted in a substantial change in modern space physics. Besides being a philosopher, Marx was the founder of scientific socialism, in which the interpretation of dialectic materialism is applied to the historical and economic processes of mankind. But whereas Einstein's contribution can easily be classified within the field of physics and mathematics, and that of Marx within a social, political, and economic ideology, doubts still arise as to the position to be assigned to the body of theories, hypotheses, and methods discovered and developed by Freud.

Among those authors who have dealt with this problem, some have concentrated their efforts on the scientific validation of the psychoanalytical theory (Brosin, 1955). Others have sought to include it within the domain of philosophy (Hook, 1959). Still others have held that it should be regarded as a new psychodynamic or mental science (Guntrip, 1967). There were also some who objected to considering psychoanalysis as a science (Home, 1966).

We may wonder whether it is worth trying to assign psychoanalysis to a place within any given scientific or humanistic discipline.

Personally, I do not think it is. Psychoanalysis is a unique phenomenon, resulting from a revolutionary discovery by a genius, and its very nature meant a drastic departure from existing frameworks. It became the most important instrument of investigation elaborated *by* the human mind to disclose the secrets *of* the human mind.

Freud himself never gave a precise definition of psychoanalysis. Instead, he referred to it as: (1) a procedure for the investigation of mental processes; (2) a method for the treatment of neurotic disorders; and (3) a collection of psychological information (1923 [1922]). Later Freud stated that psychoanalytic theory did not aim at the formulation of a *Weltanschauung* but should share the views of the common scientific world (1923a). As Brierley (1951) points out, Freud did not seem to be fully aware of the way in which his work as a whole challenged the old *Weltanschauung*.

A retrospective view of the evolution of psychoanalysis from the time of its birth up to the present raises this first question: what form did this evolution take? There was an outstanding development of its basic theories while Freud was alive. Granted certain exceptions, this was not the case after his death, particularly if one compares the slow rate of evolution of recent decades with that of the initial stages of psychoanalytical theory.

It was inevitable that at the beginning psychoanalysis should remain closely identified with its creator and that, on account of

Freud's exceptional qualities, a perspective free of such an absolute identification could be attained only with difficulty. In some cases this led to an excessively rigid and idealized adherence to Freud's ideas. One of the consequences of such a position was the attitude of rejection of new concepts, which were regarded as a threat to the whole body of theories accepted by many as unshakeable truth.

The need to stimulate differences of opinion, in order to further psychoanalytical development and to guarantee its vitality, has frequently been pointed out; but, at the same time, this praiseworthy purpose has been nullified by attitudes of plain refusal to accept new concepts. Again and again it has also been stated that uniformity provokes sterility and stagnation. Yet paradoxically enough the very people who acknowledged the validity of this fact raised serious obstacles to the development of hypotheses and theories other than those classically admitted. Obviously I am referring to new prospective theories that tend to foster development, and not to just any theory at all, distinguished only by novelty.

Emotional factors played an important role in this conflict between a more conservative attitude on the one hand, and innovation on the other; and occasionally they were the most influential elements in the serious controversies and schisms that occurred in certain psychoanalytical centres.

I should like to quote here a paragraph by Robert P. Knight (1954): '[Freud's] position as a pioneer investigator is completely secure, and has no need of being jealously guarded by "followers" who quote his hypotheses as dogma to squelch the "deviant" observations and hypotheses of "heretics". . . . We have no time to waste in building a stockade around sacred ground, erecting a statue to worship, and then conducting loyalty investigations within the stockade.'

This scientific and ideological subjection to superego fathers and 'arch-fathers' was strong enough to interfere with the assimilation of new concepts and to inhibit creative capacity. The danger of misusing the transference has not been sufficiently emphasized. It is possible that, consciously or unconsciously, undue advantage has been taken of transference, in order to transmit the 'tradition' to sons–candidates–students as an immutable and sacred treasure. Brierley (1951) pointed out that 'to expect to conserve the letter of all Freud's statements, as a kind of "Bible of Psycho-analysis" is to condemn psycho-analytic inquiry to stasis and, therefore, psycho-analysis as a science to death'.

The most useful model to illustrate this kind of phenomenon concerning new concepts is Bion's 'container–contained' model (1966). He says that 'from time to time men appear in history who are variously described as mystics or men of genius. . . . Mystics have appeared in all religions, at all times, in all places and in all centres of scientific discussion. . . . But I consider it also to be the function of the society to make the mystic or the messianic idea available to the members of the group. This is done by means of the laws (society), of the dogma (religion), and of the rules and laws (science). Bion proposes the popular term *Establishment* to designate the authorities upon whom have been bestowed the executive functions in the scientific or religious society, or in the State. Since the new idea usually has a revolutionary effect upon the environment, the 'Establishment' may fail in its attempt to adapt this idea suitably, and its reaction might be, among others, that of a 'container', which suffocates the 'contained new idea', which is regarded as potentially dangerous, and thus life is squeezed out of it.

What is a new concept or theory? To my mind, it is one that enables someone to approach a given problem from a different angle, which offers a new perspective. It is contemplating what is already known with different eyes to disclose unknown facets. Susanne Langer (1942) points out that '*A new idea is a light that illuminates presences which simply had no form for us before the light fell on them.* . . . They [the new ideas] are the terms in which theories are conceived; they give rise to specific questions, and are articulated only in the form of these questions. Therefore one may call them *generative ideas* in the history of thought (my italics).

Apart from their heuristic value, new ideas or theories should have, in my opinion, that quality of 'language of achievement' in the sense given to it by Keats in one of his letters (Forman, 1931). By 'language of achievement' he means that characterized by *penetration* through time and space. On the other hand, Keats also pointed out that this language depends on what he called 'negative capability'—namely, the capacity for 'being in uncertainties, mysteries, doubts, without any irritable reaching after fact and reason'.

Applying this statement to new concepts in psychoanalysis, I think that the capability to cope with uncertainties and half-truths without feeling compelled to undertake the irritating search for certainty helps the creative mind not only to produce new theories, but also to mould them flexibly and lastingly enough to avoid their premature saturation.

I should like to mention here Rickman's (1951) interesting classification of ideas: (1) *Horizon-moving ideas,* which alter the horizon of our thoughts. They are new and original ideas that 'spring from the deeper levels of the mental experience of their author and are a tremendous event for him and for the world of science'. (2) *Rearranging ideas,* which include the vast majority of the papers submitted to our societies: new applications are made of already known ideas, or new data are presented in support or modification of theories within the familiar field. (3) *Transplantation ideas,* which are a re-examination of our everyday material in the light of concepts employed in other disciplines. This category of ideas is usually contributed by the younger generation because they are more familiar with the constant process of change in the philosophy of science than are their psychoanalytical teachers.

It is also significant that it is precisely younger people who show greater receptivity to new ideas (see Rodrigué, 1969). Seemingly, closer analogies exist between their youth, revolutionary restlessness, and readiness for change and the parallel qualities involved in new concepts. Older generations, on the contrary, respond more cautiously, due, among other reasons, to their attempt to avoid mourning for the possible loss of 'old' theories that they have assimilated into their own identity.

I have mentioned above that the conflicts between conservatives and 'innovators' were not entirely due to ideological divergences, but also to emotional situations, the consequences of which became evident at the individual, group, and institutional levels.

Freud himself, and some of his early followers, could not escape this type of conflict. It was a sort of latent endemic disease, which would break out periodically in different milieux and contexts. During those confrontations between generations, there were some who felt compelled to perpetuate childhood rebelliousness and sought paternal images to rebel against, as well as 'fathers' who could not tolerate the growth and competitiveness of capable and talented 'sons' who threatened their position and prestige.

The influence of such experiences was most probably the reason why, years later, Freud (1937c) stated that not all of the analysts had reached the degree of psychic normality that they would expect from their patients, and that training analysis could not guarantee the persistence of the positive modifications achieved. For this reason, and as a preventive measure against the 'dangers of analysis', he proposed periodical re-analysis.

In the past (Grinberg, 1963) I have dealt with the vicissitudes of the relationships between analysts and their motivations. I said then that one should not minimize the difference between the dynamics of an analytical circle and those of any other scientific, social or working group.

Occasionally, conflicts may also arise between institutions themselves, due to ideological discrepancies or other disagreements. In this connection there was once discord between two psychoanalytical societies from the same locality, which for many years maintained the rivalry that had existed between the pioneer analysts, founders of their respective societies. They simply 'had to' keep the contentious tradition alive, like the Capulets and Montagues. But, as was to be expected, discrepancies were rationalized and found their concretion in scientific or ideological differences.

How did new ideas appear?

Freud's own discoveries and his constant readiness to revise and restate his theories were the factors that inspired and encouraged the setting out and the development of new ideas.

As Guntrip (1961) points out, Freud's early emphasis on instincts gave rise to an antithetical emphasis on sociological and cultural aspects. Notwithstanding, Guntrip adds that this shift in psychoanalytical thought had already occurred to a certain extent in Freud himself when he formulated the theory of the superego.

The immense value of Freud's work lies not only in the discovery of a new way of investigating the psyche, but also in the multiple and fruitful concepts whose validity has remained unaltered and which constitute the soundest basis of our theoretical and technical armoury. Nevertheless, Freud himself introduced modifications in his theories throughout his creative life. The most important were those after 1920, when he advanced the concept of 'repetition compulsion' and the principle of 'Nirvana'. He modified the theory of instincts, now polarized in life and death instincts, thus keeping closer to a biological model (1920g). In addition, he postulated his second theory of the psychic apparatus, based on the structural aspect: id, ego, and superego (1923b). Finally, a modification was introduced in the theory of anxiety, which became a function of the ego: a 'signal anxiety' (1926d).

In the following years other investigators were also mainly concerned with ego-analysis.

Anna Freud's contribution was, in this respect, of particular importance because of her systematic analysis of the defence mechanisms (1936). Her study of the ego influenced the significant shift that took place in the evolution of Freud's theories and the consolidation of the structural approach. Hartmann (1966) undertook further investigations into ego development and the problems of adaptation, formulating his well-known concepts of primary and secondary autonomies. Rapaport, Erikson and Kris each contributed new ideas, some of which dealt with thought (Rapaport, 1950), affects (Rapaport, 1953), ego-epigenesis and its psychic and social evolution (Erikson, 1950) and 'regression in the service of the ego' (Kris, 1938). Hartmann et al. (1946) critically analysed the formation of the psychic structure as postulated by Freud from 1923 on, disagreeing with some of his views concerning the three substructures, id, ego, and superego, and the genesis of the ego.

The above-mentioned revisions and modifications introduced into Freud's work were generally accepted within the body of hypotheses that constitute ego psychology. However, other objections to some of Freud's metapsychological concepts were not so widely accepted, in spite of their being formulated by analysts of diverse psychoanalytical communities. For instance, Freud's emphasis on a quantitative approach to psychic phenomena became the target of criticism by several authors, among whom I may mention G. S. Klein (1966), Baranger (1968), Guntrip (1967), and Home (1966).

The pleasure principle was regarded by some not as a psychological concept but as a physiological and mechanistic theory that considered the mind as an apparatus in which facts were automatically regulated. As G. Klein (1966) insisted, Freud's metapsychology was rather a theory as to *how* a process operates, seeking a neurophysiological basis, than a theory of *why* a process operates. Baranger (1968) has also pointed out the inconsistency of Freud's economic point of view with the rest of his psychological concepts. But these criticisms found no response.

Further new ideas, involving wider modifications and developments of the Freudian theory, gave rise to serious controversies and to attitudes of frank rejection, as in the case of Melanie Klein's concepts.

Child analysis was the cornerstone of the development of quite a number of new concepts. Once more, it was Freud's merit to introduce the new perspective of child analysis with Little Hans (1909b). However, starting in 1920, Hug-Hellmuth (1921), Anna Freud (1927), and Melanie Klein (1921) were the pioneers of the analytical treatment of children. Melanie Klein's well-known 'play technique' was a revolutionary innovation in child analysis (1923, 1929).

There are two reasons why I shall give special consideration to the phenomenon of the singular impact of Kleinian theories: (1) To my mind, they form the most important and transcendent polemic of the last 30 years; this was clearly shown after the series of controversial discussions held in 1943 (see British Psycho-Analytical Society, 1967) significantly only four years after Freud's death. (2) In recent years I myself have been a direct witness, at international congresses and scientific meetings, of many discordant attitudes that often involved emotional factors.

Melanie Klein's concepts dealt especially with the first stages of ego-development and the existence of object relations from the beginning of life; with the importance of anxiety and aggression, based on the functioning of the death instinct within the organism; with the postulate of two fundamental stages in development (with their corresponding paranoid–schizoid and depressive positions); with the earlier dating of the superego and the Oedipus complex; and with the notion of internal objects. She placed special emphasis on the functioning of primitive defence mechanisms, particularly of projective identification, and on the significance of the concept of the reparation of damaged objects as the essential element of the depressive position. She stressed the importance of envy, innate sadism, and primary masochism, resulting from the functioning of the death instinct (1932, 1946, 1957).

Although Kleinian concepts fall within the category of new and fertile psychoanalytical ideas and constitute a real development of many of Freud's theories, her postulates aroused strong reactions, which resulted in the formation of two factions: followers and detractors.

The problem of accepting or rejecting her work still exists, not only within the British Society, but in all psychoanalytical communities. Paradoxically, Melanie Klein was criticized not only for her supposed detachment from Freud's ideas, but also for her excessive adherence to some of his theories, as for instance the death instinct, which many Freudian analysts reject. I think that the intolerance and violent criticism of her ideas and those of her followers make manifest the prejudice and emotional tensions involved in such criticism.

On the other hand, the group of Kleinian analysts, most probably as a reaction, assumed an attitude of 'counter-dogma', which in turn gave rise to further difficulties. As a consequence of this, they held off from closer contact with non-Kleinian analysts and took no interest in their scientific production. I was able to ascertain in some of their representatives an intransigence similar to that of many of their detractors.

This confrontation between dogma and counter-dogma is, in this case, an example of how the 'Establishment' failed in its attempt adequately to contain a new idea so as to facilitate its development and its incorporation into existing theories. This contributed to the increasing divergency, the lack of communication between analysts, and the obstacles that were put in the way of the development of psychoanalysis.

Nevertheless, and in spite of the rigid attitude on the part of certain psychoanalytical groups who adhere to the letter of Freud's theories rather than to his spirit, we have been favoured with various valuable and original contributions from investigators who have complemented, modified or developed those hypotheses that called for revision, or those that Freud indicated as points of departure.

Let us now consider the present.

It is not difficult to outline a geographical and ideological map featuring the different currents of today's psychoanalytical thought. These trends would correspond to three principal psychoanalytical communities: (1) the European community, comprising the Continental and British analysts—the latter, in turn, split into a 'Freudian' group and a 'Kleinian' group; (2) the American community, and (3) the Latin-American community.

This is, of course, only a rough-and-ready outline, since representatives of diverse ideologies do exist in each community. Quite a number of common views are shared by most European and American analysts; their basic theoretical and technical concepts are practically the same. Nevertheless, there might be European analysts who do not feel fully identified with the followers of ego psychology, although their views may coincide with many of its principles. And they would be right, since some of their approaches vary. Likewise, most Latin-American analysts, although basically accepting the most important theories of Melanie Klein, have also incorporated elements of ego psychology and, moreover, present original and differentiated aspects in their scientific productions, which give them a specific identity.

Each analytical community characteristically adopts frames of reference based on different ideological conceptions. It might be inferred that such differences are the logical outcome of the evolution of the psychoanalytical movement in each country or continent, as well as of the cultural and social influence of the respective environments. Nevertheless, such an explanation is not fully convincing, particularly if one considers that in spite of common cultural and historical factors, two groups have been formed in England sufficiently extreme to split the British Society practically in two, although a formal separation has not occurred. Neither would the confrontation of scientific arguments account in itself for such sharp antagonisms. Once more, the reasons should be sought in emotional and personal conflicts.

Again, each regional group regards itself as possessing the truth and having 'better and more authentic' knowledge, rejecting the other group's theories as erroneous and lacking a scientific basis. Should not doubts be awakened merely by the fact that a given discipline is developed according to certain canons valid *only* for those who live between its geographical and/or ideological boundaries? To illustrate this, I should like to mention a fact that is well known in the analytical world—namely, that the great majority of American analysts firmly support the concepts of ego psychology, whilst most Latin-Americans are followers of Melanie Klein's ideas. Does the same phenomenon occur in other scientific fields? Perhaps it does, but certainly not to the same extent. I doubt that South African doctors apply surgical techniques that are sufficiently different from those of Australian surgeons as to be given labels equivalent to 'Freudians' and 'Kleinians'. Nor do I think that they reject systematically other techniques or theories from different sources, as happens in the psychoanalytical field. They will at least study, try out, and test such techniques in order to decide finally whether they should be accepted or rejected. In any case, although there may be individual or group differences, they will not weigh upon the identifying features of the Australian or South African surgical community *as a whole*. [I realize that by the nature of this example I am simplifying the issue, but the main argument remains.] The influence of transference upon the maintenance of analytical ideologies may be another of the factors that determine that such a phenomenon occurs with greater intensity among analysts.

We must pay rather a high price for adhering too strictly to our ideological partisanship: we run the risk of lack of communication between analysts, in spite of the frequent congresses, panels, and symposia held at an international level. It would seem that occasionally dialogue is established, but in one direction only: one speaks but does not listen. This difficulty in overcoming past theoretical discrepancies and achieving adequate comprehension and assimilation of the different expressions in psychoanalytical thought will inevitably lead to stagnation. The possibility of opening up new vitalizing fields is thus hindered.

However, a fruitful dialogue was established upon certain occasions. In this respect I wish to refer now to some conclusions drawn from my own personal experience. Thus, for instance, a positive balance has resulted from the sequence of three first Pan-American Psycho-analytic Congresses that have been held.

It is true that at the first Congress the participants fell into two opposing camps, and a sterile confrontation followed, which produced a reply, but certainly no dialogue (Litman, 1966).

The fact that was most often resented by Latin-American analysts was the *a priori* attitude of American colleagues, who obstinately rejected their concepts with stereotyped criticisms such as 'premature interpretations', 'extremely regressive or non-analysable patients', 'excessive emphasis on the inner world and on unconscious phantasies', 'excessive use of transference interpretations', 'wrong conception of the psychic life of the newborn', and so on. Nor were Latin-American analysts free from prejudice. They complained that their American colleagues practised 'superficial analysis', that they 'seemed to be unaware of the value of transference', that they 'took only the external reality into account', that they 'questioned the existence of psychic life in children under two', that they 'seemed to reduce everything exclusively to the oedipal conflict', that they 'disregarded the dynamics of the transference–countertransferance relationship', and so forth.

I must admit I had my doubts about including these remarks, which, while (almost) absent from the papers, circulated freely in the Congress corridors. It was the desire to transmit *in vivo* the atmosphere in which that experience took place that led me to do so.

There was a significant improvement at the second Congress (Grinberg et al., 1968): expositions were made at a higher level of mutual respect, and the participants who submitted their papers made use, explicitly or implicitly, of their respective frames of reference on a sounder basis. There was an even more evident rapprochement at the third Congress, especially during the discussions and exchange of ideas resulting from the consideration of clinical papers. Significantly, on that occasion both groups realized—perhaps for the first time—that they were speaking the same language, namely a language based on clinical experience.

Since, in my opinion, Latin-American analysts are less known than their colleagues at an international level, I wish to deal with certain aspects that determine their scientific characteristics as a group.

The image of the Latin-American group is that of a younger community, one that shows a remarkable rate of growth. Because of its geographical site, as well as for historical reasons, the source of its analytical knowledge is both Europe (particularly England) and the United States. In its theoretical and technical approaches it has basically made use of Freud's most important theories and, at the same time, has not unsuccessfully integrated the fundamental ideas of Kleinian theory with concepts of ego-psychology.

If I wished to indicate any distinctive theory held by Latin-American psychoanalysts, I should mention the specific concept of *countertransference as a technical instrument*. I think it is worth while to include here a brief account of the way in which the evolution and incorporation of this concept took place in the theoretical and technical work of Latin-American analysts, particularly as it stood as a polemic issue *par excellence* at a number of congresses and scientific meetings and, in addition, falls within the category of controversial 'new ideas and theories'.

Formulated by Freud for the first time in 1910, the concept of countertransference has since been regarded by most analysts as a symptom corresponding to the analyst's own pathology. The use of countertransference as a technical instrument has had a significant historical evolution. It appeared almost simultaneously in London and in Buenos Aires. Racker (1953a) and Heimann (1950) were those who established the basis of its application. Racker, of Buenos Aires, contributed the most systematic and fertile study on this topic. He considered countertransference as the whole of the psychic and emotional reactions of the analyst to his patient's transference. He also regarded countertransference neurosis as a pathological expression involving the analyst's neurotic response to his patient's transference neurosis, in agreement with the classical criterion as far as this respect is concerned. In addition, he dealt particularly with the psychoanalytical attitude of *comprehension* towards the patient, based on conscious countertransferential feelings. That is to say, the analyst increases his therapeutic capacity by utilizing countertransference, which is transformed into a useful instrument for detecting, comprehending and interpreting the patient's conflicts (Racker, 1957).

Let me add now, to round off this conceptual and technical panorama that is specifically characteristic of Latin-American analysts, that their mode of work can be summarized in the following statement by Baranger and Baranger (1961) in connection with *the analytic situation as a dynamic field*: 'The analytic situation is that of two people infallibly linked and complementary . . . or involved in the same dynamic process. Neither of the two is intelligible in the situation without the other. . . . This is precisely the meaning conveyed by the opportune recommendation to utilize countertransference as a technical instrument.' [Other important research work developed by Latin-American analysts dealt with psychosomatic medicine, foetal psychism, mourning and depression, dreams, filicide, communication, lethargy, psychotic mechanisms, symbiosis, female sexuality, phobias, symbolism, acting out, research in child analysis, free association and words, etc.]

To my mind, the concept of countertransference is *a border and a bridge between the clinical and theoretical aspects*. It has the advantage of stimulating observation of what happens in the analyst–patient relationship, by detecting the latter's unconscious phantasies with their corresponding emotional content, by means of the analyst's own emotional reactions. Thus theoretical conclusions may be drawn from the data obtained through observation, which may be corroborated by the material observed in subsequent clinical experiences.

This emphasis on the clinical and theoretical aspects increases the possibilities of a greater *exchange of ideas* on a more objective and fertile basis.

Up to this point it has been my purpose to present a panoramic view of past psychoanalytic development, whith the principal modifications introduced into some fundamental hypotheses, the objections to certain aspects of metapsychology, the rejection of new theories and the heated controversies this gave rise to, with their corresponding emotional content. I then touched on the present situation, according to the geographical and ideological distribution of analytical communities, emphasizing the specific characteristics of Latin-American analysts.

I shall now attempt to develop some ideas as to the future of psychoanalysis. For the sake of consistency, I shall try to deal especially with the conditions required for improved exchange between analysts of different trends, and for more fruitful investigation.

Theoretical divergences have almost inevitably caused trouble. I believe that in future much of this could be avoided and opposing concepts reconciled, if the following propositions were kept in mind:

1. acceptance of priority for *a common clinical denominator (clinical language)* on the basis of psychoanalytical clinical experience, which, according to G. S. Klein (1966), may be regarded as a theory in itself;

2. less strict adherence to psychoanalytical theories, in order to diminish their rigidity and dogmatism, and give them greater flexibility, thus making possible their wider application;

3. reduction of theories to a suitable minimum number, as Bion (1962) proposed, so that these few may be applied to a wide variety of situations;

4. setting up research teams of analysts with different frames of reference to study the means of tapping the latent unexplored wealth of psychoanalysis to the full.

I feel sure that if these proposals were followed through, it would lead to a genuine interchange among analysts at a deeper level of communication, which in turn would greatly stimulate psychoanalytical investigation.

G. S. Klein, in his very thought-provoking paper 'Perspectives of change in psycho-analytical theory' (1966), states that the opinion, widespread among analysts, that clinical concepts are descriptive rather than theoretical, is erroneous and harmful for the future development of psychoanalysis. According to him, 'the clinical concepts are, hopefully, more responsive to pressures imposed by data and hence potentially more capable of systematic modification. Moreover, being a theory of man's behaviour and experience, *the clinical concepts are a general theory of behaviour,* no less than metapsychology' (my italics).

He also holds that within clinical theory, a distinction can be made between experiential or intraphenomenological concepts, based on data inferred by the analyst during the analytical session, and extraphenomenological concepts that illuminate and elucidate the meaning of such experience. The strategy of inferring from clinical data until laws have been formulated is regarded by G. Klein as essential.

Similarly, Bion (1968) has also insisted on the importance of clinical observation as the basis for psychoanalytical development. In his opinion the 50 minutes of an ordinary session are extremely valuable, since this space of time is the only chance the analyst has of obtaining the necessary material directly. By comparison, nothing else is so important; hence theory would be subject to clinical observation.

Clinical language—that which conveys the experience with a patient—usually underlies meaningful communication between analysts. It has the advantage of having factors in common that enable each interlocutor to acknowledge the subject that is being discussed, to imagine the situation and to place himself in it, regardless of whether or not he agrees with the other party's views.

To illustrate this point, I should like to mention a personal episode that enabled me to ascertain that, at an international congress, clinical language found greater receptivity and comprehension than theoretical conceptualizations. It happened when I presented my official paper 'On acting out and its role in the psycho-analytical process' (Grinberg, 1968). After the paper was read, some of those participating in the official discussion, as well as members of the different discussion groups, focussed their attention mainly on clinical aspects, of which they seemed to have a better grasp than of theoretical ones. So for example, from one of the groups whose members had different frames of reference from my own, V. Calef stated: 'Dr Moore [1968] thereby reconciles his definition . . . with Grinberg's discussion, showing that Grinberg's [clinical] description uses body function as a model for psychic functioning. Moore's opinion is that what was corrected by the therapy of Grinberg's patient was a ready tendency to displacement. Moore agreed with Grinberg's emphasis that an object-relationship is indispensable for acting out. Though Moore wishes to differentiate between acting out and psychosomatic states as well as dreams-while-waking (which were all brought in relationship to each other in Grinberg's paper), *he finds ways of translating* Bion's and Grinberg's ideas about the need for an object, the need for projection and finding a so-called container, *into his own* concepts about object need, individuation, and identity *as similar and compatible concepts*' (V. Calef, 1968, p. 226; my italics).

Bion (1962) has also emphasized the advantages of working with the least possible number of fundamental psychoanalytical theories, sufficiently abstract to allow greater generalization, wide enough to cover the different problems that may be encountered during the analytic process. He further says that it may be helpful for the analyst to build up models that enable one to maintain the structure of psychoanalytical theory and that are sufficiently flexible to be applied to diverse situations in psycho-analytical practice. A model fulfils a very important function, so long as it is regarded as such. It is transient and in this respect differs from theory. As soon as it has succeeded or failed in its purpose, it can be discarded. The advantage of a model (be it biological, mathematical, physical, etc.) lies in its enabling inves-tigation to go forward.

In a recent contribution J. Sandler and W. G. Joffe (1969) propose precisely a 'basic psychoanalytic model' whose aim is to clarify diverse psychoanalytical concepts and, at the same time, to give concrete form to a frame of reference. Among other things, it represents a kind of unifying scheme that allows the reciprocal linking of different concepts or models and stimulates new for-mulations and further developments. A sentence by Rapaport (1951), quoted in this paper, may well be included here: 'The disagreements between model makers dwarf all their agreements except one: *that model making is necessary*' (my italics).

Freud himself used provisional models on which to develop his fertile ideas on the functioning of the psyche. He developed his models until they could be replaced by more adequate ones.

In my opinion, using few theories and complementary models stimulates the analyst to more creative thinking in situations that occur in his practice. Moreover, the fact of working with a mini-mum of psychoanalytic theories will counteract the widespread tendency to create new *ad hoc* theories and sub-theories. It also stands as a sort of barrier against the danger of chaos in scientific communications between analysts. The Babel myth describes how man, in his desire to reach heaven and to acquire knowledge, was punished by the destruction of the integrity of his language, since a common language bestowed on him the capacity for reciprocal co-operation. As integrity was destroyed, each fragment became a new language: confusion prevailed, and the different groups were dispersed.

Both Bion and G. Klein oppose the principle of causality, which asserts that a phenomenon Y must originate in a cause X, and point out that the problem is one of *relations* rather than of cause and effect.

Very significant is the fact that two psychoanalysts of such different analytic trends of thought share essential views in their respective approaches. These common elements are: (1) the priority assigned to clinical experience, which they consider as a theory in itself (G. Klein's 'clinical theory'; Bion's 'theory of observation'), and (2) the advantage of handling a limited number of subsidiary theories to elucidate clinical facts. Their respective theories may differ in formulation and content, but their goals are similar.

The possibility that representatives of different theoretical trends could perform joint research work, on the basis of common elements (clinical–theoretical common denominator) is more feasible than is usually assumed. Moreover, I think that once intransigence, prejudice, and ideological partisanship have been overcome, the multiple advantages of working together *for relatively long periods* will be truly appreciated. There will be mutual stimulus as the result of considering different approaches and perspectives; profitable reviewing and restatement of respective frames of reference will be encouraged by constructive criticism, conferring pristine freshness on many concepts already 'worn out' by use and routine. However, in my opinion, the most important aspect is the possibility of finding new lines of investigation. (We have had some experience of this in workshops at a number of congresses, and in small discussion groups, for instance at the pre-congress conferences on training).

In line with the fourth proposition suggested at the beginning of this section, means should be sought to enable representatives of different analytic trends of thought to contact each other more frequently and for longer periods, at scientific meetings scheduled on a more systematic and continuous plan. In this connection, I think the International Psycho-analytical Association has recently adopted a very positive initiative as regards the functioning of seminars and permanent study groups at international levels, integrated by analysis from diverse latitudes.

I should like now to give some views on the position of psycho-analysis in relation to the social and cultural problems of our time.

To my mind, the valuable knowledge that may still be derived from psychoanalytical investigation is far from being exhausted. In fact, what we do not know far exceeds what we do know, and what we know outweighs what we apply. If we acknowledge the existence of such potentialities, we should make every possible effort towards their accomplishment, not only for the sake of psychoanalytical theory and practice, but also for their application in extra-analytical fields.

Faced with the increase of anxieties characteristic of the space era, of group tensions, racial prejudice, class confrontation, violent repression of juvenile rebellion, juvenile delinquency, waves of crimes and suicides, and, fundamentally, war in all its aspects, what is the role assigned to analysts? Some emphasize the danger involved in detaching ourselves from our specific field, the analyt-ical situation, and remind us of the risk of losing our scientific integrity and the relatively minor value of expanding our know-ledge into the social field.

On the other hand, others point out that one of the greatest hopes for the future of mankind lies in the continuous and ever wider application of psychoanalytic comprehension to the com-plexities of the human mind and its contradictions. In this respect they hold analysts' contributions to be unique and essential. [J. Bleger (1958) points out: 'the problem of the intellectual and the sci-entist beckoned and challenged by a social and political reality into which he is drawn by conscience and the responsibility of a citizen and a thinker to participate and reform; and on the other hand needing to keep a certain distance from immediate and day-to-day facts, dealt with strictly by method, not in order to shut his eyes to reality and ignore it, but precisely the contrary, to investigate it and deal with it in its true historical and scientific perspective.']

Confronted with such a dilemma, I prefer to pause for reflection. Maxwell Gitelson's (1963a) words come to mind: he advised mod-esty when faced with the impulse towards excessive therapeutic ambition that tempts us to reach out into the social field under the pressure of the conditions of our era. But at the same time I realize that he was actually referring to the unconscious repercussion of collective anxieties that may give rise in us to anxiety and guilt-feelings. (Gitelson mentions the well-known sequel to the making of the atom bomb: the re-awakening of the scientists' social conscience). He added that his call to modesty—which was also a call to self-respect—'should not leave us with the impression that we should adhere to the *status quo*. The self-respect of which I have spoken is the security of knowing and accepting intrinsic potentialities and limitations'.

In this sense, and so as not to cling to the *status quo,* we should explore to a greater depth both our potentialities and our limitations and seek a fruitful way to apply the former.

In connection with the role of psychoanalysis in our culture, Meltzer (1968) points out that, from the standpoint of its historical context, 'we may have unwittingly involved ourselves in a revolution . . . and we should be prepared for it and recognise its implications'. Meltzer has recently studied a certain aspect of anxiety, namely terror, which is manifested in the form of tyranny in the individual's perversions and addictions. But he extended this concept to cover the social context and considered tyranny as a specific social phenomenon. In his view, 'the apparently unending proliferation of tyrannical modes of social relationships seems to be the equivalent in social relationships of perversions in sexual activity'. He therefore holds that our contribution to the solution of cultural problems should be an understanding of the anxieties that hold sway over people and their cultures, and the practical methods for diminishing these anxieties. He finally adds: 'if that is so, we are under an obligation to *do something* about it' (my italics).

It is then legitimate to speak of the psychopathology of society when it appears with negative characteristics that are both cause and consequence of serious disturbances in object-bonds between individuals. Sometimes society sets up superego-type standards to which it subjects people in a strict and violent way. On occasions, a certain 'progress' of civilization and culture has the paradoxical effect of unleashing regressive processes that lead to greater isolation of the individual and a gradual loss of the capacities of his ego. Society can act against its members in such a negative way that it restricts every kind of aspiration, increasing frustration and anxiety. The tenacity with which certain societies cling to rigidly conservative standards, not tolerating change or evolution, reveals the existence of sick elements leading to actions and defences that are also pathological.

If we considered carefully the painful panorama unleashed by the problem of war and the increase of aggression and violence, we should feel that the urge to do something about it is fully justified. But as analysts, all we can do is to study these phenomena as deeply as possible, throw light on their motives and the roots of their underlying anxieties, and also consider our role and our ideology in this respect. I have not the slightest doubt that ideology is an important part of every analyst's countertransference. [In her article, 'Analysis in the year 2000', M. Langer (1968) deals with different aspects related to the future of analysis. She mentions among other things the concept of anomia applied to the field of analysis and specifically related to civic and political convictions. 'Many of us', adds Dr Langer, 'cannot integrate our political conscience with our scientific knowledge, nor with our everyday professional work'. She quotes various contributions on the subject of integration which in their time aroused much interest and then were left to one side: that of J. Bleger in his book, *Psycho-analysis and Materialist Dialectics* (1958), the research carried out at institutional level by R. Serebriany et al. originating in the Symposium on Antisemitism (1963), and W. Baranger's article on 'Interpretation and ideology' (1957), in which he discusses the rule of ideological abstention on the part of the analyst. We have to recognize that society acts as a mother–container that has not been able to contain nor metabolize the growing anxiety underlying all protest and youth movements. These must also be understood as an alarm signal and sometimes, under the surface, as a cry for help.

It is significant that more than thirty years ago Einstein (see Freud, 1933b [1932]), wrote to Freud in an effort to discover the means of setting humanity free from the 'curse' of war. His genius enabled him to perceive distinctly the existence of those powerful psychological factors that invalidated any attempt to eliminate the mutual destruction of mankind. He ventured the following explanation: 'Only one answer is possible: Because man has within him a lust for hatred and destruction. In normal times this passion exists in a latent state; it emerges only in unusual circumstances, but it is a comparatively easy task to call it into play and raise it to the power of collective psychosis. Here lies, perhaps, the crux of all the complex factors we are considering, an enigma that only the expert in the lore of human instincts can solve.'

Freud could not help but admire Einstein's keen intuition, which anticipated a great deal of what Freud himself had to say on this subject. His well-known reply, 'Why war?' (1933b [1932]), summed up the conclusions of a former paper, 'Thoughts for the times on war and death'. Freud felt discouraged and pessimistic with regard to war, which then seemed even more implacable than in the past; and he admitted he was unable to propose any practical and immediate solution to bring it to an end. But he added that perhaps it would not be an entirely utopian hope that the 'cultural process' and the logical fear of the consequences of a future armed conflict (which would threaten total destruction) might eliminate wars.

Both Einstein and Freud opened up unsuspected paths for investigation in their respective fields. Teams of physicists pooled their efforts and knowledge to further the developments started by Einstein. Why should teams of analysts not be formed to continue the research suggested by Freud into territory as yet unexplored?

We carry the desire for reparation within our vocational choice. Although the therapeutic goal may be narrower, or different from what it was conceived to be years ago, the curing of ills has not been eliminated from our specific task. In my opinion, such a desire manifests itself not only towards the individual, but also towards society, which we unconsciously regard as an extension of our own family.

Einstein stands as a symbol of what at the present time is the hopeful claim of so many who seek help from psychoanalysis. Nothing could be more appropriate to the assumption of our responsibility than to set up teams specifically for this purpose, made up of analysts who can each contribute with his own approach. This would be the best way to bring together the analytic knowledge that is at present so widely scattered and to resolve not only the psychic disturbances of the individual, but also the mad and desperate behaviour of society today. Psychoanalysis, by its very essence and its objectives, does not reject but rather integrates the social dimension in the life of mankind.

CHAPTER THIRTEEN

The 'razor's edge'
in depression and mourning

I n this chapter I am attempting to pinpoint the most salient aspects of the painful feelings that are grouped together under the term 'depression', and also feelings of mourning for a lost object and of mourning for the parts of one's own self involved in this loss.

In certain forms of depression the individual feels that he cannot satisfy the demands of his ego-ideal. He then has recourse to omnipotence and megalomania as attempts to counteract his depression. In such cases there may be sudden changes from depressive to manic states and vice versa, giving rise to the phenomenon I have called the 'razor's edge'. On other occasions the depressive emotions are mixed with feelings of persecution. The patients usually experience rather abrupt emotional changes, moving rapidly from deep sadness to feelings of persecution, hostility, and an excessively critical attitude, which may surprise the analyst and cause sudden changes in his own counter-transference reactions. This shows the narrowness of the intermediate zone between different types of feeling; it is as narrow as a 'razor's edge'. Something similar may occur with the abrupt changes between different modes of mental functioning, such as those of the 'psychotic personality' and those of the 'neurotic personality', as can be seen in borderline patients.

In these patients there is a marked intolerance of the absence of the object, the lack of meaning, and the psychical suffering. This intolerance is due to childhood experience of losing the mother, either by real absence or by the failure of the mother to give back in a mitigated form the painful affects projected by the child. They then bring into play different defensive operations to neutralize psychological pain, among which are splitting and pathological projective identification, acting out, omnipotent control, omniscience, 'reversal of perspective', conversion hysteria, and so forth.

I am also concerned with creative experiences based on the working out of depressive phantasies and painful feelings that attempt to restore the object and the damaged parts of the self. I believe that the act of creation is the result of a process during which the individual has inevitably to pass through states of temporary 'disorganization' and the breaking of his acquired structures and links, with transient blurring of the limits of the ego; then he will reintegrate himself and 'organize' himself in a different way, from which the created product will emerge.

Depression usually means a set of painful emotions and concomitant thoughts with which the individual responds to experiences of loss or failure of achievement. It may form part of what we know as the psychopathology of everyday life, giving rise to what I have described as 'microdepression' or 'micromourning' (Grinberg, 1963a) or, due to the intensity of its manifestations, it may turn into a long and severe illness.

The problem of painful emotions (including different types of guilt feelings), together with mourning for object-loss and the loss of the parts of the self involved with the object, the experience of change, triggering off depressive reactions, and the rallying of specific defences against pain and psychic suffering, sometimes shaping the phenomenon I have called the 'razor's edge', are the main aspects with which I try to deal in this chapter.

Depression is closely related to the concept of mourning as part of the psychopathological process triggered off in the individual by the loss of a loved object. But in my opinion this loss implies, for the person who suffers it, the need to face at the same time the threat of loss of the ego-functions the ego and the parts of the self linked with the lost object.

I think that, in the well-known account by Freud (1920g) of the little boy and the wooden reel, with its corollary the mirror game, the child was expressing the relationship between the disappearance of the object and the disappearance of his own reflection; they are co-existing aspects of the same phenomenon. My hypothesis is that the temporary or permanent loss of an object causes in the individual a painful feeling that he has lost at the same time something of himself. The child's game with its two scenes, the reel and the mirror, is in my opinion a vivid dramatization of what happens in every kind of mourning: in other words, and as I have maintained in various works (Grinberg, 1963a), faced with an object-loss 'one rushes to the mirror' to check what has happened to one's own image. For this reason I suggested several years ago that in every significant experience of object-loss we should take into account not only mourning for the object but also mourning for the lost parts of the self (Grinberg, 1963a).

Depression does not consist of a single emotion, but embraces a group of complex and painful manifestations unleashed by the meaning or 'meaninglessness' that the experience of loss may have for each individual. Every loss, either of an object or of aspects of the ego, may bring with it the feeling that the fulfilment of the wish to recover the loss is impossible. This depressive feeling entails the failure of love for oneself, or narcissistic love, which is accompanied by feelings of deprivation, helplessness, and the collapse of self-esteem, thus causing a 'narcissistic wound'. When this happens, the development of love for the object is disturbed. Instead, hostility and guilt rise up against the object and against one's own ego. This causes a vicious circle in which both currents of hate and guilt, against the object and the self, respectively, feed each other and sometimes give rise to 'no-exit situations' or 'closed systems'.

The narcissistic collapse resulting from the loss of the valued self-image, which is close to the ego-ideal, produces a painful state, sometimes felt as an actual disaster.

In narcissistic depression, the subject feels that he cannot fulfil the aspirations of his ego-ideal, which means he cannot ensure his self-esteem and simultaneously loses the love and respect of the object. As a defence there may be an increase in the pathological infantile narcissistic organization reinforced by omnipotent and destructive aspects of the self that attack every libidinal link with the object and tend to make it appear worthless. Furthermore, the breakdown of omnipotence usually unleashes in its turn painful feelings that are hard to bear.

We know of the existence of a normal useful narcissism, based on healthy self-love, which facilitates the development of healthy object-love and involves psychic and somatic protection. In this type of narcissism the ego shows the ability to gratify and be gratified, and to repair and work through mourning for objects and for the lost parts of the self. On the other hand there is a type of narcissism that is like a pathological organization in which envy and aggression against the object and against the self predominate, and whose reinforcement depends on the family's attitude to the child. When this attitude is mainly negative, the narcissistic wound is deepened, and the pathology is intensified, with a decline in self-esteem, the appearance of depressive and persecutory emotions, humiliation, denigration, and helplessness, which the child tries to counteract with omnipotence and megalomania. In such circumstances there may be sudden shifts from depressive states to the manifestations of megalomania or vice versa, giving rise to the picture I have described as the 'razor's edge'—the rapid change from one situation to another.

Depressive personalities show a marked intolerance to frustration, separation, loss, and experience of change in general.

The ability to go on feeling the same person throughout successive changes is an important factor in the working through of mourning and lays the foundation for the emotional experience of identity. It implies preserving one's stability in different circumstances and through all the transformations of life (Grinberg & Grinberg, 1974).

But the development of each individual is an unbroken series of changes, large and small, which we must work through and assimilate if our sense of identity is to be established. The lack of mental growth and change is equivalent to psychic stagnation and emotional sterility; in other words, it means the paralysis or death of the psyche.

In the course of development various situations of change occur; they may be perceived as threats to one's integrity and self-identity, exposing the individual to deeply painful feelings through the experience of losing parts of the self, with openly depressive reactions. Living necessarily implies the need to pass through a succession of experiences of mourning. Growing through maturation means the loss of certain attitudes, ways of behaviour, and object-relations, which, although they are replaced by other more developed ones, have an impact on the ego, triggering off mourning processes that are not always sufficiently worked through. Paradoxically, it usually happens that the same defence mechanisms used by the ego against anxiety and psychic conflicts are transformed into factors against the structure and integrity of the self, causing it to weaken. This happens especially with the mechanisms of splitting and projective identification. In its struggle against anxiety the self becomes dissociated or fragmented, and its parts are separated and projected away, usually on to external objects. Very often the ego fears that these detached parts or aspects will never return; they are felt to be lost for ever. These phantasies can cause an intense depressive reaction with very painful feelings for the condition in which the self has been left (Grinberg, 1963a).

The process of development, when it occurs normally, gives time for the ego to work through its losses and recover from the transient and well-tolerated moments of identity-crisis that, in most cases, pass unnoticed. In pathological cases, through failure to work through the experience of mourning, there are serious identity disturbances.

There are important changes in life that can trigger off deep depression reactions because they are felt partly as experience of loss. We all know the depressive reactions following certain achievements that are really successful. Generally that depression is interpreted as corresponding to the guilt feeling for the success achieved and its implications in relations to the object. I believe that in certain circumstances this depression may also be the consequence of experiencing the loss of the part of the self that contains the desire or expectation of success. In other words, when something is deeply wished for and the wish is satisfied, obviously pleasure is felt; but this can co-exist with a feeling of depression due to the disappearance of the desire for, or the expectation of, that achievement. There are individuals who tend to postpone pleasure continuously so as not to expose themselves to the depression that follows once success has been achieved. There are some who, for the same reason, constantly put off everything in life.

I should like to stress the fact that depressive feelings with regard to the self are much more frequent than is generally admitted. What is more, I believe that their existence can be postulated—even as mild states of depression—among the phenomena of the psychopathology of everyday life. I think that if we took into account the occurrence of these 'microdepressions' and 'micromournings' for the self, it would help us better to understand the *raison d'être* of many states of mind which, without being noted as obvious depressions, are seen as bad temper, apathy, tiredness, boredom, irritability, and so forth. A project that does not come off, an unremembered dream, an unfulfilled aspiration, an unlucky meeting, a journey, a change—any type of vicissitude or frustration in which an aspect of the self can be included—are some of the many situations that daily trigger off 'depressive microreactions', as do also transient threats to the feeling of identity. Whether they are mild processes with a favourable issue or turn into more severe depressions depends, among other things, on how the corresponding depressions were resolved in the first stages of life (Klein, 1940).

A brief clinical fragment will serve as illustration. A patient who was usually careless and untidy in her appearance and dress, in a period of her analysis in which she had made fairly good progress, arrived at the session ostensibly changed, elegantly dressed in a modern style. Her feelings, nevertheless, contrasted with her appearance: she said she felt very depressed and anxious. She had been told that her smart dress and hairstyle made her look like 'another woman'. But she was distressed that she looked 'so different' since she believed that by this change she ceased to belong to her family, which was known for its 'messiness' and disorder. In this way she assimilated her own identity and that of her family, reacting to change with anxiety and strong depressive feelings. She had deep guilt-feelings (both persecutory and depressive) towards her family and herself because she had become different from them by improving herself. In her depressive reaction, her superego was demanding that she should not change, but should remain always the same and oppose any kind of progress.

Among the painful affects of depressive reactions, the feeling of guilt is one of the most frequent and intense. The individual may respond to an experience of loss with a guilt in which anxiety and retaliation phantasies predominate, forming the type of guilt that I have called 'persecutory guilt' (Grinberg, 1964). This guilt corresponds with the functioning of a labile ego with a very strict superego, and occurs in states of depression in which envy and aggressive impulses predominate; these incline towards manic reparations and in my opinion would form part of the emotions of the 'paranoid–schizoid position' (M. Klein, 1940). On the other hand 'depressive guilt' (Grinberg, 1964) appears later, with a more mature and integrated ego that can feel pain, responsibility, and a genuine wish for object-reparation; it would correspond with the guilt of the 'depressive position' described by M. Klein (1940). Both types of guilt can also be experienced in relation to one's own self.

Depressive affects are often mixed with feelings of persecution. On occasion depressive patients pass rapidly and unexpectedly from an emotional state of sorrow and pain to one of persecution and hostility, causing disturbance, fear, and irritation in the analyst's countertransference. The lability of the limitrophic zone between the two types of affect and the frequency with which I have observed these kaleidoscopic reactions in clinical practice, especially in borderline patients (Grinberg, 1976a), suggested to me the term 'razor's edge' for such situations.

These patients sometimes show the predominance of the so-called 'psychotic personality'; but they keep within the limits of the ego and do not lose contact with reality. The notion of 'psychotic personality' does not imply a psychiatric diagnosis but, rather, a mode of mental functioning that manifests itself in the individual's behaviour and language and in the effects it produces on the observer. This mental state co-exists with another, conceived of as the 'non-psychotic personality' or 'neurotic personality'. [This approach to mental functioning harks back to Freud's (1927e) article on 'Fetishism', in which he shows how the ego can, at times, keep up two different attitudes: a more normal one, through which contact with reality is preserved, and a more pathological one, that tends to withdraw from or deny reality. Freud applies the term 'disavowal' (*Verleugnung*) to the child's or the fetishist's rejection of the fact that women lack a penis; such rejection necessarily implies a splitting of the individual's ego.] Among the most significant components of the 'psychotic personality' is the intolerance to frustration and mental pain. Personalities that are particularly incapable of coping with frustration tend to *avoid* psychic suffering by means of evacuative mechanisms, especially pathological projective identification. Such an avoidance may endanger contact with reality; in extreme cases it may even bring about transient psychotic manifestations. Greater tolerance to frustration, on the other hand, sets in motion the mechanisms that tend to *modify* the frustration and to preserve contact with reality. On some occasions there is a rather abrupt swing from one kind of mental functioning, the 'neurotic personality', to the other, the 'psychotic personality', producing the phenomenon of the 'razor's edge'.

These personalities have a remarkable sensitivity combined with a certain developmental backwardness due to their conflict-ridden links with their earliest objects. These conflicts originate primarily in a lack of emotional contact with a mother who has failed as a receptive figure and was incapable of containing adequately the projections of the child's mental suffering. Besides, the very limited tolerance to frustration and separation from the object sparks off intense depressive reactions, feelings of hopelessness, and a sense of inner emptiness, which, at times, are experienced in a catastrophic way. These individuals have a great ability to grasp the mental states and emotions of the people with whom they are linked. But they expect the object to be equally sensitive towards them; any proof to the contrary is felt as an indication of rejection or of not being loved. The slightest frustration exacerbates their feelings of depression and persecution. They are therefore extraordinarily susceptible and very demanding of affection. At times they obstinately seek for a kind of 'skin-to-skin' contact with objects, showing a link of a very primitive and sensory nature.

During psychoanalytical treatment these patients change abruptly, as I mentioned above, from a depressive state to one of persecution, critical and excessively demanding, putting pressure on the analyst to find an immediate solution to their problems. They show, in this way, the narrowness of the intermediate area between the two types of feelings—as narrow, in fact, as the 'razor's edge'. These abrupt swings on the patient's part can surprise the analyst who, in turn, feels rapid changes in his own countertransference reactions. Thus, for example, he can change from a feeling of sorrow and sympathy for the patient's suffering to finding himself overwhelmed by the requirements and demands of the patient, with phantasies of defeat, failure, guilt, impotence, or irritation, or feel trapped in a *cul-de-sac*. In other words, the analyst suffers a reaction of 'projective counteridentification' (Grinberg, 1962), by being a receptacle into which the patient has emptied the feelings he cannot accept, by means of projective identification.

One of my patients used to produce this kind of material in his sessions, with utterances like: '. . . the only thing I know is that I feel overcome by complete desperation. If only I could lean on reason, with the complete and irreversible suppression of my emotions; the only thing they are good for is to make me a martyr. . . . [he cries miserably]. I am a complete and utter failure. I think of a weeping, sentimental woman. If only I could die. . . . I imagine a beautiful sunny afternoon, a friendly sun that would wrap me in its rays, giving me warmth, so that I could spend my last moments pleasurably. Afterwards . . . nothing . . . a void, but a void without suffering. But I would be sorry to leave my mother. I would ask you to explain to her and wash away all baseness from me. [He abruptly changes his tone; he laments more shrilly, and his cry becomes very demanding and threatening]. You are guilty of my downfall, you, my mother, and all the rest of the bastards. Do something! Make me into a machine, now, at once, into whatever you like, so long as we finish with this hell. But I'm turning on the tears . . . it's a blind alley.'

Through this fragment we can appreciate the changing phantasies of the patient. Besides his homosexual transference phantasy, we can also observe his desperate attempts to be free of the painful affects, evacuating them into the analyst by means of projective identification, which would convert him into a 'void', a being without feelings or life and, as a result, into a 'machine'. In the same way, he wanted to be free from the 'bastard' objects and from the damaged maternal object, that of the weeping sentimental voice (corresponding to another transference image), which he has transformed into a persecutory object. He was also seeking, through his projections, to be forgiven and to 'wash away his baseness'. In another way his death phantasy corresponds to his unconscious desire to enter into the analyst so that, with his function of mother and father, he could wrap him in his solar rays and give him warmth and life. But these phantasies failed because he felt that even when he tried to get rid of the powerful affects and of the hurtful persecutory objects, these were re-introjected into him with the same characteristics, sentimental and depressive (tearful voice); the cycle came round again and placed him once again in his 'cul-de-sac'.

It goes without saying that the analyst suffered a sudden change from positive countertransference feelings of sorrow, empathy, understanding and a desire to help, to sudden unexpected reactions of surprise, discouragement, guilt, and irritation, due to projective counteridentification.

As we have seen, depressive patients have often had early experiences of separation and loss, that they have been unable to deal with and that are reactivated by every present loss, bringing about increasingly more painful depressive feelings as well as a sensation of helplessness and inner emptiness.

The experience of loss of a mother, whether a real absence or because of the failure of his mother in her function of returning, in a mitigated form, the painful affects projected by the child, along with intolerance to frustration, is at the basis of the depressive structure. The upheavals that appear in the relationship between the child being weaned and its mother, and more particularly with the breast, have an influence on the pathology of his later object-relations, because he has the feeling that the breast is the source of fundamental emotional experiences such as love, understanding, and meaning. The baby, as well as looking for the satisfaction of his nutritional needs, projects his affects of fear and pain on to the breast of his mother with the hope of feeling loved and understood, and therefore receiving these feelings back again 'detoxicated' and stripped of their intolerable painful quality; if the breast fulfils this function, it gives him meaning (Bion, 1965). If it is absent, the fear born of the phantasy of having destroyed it implies not only that he will cease to exist, since without the breast he cannot live, but also that the meaning, as though it were material, has ceased to exist.

In these patients there is a marked intolerance to the absence of the object (and the absence of the aspects of the self involved) as well as intolerance to what this absence presupposes: intense psychic suffering. The absent object then becomes a present per-secutory 'non-object', which must be promptly got rid of. For the same reason these patients cannot bear separation from their analyst; moreover, when the analyst thwarts certain transference phantasies, he instantly acquires, even when he is present, the characteristics of an absent object through non-fulfilment of the gratifying aspects they want, and becomes a threatening, persecu-tory 'non-object'. In such cases these patients seek interpretation merely as evidence that the analyst has neither gone nor has been destroyed. They seek ceaselessly to arouse countertransference feelings or reactions of projective counteridentification, which may provide evidence that meaning still exists. Interpretation is sought not as useful enlightenment but as reassurance and an antidote for psychic pain and anxiety, especially when they are afraid of facing the unbearable thought that everything is mean-ingless.

In such cases, every time the analyst interprets they appear to hear the word 'because', with its connotation of causation. In this way things incomprehensible to the patient acquire some mean-ing, whether it is the right one or not.

These patients cannot bear pain. They feel it but they do not 'suffer' it. They take the sensation of pain for the actual 'suffering' of pain (Bion, 1970). They complain of how 'painful' certain experiences have been to them, but, in fact, they have avoided suffering. One of my patients used to cry during his sessions as if he were suffering, until I came to see that, for him, crying was a way of releasing pain without actually suffering it. This was brought home to me later when once he said that weeping relieved him because it was a way of 'letting off steam' and thus 'eradicating' his emotions. At times, in order to avoid pain, certain individuals tend to sexualize it, as may be seen in some perversions, in which pain is either inflicted or sought. [B. Joseph (1978b) has described a particular type of psychic pain that belongs to the emergence from schizoid states of mind, and discussed it as a 'borderline' phenomenon between mental and physical, between anxieties felt in terms of fragmentation and persecution and the beginnings of integration and concern.]

I shall add another clinical vignette to illustrate this avoidance of psychic suffering. This concerns a 37-year-old divorced woman who was very successful as an architect. However, this did not compensate for her depressive state and her role as victim, which she used to assume in her relationships with others. This was due, to a large extent, to her identification with a mother who was apparently self-sacrificing and who 'made suffering a virtue' (as the patient said), but who had never loved, looked after, or understood her. Her father had nearly always been away on business, and she felt she had never been able to enjoy his company nor indeed get close to him, because later on he suffered a manic-depressive psychosis. She was the eldest daughter; her only brother was killed in an accident when she was only six years old, and, according to the patient, he had been her mother's favourite. She felt responsible for his death because of the rivalry and jealousy she felt towards him. She had sought treatment because of her depression, the breakdown of her marriage, and also for her frequent feelings of persecution, hostility, and rejection on the part of others.

I intend to present fragments of two sessions in order to show some aspects of her pathological mourning, her persecutory and depressive feelings, and also the fluctuation between the psychotic and neurotic parts of her personality.

She started one session with the following words: 'I don't know why, but I find it difficult to speak today.... I've been very anxious the last few days. I worry about anything ... My friend, Pauline, paid me a visit yesterday. She's hard to bear. She keeps making demands that no one can ever satisfy. She's permanently dissatisfied. She finds objections to everything. Nobody can help her. Yesterday I went with my father to an interview with his psychiatrist, and this made me very anxious. I felt that my father was excluded, and that the communication between the psychiatrist and me was totally inaccessible to him.'

I pointed out her hopelessness of being able to save a part within her that she considered to be beyond reach and very demanding, and that she felt neither she herself, nor I, nor analysis, nor indeed anyone could change. I added that she had partly lodged this sector in me, and she was afraid that I might demand too much of her.

We may suppose that this sector contains the injured or dead objects as part of her injured self that cannot be repaired and that jointly take on the role of an inexorable and cruel superego that cannot be satisfied. It is as if the accident that killed her brother, and her father's psychosis (which she also saw as an accident), had brought about an internal 'accident' in her psychic organization.

In the following session the patient said: 'Yesterday I felt I would like to be hospitalized like those people who go in to lose weight and go on a diet. My idea was to come to the session and then to stay on. Last night I couldn't sleep. I had some strange thoughts. Who would I like to be? I realized I didn't know what other people were like, especially inside. There must be other ways of living that even I have never thought of. I remembered Elena [a friend of hers who had had an accident in which her husband died] and how she was after the terrible operation she had. She was always very vital.... She was able to survive the dreadful experience thanks to her strong will to live. Will it be any use to her? How can she live now? I thought once again of the possibility of changing myself. I don't think it's possible. Even supposing I change, how can I assimilate these changes to all that is already established? Once all the important things in life have been done, getting married, studying for a career, what can you do with all the things you want to get rid of and all the things you acquire? Yes, I should like to go into retreat.'

I believe the patient at that moment was expressing a regressive phantasy coming from the psychotic part of her personality, of having got inside me and the analysis, disconnecting herself from all exterior reality and also from all changes experienced as 'catastrophic' (like the 'accidents' that could not be remedied) and in that way was trying to avoid her psychic pain. But the phenomenon of the 'razor's edge' appears again.

The patient went on to say: 'I would like to begin my life all over again, go back to the mother of my infancy and of my adolescence, but to a different mother. I would like to have a different way of going about things, but it is so difficult to imagine myself being any different. I would like to undo all the parts of me that I don't like: my arrogance, my boastfulness, my competitiveness, and so many more things. But if I were to do it, I would feel too impoverished, diminished, empty.'

I told her that she was trying to retreat into analysis to distance herself from her suffering, or hoping that analysis would give her the chance to be born again, as though to another mother who had a different relationship with her, one that allowed her to survive, freeing her not only from the aspects she had mentioned, but from all that was dead and mad within her. However, this put her in the position of losing aspects of herself as if she were on a diet that would leave her empty or hollow.

The patient replied by saying: 'I don't know why, but I have just remembered a dream that I had forgotten about. You told me in the dream that you were not going to treat me any more. I thought it was Pauline's situation all over again when the doctor stopped her analysis. You told me I couldn't go on because I hadn't brought Pauline with me. It seemed odd. Then I saw a sick child who was crying, and her father was singing to her. When I came out of the house, I saw some children playing, and they seemed happy. I imagined they were your children, and I said to myself, "he is a good father, I must ask him to let me go on with the analysis".'

The patient was anxious and afraid that she might really have to stop her analysis. She showed through her associations that she had been worried about the episode of Pauline (who had suffered a psychotic breakdown). It seemed odd to her that, in her dream, I should tell her she should have brought Pauline (who represented her psychotic part), since this implied the risk that I would not put up with this psychotic part, and so I would end by asking her to leave.

The dream could also indicate that both she and I were 'singing' to quieten the child who was linked with the extremely sick part of herself that she did not want to bring along to the session because that would mean anxiety and psychic pain. But at another level of the dream there seemed to be an indication of hope that I was a good 'father–mother–analyst' who 'sang' interpretations and who was dealing with her sick depressive part, making it more accessible and turning her into a child who could 'play' and begin to communicate.

Certain kinds of patient react to the experience of separation and loss of object in a specific way; their depressive reply is of a catastrophic nature: they feel as if they were breaking up or falling to pieces. They usually spend hours and hours in bed, wrapped up in blankets, in order to feel contained. From childhood onwards they have had difficulties with the 'container' aspect of the psychic function of their skin. Since they have lacked a maternal object with a good enough capacity to contain their evacuations and projections, they have had no possibility of grasping the notion of space. They have not learned to distinguish between being inside or outside the object. It is for this reason that one of their characteristic symptoms is confusion and superficiality in their relationships and behaviour. They also have difficulty in the learning process, since they cannot make true identifications to assimilate knowledge and therefore fall into imitative attitudes that tend to reproduce what the object does. Through their lack of the idea of inner space, in both the objects and themselves, they fail in the use of the mechanism of projective identification, which would be the mechanism *par excellence* in the three-dimensional world. These patients appear to live predominantly in a two-dimensional world using the mechanism of 'adhesive identification' described by Esther Bick (1968). This type of identification can produce an extreme dependency in which separate existence and autonomy of the object are not recognized, and they have the phantasy of being 'stuck' to the surface of the object, like a stamp; thus they become a part of the object, imitating its appearance and behaviour. They develop characteristics similar to the 'as if' personality (Deutsch, 1942) or to that of the 'false self' (Winnicott, 1955).

For these patients, not only separation but any other experience of change is felt as a 'catastrophic change' to which they react as if their 'container' skin has been perforated, and they are afraid of being 'scattered'. Sometimes they give the impression that their mental apparatus is 'falling to pieces' and they are reduced to their perceptual capabilities (Meltzer et al., 1975).

One patient whose case was under my supervision suffered a dramatic depressive reaction when her husband telephoned her from abroad to tell her that he would be arriving a day later than planned. This coincided with the fact that her mother had recently moved away from the district to another address further away, which alarmed the patient because she had a symbiotic relationship with her. She went through a hallucinatory episode, which she described as follows: 'When my husband told me not to expect him today, I felt upset, very distressed; I didn't know what to do. My mother was no longer there. I tried to sleep, but I couldn't. I saw my little son breaking up, falling to pieces . . . it wasn't a dream. It shocked me terribly. I felt very agitated and wanted to cry. I wanted to rub out the image. At the beginning I couldn't; afterwards I could. I had to think of you to calm myself down. I went to bed and wrapped myself in the blankets; finally I managed to fall asleep.'

The experience of the loss of the object sparked off the hallucinatory phantasy of disintegration, although it was projected on to the image of her son, who represented her own infantile part. She then took refuge in calling her analyst to mind as a 'container' object and used the blankets as a protective and re-integrating 'skin' to counteract the experience of the loss felt as an intolerable 'catastrophic change'.

'Catastrophic change' is the term under which Bion (1966) tries to combine certain facts characterized by violence, invariance, and subversion of the system, elements that he considers inherent in all situations of change and growth. A new situation or a new idea contains a potentially disruptive force, which violates to a greater or lesser degree the structure of the field in which it appears. Thus a new discovery violates the structure of the pre-existing theory; an experience of change can violate the structure of the personality. One structure is transformed into another through stages of disorganization, pain, and frustration; growth depends on these vicissitudes. The term 'invariance' refers to that which allows recognition to the new structure of aspects of the old one. Subversion of the system refers to those changes that appear to break up the already existing order.

But we should bear in mind that the 'catastrophic change' experience can also be found in those situations of change that involve progress, development, or acceptance of new ideas, as happens in the creative process. Every creative act is specifically based on the working through of depressive phantasies and painful affects that aim at the reparation of the lost object and the damaged parts of the self. In normal mourning, the predominance of depressive guilt, together with sublimatory and reparatory tendencies, increase creative capacity. There are people who, in mourning, become involved in writing or composing music or other creative activities. [Hanna Segal, in her article 'A psycho-analytical approach to aesthetics' (1952), establishes the relationship between the infantile depressive position, mourning and creativity, pointing out that by re-creation the lost object becomes a symbol.]

I have pointed out elsewhere (Grinberg, 1972a) that the creative act can be conceived as the outcome of a process during which the individual must inevitably go through transitory states of 'disorganization' and disrupture of familiar structures and established links and must accept the temporary blurring of the ego boundaries and become immersed in fusion with idealized internal objects through projective identification, in order to reintegrate and reorganize himself later in a different way. From this will emerge the created product, which he will feel as a new part of himself. The creative personality will need to tolerate frustration and the anxiety of remaining temporarily in a 'void', in 'disorder' and in 'chaos'; he will endeavour to draw near the truth and will be open to the impact of intuition and ready to follow it. In exactly the same way as the creative process shapes the change-situation, it will inevitably involve a mourning reaction with its corresponding painful affects, due to the loss of the old structures and the loss of aspects of the self and objects with their respective links, which will necessarily be replaced with new links and new structures.

Others have occupied themselves with a similar phenomenon—as, for example, M. Milner (1969) when she points out that certain people endeavour to break down their false internal organization by means of a temporary chaos or a 'creative fury', which destroys a compliant and conformist adaptation, allowing the emergence of a more authentic organization. This idea is in line with Winnicott's (1955) assertion about the need to replace the 'false self', which acts as a protective armour, by the 'true self'.

During the analytical process, in the face of any material which can trigger off a threat of mental pain, several defensive operations are mobilized in the patient and, occasionally, in the analyst also. Among these defence manoeuvres against psychic suffering we can mention splitting, pathological projective identification, acting out, omnipotent control, omniscience, 'reversal of perspective', somatizations and, in the case of the analyst, the 'resistential' use of psychoanalytical theories in an attempt to avoid psychic pain.

Many of the above defensive processes are sufficiently well known not to need description. Nevertheless I think it will be useful to say a few words about some of them. Omniscience is characterized by a response to the functioning and influence of a superego which opposes all search for the truth and tries to impose itself on the basis of a phantasy of total superiority. Patients who use this phantasy, instead of trying to learn, insist that they 'possess knowledge', trying to avoid the painful experience of the learning process. The meanings and emotions with which they come into contact are actively stripped of vitality and sense, so they cannot learn; nor can there be growth or evolution in their personalities.

Obsessive omnipotent control tends towards the separation of the object and the simplification of experiences, which amounts to real splitting; they are reduced therefore to a level at which psychic meaning disappears and emotions are cancelled out. It is for this reason that this mechanism is so much used as a defence against mental pain.

As for 'reversal of perspective' as described by Bion (1963), it consists in a silent and constant rejection of the premises on which the interpretation is based, disguised as apparent agreement with the analyst. There are patients who react to certain interpretations as if they were countertransference confessions, misrepresenting in this way the objective of the analysis. What the patient is really doing is denying the dynamic character of the interpretation and its investigatory aspect, which are fundamental preconditions through which the analysis can be capable of furthering change and mental growth. For his part, the analyst can also reverse his perspective, taking the patient's associations as an antidote for his own anxiety in face of the unknown and unknowable in the material, and then transforming them into the confirmation of a predetermined theory that gives some meaning to what is happening.

Another type of defensive operation that tends to counteract the suffering of psychic pain consists in the unconscious evacuation of that pain, along with the conflict that originated it, into the body. Normally, physical pain appears to be better tolerated than psychic pain. Thus the mental phenomenon is transformed into a sensory impression devoid of the feared emotional meaning, or rather it tries to change that intolerable psychic meaning into a sensory experience. [Pain, as Rosenfeld (1978) pointed out, can also mean the existence of an overwhelming depressive affect that is trying to find its way towards consciousness.]

To sum up: depression is an affective-cognitive 'constant conjunction' in which different elements that affect one another play a part. ['Constant conjunction' is a term taken from Hume, and refers to the fact that certain data observed appear regularly together. Bion uses this term in his hypotheses about the development of thought. A concept or a word is expressed which links together under its name the observed elements, which are constantly conjoined.] Among these are experience of loss (or change felt as loss), mourning for the lost object and for the parts of the self involved in the loss, painful affects (persecutory and depressive), along with their corresponding ideational representations, and an ego that, faced with the menace of psychic pain, sets in motion specific defences against it. The painful affects mentioned may, at times, alternate very swiftly, thus giving rise to the 'razor's edge' phenomenon.

CHAPTER FOURTEEN

Dreams and acting out

D reams can be used as containers that free patients from increased tension. This may be the principal function of certain types of dream, called 'evacuative dreams'. They are dreams used for getting rid of unbearable affects and unconscious phantasies, or as a safety valve for partial discharge of instinctual drives. These dreams are observed primarily in borderline and psychotic patients, but they can also be seen in the regressive states of neurotic patients during weekends and other periods of separation. Such dreams have to be differentiated from 'elaborative dreams' that have a working-through function and stand in an inverse relationship to acting out: the greater the production of elaborative dreams, the less the tendency to act out, and vice versa.

In the last two decades psychoanalysis has been faced with some new problems in the conceptualization of the dream and dreaming. The same may be said of the phenomenon of acting out.

The purpose of this chapter is to present my current ideas about these issues and about the technical approach to them. I begin by proposing a clinical classification of dreams and showing their inverse relationship to acting out: the greater the production of dreams, the less tendency there is towards acting out, and vice versa. I shall further develop a hypothesis, conceived several years ago (Grinberg et al., 1967), of the existence of evacuative, mixed, and elaborative dreams. This hypothesis originated in a study group co-ordinated by me and devoted to the investigation of dreams.

I believe that it is important to be able to differentiate between these various types of dreams in our clinical work, because it can enable us to learn more about a patient's level of regression, that is, what his capacity is for insight and for taking advantage of the working-through function of dreams. It can also add another dimension to our procedure for interpreting dreams. I consider certain dreams to be closely linked with acting out, which can precede the dream or appear after it, even though these aspects are related to one another by a common unconscious phantasy.

Freud (1900a) showed that one of the functions of a dream is to preserve sleep. According to him, the archaic psyche is reactivated in the individual who dreams, which results in the transformation of the psychic contents into visual images, condensations, displacements, symbolism, and other individual manipulations of the circumstances of space and time. Oneiric regression makes manifest the archaic levels of the psyche and establishes continuity between past, present, and future, bringing the present back to the past and actualizing the past in the present. It is probable that the regressive process that converts day residue into objects in the dream is the same one that converts experiences and day residue into memories selectively stored in the unconscious.

Freud also emphasized the functions of wish-fulfilment in dreams. A compromise is reached between the repressive and repressed forces by means of the dream-work so that the forbidden wish can find a certain form of satisfaction. Freud did not revise this theory in the light of his later discoveries. Some authors, however, have raised objections to it. Hanna Segal (1981), for example, expressed her reservations about the dream being conceived of solely as a compromise. She held that 'the dream is not just an equivalent of a neurotic symptom. Dream-work is also part of the psychic work of working through'.

The dream, therefore, is an important and complex psychic act. Melanie Klein (1932, 1946), delving deeper into early object-relationships, basic anxieties, and defence mechanisms, has enhanced our approach to the dream by enlarging the concept to include a richly complex internal world. Thus the dream can be seen as the dramatization of a conflict and as an attempt to working it through. The dream appears within the temporal limitations of a person's internal world, with its various structures, representations of objects, and reciprocal relationships.

Bion (1962) reformulated some of the concepts on dreaming and dreams. He believed that in order for a person to be able to dream, it is necessary for him to possess an alpha function capable of processing his sensory impressions in such a way that it transforms them into alpha elements. These elements are used in the formation of unconscious mental processes during wakefulness, oneiric thoughts, dreams, and memories. The alpha elements, upon uniting among themselves, form a 'contact barrier' that isolates the conscious from the unconscious and establishes a selective passage between the two. If the alpha function is effective, the individual can distinguish between being asleep and being awake and is therefore able to dream. This 'contact barrier' protects against the mental phenomena that could overwhelm consciousness and, in turn, makes it impossible for consciousness to overwhelm the phantasies. It also protects one's contact with reality, avoiding its distortion by emotions of internal origin.

This capacity to dream protects the individual from what would virtually be a psychotic state. If the alpha function fails, the patient cannot dream and therefore is not able to differentiate sleep from wakefulness. For these cases, Bion introduced another concept, the 'beta-element screen', which he used to explain those mental states in which there is no differentiation between conscious and unconscious, sleep and wakefulness. The 'beta-screen' is composed of beta elements, which are experienced as things-in-themselves; they are not appropriate for thinking, dreaming, remembering, but only for being evacuated through projective identification or by acting out.

In our study group we had thought about the possibility of extending to dreams Bion's (1962) concept of the existence of an 'apparatus for thinking thoughts'. The 'apparatus for dreaming dreams' would have a double function: to 'dream' them during sleep and later on to 'think' them during wakefulness in such a way as to be able to recall them instead of repeating them as though acting out. This apparatus is gradually formed in the infant's mind, granting it the capacity to think, through the internalization of repeated experiences of its relationship with a mother–container with a capacity for 'reverie', who has received the anxiety and other affects projected by the child, returning them in an attenuated form.

In the course of the analytic process, just as in infancy in the mother–child relationship, the analyst's capacity for 'reverie', his ability to contain and metabolize the patient's projections, returning them through the interpretation, gradually becomes assimilated by the analysand's ego. It is then possible for the patient to continue learning to 'dream' his dreams in the same way as he gradually learns to 'think' his thoughts.

Thus the analyst's interpretations continue to confer on dreams meanings previously unknown to the patient. The dream itself, in its manifest and latent contents, may be considered a fairly accurate clinical indicator of the stage of elaboration or non-elaboration that the analysand is passing through.

In classic psychoanalytical theory, the latent content of a dream is considered to be where the day residue and repressed infantile wishes and memories intersect. Rallo (1982) has suggested a second meaning for latent content, when analysis of the manifest content of a dream brings to consciousness the structure and functioning of the psychic apparatus. This second concept of latent content complements and is synchronous with the earlier one. To decipher these latent contents of the manifest content of dreams would enable us to differentiate the character and nature of various dreams. Some dreams would exhibit a lack or deficiency of processing; they would not achieve adequate elaborations of internalized reality and would have predominantly evacuative functions. Other dreams, however, in which the secondary process participates more, would have an elaborative nature and relevant functions in the adaptive integration of reality.

In accordance with the ideas put forth here, we have proposed a clinical classification of dreams during the analytic process, based either on their predominantly evacuative function (with the use of projective identification into external objects) or on an elaborative function (with a greater tendency to introjective identifications):

1. *Evacuative dreams,* which primarily seek the discharge of unbearable affects, unconscious phantasies, and object-relations into an external object that constitutes a container, for example, the analyst;

2. *Mixed dreams,* which not only seek to discharge the unwanted affects and parts of the self and objects into a container, but also possess elements of concern and guilt;

3. *Elaborative dreams,* in which the function of discharge is not primary. They contain depressive and reparatory elements with a distinct tendency towards working through.

Evacuative dreams are those in which the function of liberating the psychic apparatus from ideational and affective contents predominates, due to the dreamer's inability to tolerate the anxiety that they awaken. They are primitive dreams, dreamed essentially in order to discharge their contents into object-containers, and often appear in the initial stages of analysis when the patient has not yet built up defences against insight into his psychotic nucleus. They become more frequent during interruptions in the treatment as a result of separation from the analyst and the need to find a substitute on to whom the patient can project his painful affects. The condition of 'evacuativity' is created by the inability of the psychic apparatus to tolerate increasing tension, by the latent content of the unconscious phantasy, and by certain characteristics of the manifest content in which elements of the primary process often appear with a primitive symbolism or with scant displacements, usually representing very regressive defence mechanisms.

Animals, machines, or apparatus from outer space, non-human elements, partial objects, usually appear in the manifest content of these dreams. The dreams often coincide with gross alternations of the setting, severe acting-out behaviour, or serious somatizations.

Evacuative dreams are predominantly observed in regressive patients, in borderline cases, or in patients with psychotic personalities. We can see this in the following dream of a seriously schizoid patient: In the first part of the dream an aeroplane flies over a place and drops an atomic bomb. The patient is desperate because he cannot find any place to take shelter. The bomb falls, and there is an explosion. Up to this point there is discharge and evacuation of explosive and annihilating anal contents with massive destruction of a psychotic type and infinite fragmentation. There is no container capable of containing the discharge. In the second part of the dream the patient discovers that he is not dead, but he sees that he appears to have holes, and parts of his body are putrified from the effects of radiation. In other words, the attempt to search for a container in his own body has failed because of the persecutory nature of the contents, which end up by disintegrating the container.

Freud has emphasized the analogy between the dream world and the waking life of the psychotic. In his studies on the relationship of dreams to psychosis, Frosch (1976) expressed the idea that 'the fear of disintegration and dissolution of the self of the psychotic patient will influence his dreams both as to form and content'. 'In several patients considered with psychotic characters, the appearance of nightmare-like dreams was a common occurrence. The manifest dream content was generally of violence, including murder, rape or fire.' 'Many analysts have observed the presence in dreams of flagrant and manifest oedipal, homosexual, or more primitive material such as cannibalistic manifestations at the beginning or early in treatment. Do these dreams reflect psychosis?' To my mind, these are evacuative dreams that may also appear in the first stages of the analysis of a neurotic patient. Richardson and Moore (1963) submitted manifest dreams of schizophrenic and non-schizophrenic patients to a panel of analysts who were asked to differentiate between them. The ability to differentiate did not appear to be good, and the criteria used by the panel seemed as valid for one type of dream as for the other. Nevertheless, the authors found a significant difference between the two types of dreams. They found that the presence of unusual, strange, uncanny, and bizarre qualities in the manifest content was more common for the schizo-phrenic than for the non-schizophrenic dream.

The need to communicate the dream is especially intense in evacuatory dreams and is the primary aim of the dreamer who thus searches for a container into which to evacuate his dream. Kanzer (1955), insisting on the communicative function of the dream, pointed out the urgency of communicating the dream itself, which had already been described by Freud. Kanzer referred not only to the interpersonal communication with the objects of the external world, but also to the intra-personal communication con-tained in the dream and which is established between different aspects of the self. Baranger (1960), who also studied dreams as a means of communication, emphasized that the patient can use oneiric regression to claim a lack of responsibility for the dream and to maintain a dissociation from certain conflicts that he refuses to acknowledge.

In our paper on 'Monday's dreams' (Grinberg & Grinberg, 1960), we called attention to the fact that these dreams were very often related to the weekend separation from the analyst. In the uncon-scious phantasies of their latent content we usually found oedipal situations, jealousy, feelings of exclusion, problems involving birth and death, and separation anxieties. The common element of Monday dreams was the *search for communication* or contact with an internalized analyst in order to compensate for the separation caused by the weekend.

On occasion, patients have been observed to need to write down the evacuative dream, with the apparent justification of fear of forgetting it. In reality, the paper represents, in these cases, the intermediary container prior to its projection into the therapist.

The dream itself can be turned into the persecutory part, which the patient wants to get rid of, and not merely a representation of it. It can also happen, then, that the patient will oppose the interpretation of the dream if he feels that it would entail a re-introjection, a 'reverted' projective identification of what was projected. Blitzten, Eissler, and Eissler (1950) have given us a highly illustrative example. A patient who was at best a bor-derline case with 'paranoid mechanisms' reacted with 'panic and extreme rage . . . whenever her attention was drawn to her dreams and she was called upon to associate to them. The violence of her objection was so great that she even sometimes jumped up from the couch and huddled in a corner.'

Although with another meaning, Freud (1923c) pointed out, 'It is possible to distinguish between dreams *from above* and dreams *from below* . . . Dreams from below are those which are provoked by the strength of an unconscious (repressed) wish which has found a means of being represented in some of the day's residues . . . Dreams from above correspond to thoughts or intentions of the day before which have contrived during the night to obtain re-inforcement from repressed material that is debarred from the ego.'

In other words, as the regression deepens, the secondary process gradually loses its supremacy, to the point where it gives rise to dreams termed 'from below', where the primary process dominates. When the integrative command of the secondary process is maintained, we find ourselves with dreams 'from above', which would be more related to the problem of wakefulness introduced by means of day residues.

Freud (1900a) referred indirectly to the function of discharge in dreaming when he stated: 'Dreaming has taken on the task of bringing back under control of the preconscious the excitation in the *Ucs* which has been left free; in so doing, it discharges the *Ucs* excitation, serves it as a *safety valve* . . .' (my italics).

Segal (1981) also pointed out that 'dreams may be used for purposes of evacuation. . . . A patient can use dreams for getting rid of, rather than working through, unwanted parts of the self and objects, and he can use them in analysis for projective identification. We are all familiar with patients who come and flood us, fill us with dreams in a way disruptive to the relationship and to the analysis.'

When the patient brings this type of dream to the session, it is advisable to orient the interpretation more towards the evacuative function of the dream and its liberating objective than towards its content. On occasion, the analyst can even make clear to the patient his wish to receive and keep the patient's dream without intepreting it, in order to avoid its re-introjection.

'Mixed dreams', while they contain evacuative elements, also present depressive aspects and a beginning of working through, since feelings of guilt and responsibility arise in the manifest content, even though some of the primitive defence mechanisms, such as dissociation, still persist.

An example of this category of mixed dreams is one told by a patient who habitually passed through very regressive periods in her analysis: 'I saw a rain of fire fall as if it were a volcano in eruption, destroying everything. I was terrified and tried to run away to save myself while people around me were falling down. A man took me by the hand and a voice 'off stage' guided us. This way we were able to reach a house where it seemed that we were safe. Later the police arrived to investigate something or other, but I was not frightened.'

Among her associations, she referred to the cataclysm at Pompeii. She later mentioned that she had seen a film on television in the company of her husband and in-laws. She was greatly shocked by the reaction of the protagonist who had learned unexpectedly during a visit to her doctor that she had a malignant tumour, which required immediate surgery. She was moved by the protagonist's anxiety in the face of the possibility of death. On the other hand the patient had quarrelled with her in-laws, because they criticized the film, and she felt she had to control her aggression in order not to explode violently. She felt a great need to come to the session, even though she arrived a few minutes late because she thought she had carefully to supervise the electrician who was installing some outlets in her house.

The patient feared the unexpected eruption of a violent psychotic crisis (rain of fire) that could destroy her and the others. She had identified with the character in the film and unconsciously compared her own anxiety in the face of the dreaded emergency of an uncontrolled psychotic crisis to the anxiety faced by the protagonist who had to deal with her cancer. This anxiety was evacuated in the manifest content of the dream, and she felt the need to evacuate it into the analyst, along with the man (electrician–analyst) whom she had to check to see how he installed the outlets. In the second part of the dream the attempt at working through appears, guided by the hand and voice of the analyst to the house (analysis). She was then able to accept with less fear the need to investigate (police) what had happened to her.

Elaborative dreams show a greater intervention of the secondary process, with the appearance of depressive elements that tend towards integration. The patient who brings elaborative dreams to the sessions shows his increasing capacity to introject the clarifying function of the analyst. His external attitude towards his dreams is also modified; he has diminished his anxiety in confronting them and no longer reacts with paranoid defences that tend to hinder the reintrojection of the dream, nor does he persist in phobic avoidance mechanisms or manic mechanisms of denial to defend himself against the intolerable projected contents, which he now accepts as his own. He therefore faces this type of dream with greater collaboration and interest, which is evident through the quality and form of his associative sequence, implying a greater connection not only with the preconscious, but also with the happenings in the world of wakefulness.

The elaborative dream constitutes for the patient a hierarchical index of the state of his internal world. As he progresses, the patient acquires the capacity to recall, evoke, and work with his dreams. Ultimately, this will allow him to arrive at the possibility of analysing his dreams himself and of taking advantage of them adequately, not only during the analytic treatment but also during the therapeutic 'weaning' and post-analysis. Obviously, the attempt at working through exists in all dreams, but its intensity and context is what gives it the quality of an elaborative dream.

For Meltzer (1984), dreams must be considered as images of an oneiric life that is constantly unfolding, whether the person is asleep or awake. We could call these images 'dreams' when we are sleeping and 'unconscious phantasies' when we are awake. This implies that the internal world must be assigned the full significance of a place, a life-space, perhaps the place where meaning is generated—meaning that can then be deployed to life and relationships in the external world. For Meltzer, dreams told by patients are sometimes 'successes' and at other times 'failures'. The successful dream is one that contributes to solving the problem; the failed dream does not. He adds: '. . . what of the fruitful harvest of those dreams which do succeed in grasping the nettle of mental pain, resolving a conflict, relinquishing an untenable position?'

These reflections undoubtedly refer to elaborative dreams. By attempting to give a verbal representation to the thoughts contained in these dreams, we are also preparing them to be used in more sophisticated forms of investigation, such as the proof of reality and logical consistency. But it is the poetry of the dream that succeeds in trapping and giving formal representation to passions, which are the meaning of our experience, so that they can be controlled by reason. Lastly, Meltzer pointed out that the oneiric process can be described metaphorically as the 'theatre for the generating of meaning'. This theatre, with its various participants, implies a dramatic unity, but it also allows for a greater variety of points of view about the drama. If consciousness was defined by Freud (1900a) as 'a *sense-organ for the perception of psychical qualities*', which character in the theatre is, at the moment of dreaming, in possession of this organ? Is it the same as the recaller and narrator of the dream during the analytic session?

Fairbairn (1952) also viewed dreams as 'essentially, not wish-fulfilments, but dramatizations of 'shorts' (in the cinematographic sense) of situations existing in inner reality. . . . The situations depicted in dreams represent relationships existing between endopsychic structures. . . . All the figures appearing in dreams represent either parts of the dreamer's own personality (conceived in terms of ego, superego and id) or internalized objects.'

An example of these successful dreams of an elaborative type is one that a patient told in his fourth year of analysis, after having analysed the conflict with his wife and problems related to his possible future paternity: 'I dreamed that I was the father of a little infant, and after looking around I found a receptacle with water so that I could bath the baby'. In this dream there arose, among other meanings, different representations of the self and object-relationships, feelings of responsibility, the search for and finding of a maternal container, and attitudes of preservation and reparation.

Relationship between dreams
and acting out

I have observed (Grinberg, 1968) that one of the essential roots of acting out is frequently an experience of separation and object-loss that precipitated mourning that has not been worked through. This mourning generated extremely painful affects (sorrow, depression, rage, frustration, anxiety, etc.), which the patients were unable to cope with. Moreover, the experience of separation could touch off a particular fixation in the stage of muscular discharge, creating confusion between the normal, verbalized models and the action models.

An image that eloquently reflects the reaction to this type of loss is that of a child who loses his mother; before finding the father as a substitute, the child suffers marked anxiety when 'in the middle of the road'. The child suddenly feels alone and helpless before the 'void' and has a tantrum to keep from falling into the void. This attempt at discharge in the form of a tantrum would follow the primitive model of alleviating psychic pain through the projection of parts of the self and objects in conflict into an external object.

In my opinion, acting out can be regarded as a process that calls for two participants. There must be an object-relationship, even though it may generally be of a narcissistic nature. A clue to the understanding of the dynamics and vicissitudes of acting out can also be found in the model for the early conflictual mother–child relationship. I have already pointed out that, according to Bion (1962), when the infant feels very acute anxiety (for example fear of dying), he needs to project it into a container (his mother) capable of holding it and returning it in such a way that the anxiety is lessened. If the mother is not capable of metabolizing this anxiety, and even deprives it of its specific quality (the fear of dying), the infant will receive back in return a 'nameless dread' that he cannot tolerate.

According to this model, the patient's need to find an object in the external world that could take on both his pain and his separation anxiety is a significant element in acting out. This object is, obviously, the analyst, into whom the patient evacuates his unbearable feelings. The absence of the analyst for regular intervals, such as weekends, makes him appear as a persecutory 'non-object'. The relationship with this object must be evacuated by means of projective identification into other objects that are substitute containers. For this reason, separations during analysis ('voids') can often trigger episodes of acting out.

Sometimes the 'container–object' can be represented by the patient's own body, giving rise to psychosomatic or hypochondriacal disturbances, or by a dream with evacuative characteristics. The somatic or hypochondriacal bodily symptom becomes the concrete 'presence' that annuls or counteracts the unbearable effects of pain and separation anxiety. Freud (1926d [1925]) clearly established the relationship between the physical pain of a bodily symptom and the pain of object-loss. In these cases, the part of the body affected is perceived as alien, and the patient maintains a kind of object-relationship with it. I have termed these psychosomatic disturbances 'acting-out equivalents'. S. H. Frazier (1965) also described psychosomatic illness as a form of acting out expressed in body language.

At other times, a dream may function as a container that tends to free the individual from increased tension. As we have seen, acting out seeks to discharge unbearable impulses and emotions, but this objective is not always entirely accomplished and must be complemented through evacuative dreams.

An interesting manifestation of behaviour related to dreams was provided by Sterba (1946), who reported acting-out behaviour in patients, which preceded the narration of a dream of the night before. Clear examples demonstrated that this acting out was closely related to the dream content. Sterba stated: 'The close connection between the acting out and the dream gives the impression that the acting out functions like an association to the dream. . . . Actually, the acting out as well as the dream [report] which it precedes are both the expression of the same unconscious instinctual dynamism which succeeds in breaking through the repressing forces of the ego, particularly when the defences are loosened up through the analytic work.'

Acting out sometimes appears after the dream as an evacuative complement to it. In this sense, I agree with Segal (1981) in her remarks on predictive dreams. Apparently these dreams do predict the action, in that what has been dreamed has to be acted out. The acting out repeats almost literally the content of the dream. Possibly we are dealing here with dreams that have not been entirely successful in their evacuative function, and, as a result, conflicting aspects are retained in the patient's psyche, which he seeks to evacuate altogether through the acting out process.

An adolescent patient, whose case I supervised, reported the following dream at the end of a session, the day before an examination at the high school where she studied: 'I go into a bar with my sister and some friends. They sit at a table, and I try to buy a packet of cigarettes from a vending machine. The machine does not work, and I keep on putting in more coins and taking them out uselessly. I waste a lot of time. Meanwhile the others have finished their drinks and have gone away. My sister tells me not to waste any more time and says we should go to a high-class restaurant to eat, but since it is very expensive, she suggests that we eat our own food that she brought with her.'

During this period of analysis the patient felt as if she were a 'robot', incapable of thinking, feeling, or living up to the expectations that she and others had for herself. She wasted her time on sterile efforts to obtain unnecessary things, while she wasted opportunities to establish positive links sitting at a table with the others. She rejected the food of the restaurant (analysis), thinking it was more beneficial to eat her own lunch and not the one that the analyst offered her.

The dream attempted to evacuate into the analyst her feelings of anxiety and depression, because she felt that she was a machine that did not work, with a masochistic tendency towards failure, in spite of having resorted to manic and omnipotent defences that placed higher priority on 'her own food' in deprecation of the analytic meal. Thus she told the dream at the end of the session to avoid having the analyst serve her up a meal-interpretation. In any case, it seems that the evacuative purpose of the dream was not successful, since the following day her anxiety continued and she acted out, failing the examination, like the machine that did not work in the dream.

For Greenson (1966a) acting out is similar to dreams. It would be a form of sleep-walking, a dream in pantomime. It affords the patient not only the opportunity to repeat his past, but also to modify it.

In patients with a tendency to act out, it is possible to discern, paradoxically, a fairly good perception of reality, which enables them to grasp with accuracy what happens in the depository objects. We might say that they 'transform' reality in elements of the primary process with elements of the secondary process. Acting out would be a dramatization of a dream through which the patient tries to modify the object alloplastically in order to transform it from something autonomous into a depository. Acting out would then be a dramatized dream acted out during wakefulness, a dream that could not be dreamed.

The term 'acting out' usually suggests the pejorative connotation, indicating the resistant behaviour that attacks the analytic process and that is characteristic of some patients in analysis. Its communicative and adaptive nature is not always sufficiently taken into account. Acting out, like any verbal or non-verbal expression furnished by the patient, is also a source of information and should be viewed with the analytic attitude we reserve for dreams. Naturally, we cannot overlook the obvious differences between the two phenomena, particularly regarding the possible dangers of acting out and the tactical changes it may require in therapy (Grinberg & Rodriguez-Perez, 1982).

In conclusion, we should not forget Freud's (1911b) discovery that action makes thinking possible. Thought appears in the mind after motor discharge can be delayed. For this reason, all thought retains as aspect of action. In certain patients, some psychic elements can become recognizably mental only through actions that later become thoughts.

The model for discharge by means of projective identification is the one that best expresses the essence of the psychic phenomenon of acting out. Patients who cannot bear the increase in psychic tension seek its evacuation in external objects through intense projective identifications that erupt in them, triggering, at times, 'projective counteridentification' reactions that reveal themselves as acting out with the analyst himself.

In several articles (Grinberg, 1956, 1962, 1965, 1985), I have studied the nature and evolution of the phenomenon of projective counteridentification. I have used this term to mean the specific response of the analyst in succumbing to the effects of the patient's pathological projective identifications. In this response the analyst 'sees himself carried along' passively to play out roles and experience affects that the patient, in an active though unconscious way, 'forced' into him.

Bird (1957) pointed out a specific peculiarity common to all acting out that includes a bipersonal interaction. He stated: 'An acting-out patient always tries in every possible way to get the analyst to act out with him, and in some measure will invariably succeed' (p. 635).

I shall now present clinical material of a patient who showed a strong tendency towards massive acting out. During the first period of his analysis he seemed to be identified with an idealized, omnipotent object. His ego-syntonic acting out consisted in attacking the analytic relationship in the belief that our respective roles would thus be distorted and reversed. He could not tolerate his therapeutic dependence, which he felt cruelly humiliating. He therefore denied it and projected it on to me.

During this period I had to be very careful not to fall into projective counteridentification reactions. In the course of the sessions the patient would deliberately conceal and distort the material. Later on, he himself called this behaviour 'attacks through omission'. 'Attacks through silence' were also frequent. He would then keep stubbornly silent for some time, thus testing my ability to tolerate waiting and frustration. He sometimes responded to my interpretations with apparent 'deep understanding'. It was not, however, genuine insight but intellectual understanding or pseudo-insight, of which he availed himself as another form of acting out in order not to face the truth. Acting out outside the sessions took place usually at weekends and other intervals, due to the reactivation of his separation anxiety. This consisted mainly of extra-marital sexual relationships. He sometimes spoke of his episodes of acting out as if they were dreams, with overtones of the dreamlike atmosphere that prevailed in them.

He alternated his acting out with somatic illnesses, generally renal colics, feverish states, and precordial pains. As regards the latter, he said that he had been greatly disturbed to learn that the cardiovascular apparatus is the only system that is 'entirely closed and does not allow evacuation'. His acting-out somatizations grew worse after his father's death. This, in turn, threatened him with death. To protect himself, he felt the need to resort again to acting out in search of containers (other than his own body) for his destructive impulses. But ultimately somatizations as well as acting out would turn out to be catastrophic, because they would lead him to death or to murder. If he could not resort to either of them, he found he was at a 'dead end'. This made him feel a claustrophobic anxiety because of his massive identification with the contents and feelings that were 'under pressure' in his psychic apparatus. His acting out was then experienced as an attempt to break away from this no-exit situation.

I shall now discuss the circumstances in which this patient had one of his 'evacuative dreams' in order to protect himself against his intolerable affects and phantasies.

The patient told me about this dream after a sexual acting out due to his failure to tolerate frustration when faced with the separation of a long weekend, which reawakened previous experiences of abandonment and deprivation. His reaction had been intensely persecutory, with aggressive phantasies that sprang from jealousy and envy. He had this dream during the weekend. As I had already told him I would be away for Monday's session, everything was related to the transference situation at that time. He fancied I was going on a trip with my wife. He reported the following dream in Tuesday's session: 'I dreamed of a combine harvester, which, as if it had suddenly gone wild, ran over two pigs. I heard the noise and horrible squeals. I saw their bodies and bellies cut open by the reaping blades. It was really ghastly. They looked like human pieces. I picked up some of the torn pieces. They looked like a child's buttocks.'

Analysis of the associations to the dream showed that the combine harvester represented an aspect of himself that had harvested the nourishment and love provided by his mother's breasts and by his parents. But driven by his frantic greed, envy, and oedipal jealousy, aroused by exclusion from the parental couple (my wife and me on a trip), he had projected his excremental phantasies on to the couple, thus turning them into a couple of pigs (as in the myth of Circe), which he degraded and tore at with his teeth. The noise and the terrifying squeals also corresponded to his phantasy of a sado-masochistic primal scene. The pigs represented, in addition, the two breasts attacked by his oral-sadistic and anal-sadistic phantasies and were transformed into buttocks in the same way as the milk was transformed into excrement. Some parts of his self had also suffered the consequences of his degrading and sadistic attacks, so that they too appeared as pieces of buttocks.

Unable to cope with a longer weekend separation, he had impulsively fallen into a sexual acting out before the dream. He reported that he had been struck by the way intercourse had developed, laying emphasis on how roughly he had taken hold of the woman's buttocks. He was thus reproducing a phantasy of anal coitus through which he had dramatized his phantasy of the primal scene.

As we can see, the dream shows evacuative characteristics and belongs to the primary process in which magical thinking and the pleasure principle prevail.

As his insight into the nature of his acting out episodes deepened and the effort to overcome them increased, there was an attempt to deal with his conflicts at the level of thought and emotion rather than action, as was revealed in the following elaborative dream: 'I was in your consulting room and saw my car in your waiting room. I started the engine and realized something had gone wrong with the "head" valves. I got out and looked to see if there was smoke coming out of the exhaust pipe. But, to my distress, I saw black oil coming out, messing up everything and burning the carpet. Then I went out and met some workers on the street who were trying to raise a car placed on a scaffold to the highest part of the building. I wanted to help the workers, and so I did.'

It was clear from his associations that the car stood for himself, with his damage–illness in the head expressed by his acting out, experienced as uncontrolled anal activity. Due to his identification with the image he had of the analyst, he used his 'powerful mind–motor producing flatus–exhaust interpretations'. But when the omnipotence was curtailed by his being made to see the mess he made of the analysis, his adult part resumed control and was able to help in the work of lifting the 'car' to the highest part, thus restoring the connection between his and the analyst's mind and the mother's breasts, not her buttocks. In this way he offered to co-operate with his analyst so that his conflicts might be treated and finally resolved at the 'higher' level of mind and thought instead of at the 'lower' level of acting out.

Elaborative dreams like the one I have just described show, as Bion (1962) held, that dreaming is the equivalent of thinking. It is the ability to pour one's attention into the internal world. The creative process contained in this type of dream generates the meaning, as Meltzer (1984) pointed out, that will later be unfolded in life and in relationships with the external world. Elaborative dreams show how problems are posed, elaborated and solved.

In short, this attempt to classify dreams has two primary vectors: the associative sequence of the transference–countertransference context, and the correlation between the manifest and latent contents studied comparatively throughout the analytic process.

The difference proposed by Merleau-Ponty (1957) between 'spoken' words with a coagulated sense, proper to verbal actuation, and 'speaking' words, alive and assumed and created by the patient in free association, is similar to the distinction we wish to establish between dreams 'already dreamed' (evacuative) and 'dreaming' dreams (elaborative).

CHAPTER FIFTEEN

The goals of psychoanalysis: 'the search for the truth about one's self'

> Psychoanalysis is, in the first place, a science, and, as
> such, it shares the ethics of science in general; its
> highest value—'the good' that rules it—lies in the
> *knowledge of truth,* or, more precisely, the *search for and*
> *discovery of truth, its affirmation and its defence.*
>
> [Heinrich Racker, 1966]

I n order to understand better what happens in the psychoanalytical process and in its terminal phase, it is important to
know not only the personality of the analysand but also that of
the analyst, and especially the interaction between the two.

The criteria for the termination of analysis have lately been
modified. For my part I accept that the search for truth, mental
growth, and integration through analysis and later self-analysis is
interminable. But on the other hand I am convinced of the necessity of the logical termination of a cycle of fruitful interaction
between the analysand and the analyst, which would enable the

former to continue and control by himself his own mental growth and development.

Freud has pointed out that the analytical relationship is based on a love of truth. But this love of truth, one of the main objectives of analysis, arouses powerful resistances. The capacity of the human being to tolerate the truth about himself is precarious, for truth is a permanent source of pain. This fear of knowing the truth is implicit in resistance to change and the fear of growing up and growing old.

The successful working out of feelings inherent in mourning, the overcoming of resistances and defensive mechanisms, together with increased tolerance of psychic pain, will make it possible to achieve *insight* and come closer to the truth. It is then that the analysand will try to rid himself of his 'false self' and help the emergence of his 'real self', which will give him the investigative power that enables him to end his analysis and to continue with his self-analysis.

Psychoanalytical literature, which has dealt with the theoretical and technical problems related to the termination of analysis and its closing phase, has listed a series of criteria and goals that take into account the patient's development and the achievements he has made in different areas. These criteria are sufficiently well known not to need giving in detail (Symposium, 1937, 1948, 1950; Pfeffer, 1963; Firestein, 1969; Hurn, 1973; Balkoura, 1974; Robbins, 1975).

Firstly, I would like to state the doubts I have regarding such criteria and goals as being the expression of the essence of the psychoanalytic process. Perhaps we do not realize that we 'saturate' the development of the analytical relationship with the aprioristic idea of 'leading' our patients to achieve the 'therapeutic goals' that we had already fixed for them from the very beginning. If this topic is today under review, we should question ourselves whether these 'therapeutic objectives' correspond to what should be our 'psychoanalytical point of view' with its search for truth.

Secondly, I would like to draw attention to the fact that when considering these criteria for the closing point of analysis, the accent has been almost exclusively put on the personality of the analysand. I believe that for a better understanding of what happens in the closing phase, it is important to take into account also the personality of the analyst and the interaction that takes place between the two members of the analytical couple.

Finally, I shall discuss the disadvantages caused, in my opinion, by bearing in mind *too much* the idea of 'termination' during the carrying out of our task within the analytical situation and in the closing phase.

Regarding the first point, the primordial function of the analyst is to try to grasp through intuition and understanding the patient's communication through his verbal and non-verbal messages, and interpret them to help him to understand and also to use his own understanding so that he may know more about himself. This is one of the fundamental differences that exist between psychoanalysis and medicine in which the main objective is the 'cure' of the 'patient'. In the last few years, we analysts appear to have understood better Freud's warning against our deep-rooted tendency to try persistently to 'cure' our analysands. The threat that the medical model has implied for the development and future of psychoanalysis was pointed out by Eissler (1965), who stressed the generalized tendency among some analysts to consider psychoanalysis as a medical speciality through being over-motivated by the therapeutic goal.

In spite of its tremendous impact on mankind, paradoxically enough, it has not yet been possible to place and classify psychoanalysis within any of the existing fields of knowledge. Attempts to categorize it have given rise to a great deal of controversy between those who have thought it to belong to the field of natural sciences and those who have preferred to include it within the realm of humanities. By my criterion, psychoanalysis is a unique and peculiar phenomenon. This affirmation in no way discards the concept of psychoanalysis being a science: however, it is a science with specific and singular characteristics resulting from a revolutionary discovery that disrupted existing frameworks; a science that is not restricted by the sensory background. Bion (1970) proposes to use the term 'intuit' as a parallel in the psychoanalyst's domain to the physician's use of 'see', 'touch', 'smell' and 'hear'. The realizations with which a psychoanalysist deals cannot be seen or touched—anxiety, for example, has no shape or colour, smell or sound. Therefore, psychoanalysis should not be confused nor equated with medical science, nor with any other natural science. It is a totally different discipline consisting of the most important method of investigation carried out *by* the human mind to disclose the secrets *of* the human mind.

This problem is closely linked with the identity of psychoanalysis and that of the analyst, and also with the different philosophies as to how to deal with the closing phase of analysis and its termination. These philosophies derive from the different ways of understanding the psychoanalytic process, the goals of psychoanalysis and the analyst–analysand interaction. I have pointed out elsewhere (Grinberg, 1976b) that the central aim of psychoanalysis, the search for truth, could provoke reactions of fear and hostility that might endanger its future.

If we want to discuss the goals of psychoanalysis and of its closing phase, we should first try to relate them to what we understand by psychoanalysis—that is, its nature. The analytical experience is unique and ineffable and cannot be compared with any other experience. Only people who have taken part in it know what it is all about. But sometimes the great problem we all have is to be able to differentiate an experience that *is* psychoanalysis from one that only looks like it but ends up by being no more than 'pseudo-psychoanalytical'. This is due to the fact that both the analysand and the analyst, either separately or through an unconscious defensive collusion, have tried to avoid authentic insight for fear of facing the painful nature of such knowledge. Sometimes the fear of psychic pain and depressive suffering can awaken strong resistances in both parties of the analytic couple.

This problem of facing up to psychic pain will influence the development of the closing phase of the analysis and its termination in an appreciable way. Perhaps it is advisable to reconsider what is meant by termination of analysis: when it should terminate, how, and who should decide on the termination. Does it depend on the limits to which the analytical experience can go, or does it depend more on the serious difficulties that prevent an adequate termination of the analysis? Should we be guided by the classical criterion of 'cure', or should we wait until the analysand feels he has achieved the capacity to continue autonomously the painful learning that he has initiated with the help of his analyst, getting closer to the truth about himself?

Some authors, like Szasz (1965), assert that we should let the patient take on the responsibility of terminating the analysis in the same way as he took on the responsibility of starting it. In this way the analyst would refrain from exercising a dominant attitude and imposing his own criteria in an authoritative way. This would appear to be consistent with the fact that psychoanalysis is different from all the other psychotherapeutic techniques in that it does not use suggestion or advice, nor does it try to persuade, dominate or direct the analysand. Other authors (Bianchedi et al., 1978) hold the view that it is the analyst who should decide the termination of the analysis. They point out what they call 'the decision of separation' as being of a specific and mature capacity, which is related to the depressive position and characterized by the tolerance of solitude, the possibility of subject–object separation, the giving up of the phantasy of timelessness, and the capacity for gratification and recreation.

In my opinion, the 'decision of separation' should be a product of the interaction between the analyst and the analysand. In other words, the decision should arise as the result of the process of change and mental maturation that will have been operating throughout the analysis and will be reflected in the transference–countertransference link. Both members of the analytical couple will experience, although in a different way, an increase in their capacity for separation, and they will be able to face up to the termination of the relationship in a more depressive manner, with greater tolerance of frustration and loss. Later on I shall return to this point.

Lately it has been held that there is no such thing as an ideal termination; that the symptoms never all disappear completely; the patient does not achieve all the structural changes one would like, nor does he manage to acquire a totally integrated personality. The literature of these last few years has dealt with interruptions, situations of 'impasse', and re-analysis. This would possibly indicate that the classical criteria regarding termination have undergone a modification, or that the patients do not achieve the expected therapeutic changes that respond predominantly to the medical model, or that we should consider the problem of the psychoanalytical goals from another angle.

I believe that analysis does not terminate with the separation of the analyst and the analysand. The only thing that ends is the relationship between them, giving way to a new phase of continuation of the process through self-analysis. In this sense, I agree with Ekstein (1966), who maintains that the closing phase of analysis constitutes a synthesis and also a preparation for a new era. According to him, the epilogue is thus transformed into a new prologue; he used in this case the words of Shakespeare: 'What is past, is prologue'.

My point of view coincides with that of those who maintain the *'interminability'* of the process of searching for mental growth and integration through analysis and subsequent self-analysis. This process, once it has been started, goes on forever, and use will be made of it in all future experiences, although, for different reasons, it may need the help of a new psychoanalytical experience. I think, on the other hand, that what ends is the relationship between the analyst and the analysand—that is, there is a *termination* of the cycle of dynamic interaction between the two, which will allow the analysand to reach a new 'take-off point' from which he can continue and control the development of his mental growth and maturation by himself. In other words, the psychoanalytic relationship is ended, or is about to end, when the psychoanalytic process has been internalized by the analysand.

In the course of an analysis there may be obstacles that threaten its adequate terminability. This leads me to consider Freud's (1937c) classic article on 'Analysis terminable and interminable' from a present-day perspective. I have already referred to the problem of terminability. The problem of 'interminability' could be posed at two different levels: one I have mentioned before, which corresponds to the process of learning from experience and growing towards mental maturity, a process that never ends. The second is stated by Freud in his article, where he relates the 'interminability' of analysis to certain 'prejudicial factors' to the effectiveness of analysis, which may make its duration interminable. On examining this second concept of the 'interminability' of analysis, I think that we could better understand this apparently pessimistic attitude of Freud if we relate the 'obstacles' and the 'prejudicial factors' to the characteristics of the 'psychotic personality' (Bion, 1957), which predominate in the mental functioning of the most regressive patients and which can arise sporadically in neurotic patients as well.

Among these characteristics of the so-called 'psychotic personality' we find precisely the intensification of constitutional aggressive impulses, and a strong envy that manifests itself as hatred of reality, internal and external; such hatred is extended to all the psychic functions, which are linked to these realities. Freud must have felt by intuition the harmful influence of the predominance of a 'psychotic part' of the personality in the course of an analysis, since, in his article, he reiterates the importance of the constitutional strength of instinct, unfavourable alteration of the ego, and the fundamental role that envy plays (although he referred more specifically to penis-envy in the female) as 'prejudicial factors' that could threaten the adequate termination of an analysis.

Until fairly recently there were many analysts who considered that narcissism and borderline personalities were not analysable. This criterion has lately been modified. However, we know the technical difficulties that these patients present due to the functioning of their transference psychosis and the effects that this tends to produce. Precisely such difficulties can increase on occasion because of the unconscious participation of the psychotic modality of mental functioning in the analyst, whether because of the reactivation of his own conflicts and psychotic anxieties at a countertransference level (sometimes due to a deficiency in his own personal analysis), by states of extreme fatigue, or by reactions of projective counteridentification determined by the pathological projections of the patients (Grinberg, 1962). This can last for shorter or longer periods, during which the analyst will function with 'impatience', 'intolerance', and 'insecurity', placing a serious strain on his objectivity, neutrality, and understanding in the relationship with his patient. He may then use various defensive attitudes when facing the unknown and incomprehensible in the patient's material, trying to transform it, for example, into the confirmation of a specific theory that gives some meaning to what is happening; or perhaps he may resort to omniscience, making interpretations that he will try to impose as the only 'truth'; or he may act out by colluding with certain phantasies of his patient, playing different roles that were projected into him by the patient. Without doubt, our patients, through their pathological defences, can provoke irritation, intense anxiety, extreme courtesy, and over-protection as specific responses in us. They may also make us feel deeply depressed, so that we take on ourselves the mourning that they cannot stand; or confuse us with an intellectualized attitude of pseudo-collaboration, and so on. With regard to the theme we are dealing with, it would be useful, for example, to be able to detect the unconscious motives we have for wanting to 'retain' a patient and so prolong his analysis excessively or to bring about a premature termination. Generally, these defensive attitudes find their strength in the interaction between the analyst and the analysand.

So, faced with the emergence of material that means a threat of intense psychic pain, both partners could resort to an unconscious defensive collusion, which, in turn, could become the equivalent of what Freud described as the 'bedrock'—that is, the limit that indicates the end of the analytical possibilities. Such collusion under the influence of the 'psychotic personality' in both will determine, in the end, the lack of 'insight' and mental growth and will produce an inevitable stagnation in the psychoanalytic process.

The transference and countertransference problems that I have described above illustrate some of the 'dangers' of analysis mentioned by Freud (1937c) which can threaten the terminability of the analysis. Naturally, we should try to be aware of these unconscious processes and face up to the truth about ourselves, however difficult this may be, since the patient should be helped to know the truth about himself.

In the closing phase of all analyses, even with neurotic patients, similar moments can arise as a result of the peculiar kind of interaction that happens between the analyst and the analysand during this period (Alvarez de Toledo et al., 1966). The splitting mechanisms in the patient tend to become reactivated, alternating the phantasies of idealization with those of persecution in the transference relationship. The manic phantasies, with feelings of triumph over the analyst, and the depressive phantasies, in which the analyst, felt as attacked and hurt, is introjected, giving rise to catastrophic phantasies, will both gradually disappear and will give way to the reparatory tendencies, to the gradual increase of integration, mental growth, and autonomy of the patient, with the accentuated predominance of the reality principle (Freud, 1911b) and progressive recognition of the changes that have been taking place. Nevertheless, such changes can recreate a new wave of anxiety and persecution involving both members of the analytic couple. This resistance to change, with the fear of growth and of growing old, forms part of the unconscious death anxiety that can appear in both parties in the dramatic experience developing at this time. Such a death anxiety would also be linked to the mourning for losses that they feel are irretrievable, and to a closer approach to truth through a more real type of thought. It is a painful truth and one that has been avoided until then: the full recognition of the passage of time, as much in the analyst as in the analysand; illusory timelessness is transformed into a real temporality, and the omnipotent phantasies and those of immortality are limited. These limitations are experienced, many times, as a partial death.

The successful working through of these feelings, with the tolerance of psychic pain that is contained in them, will help the consolidation of insight, will aid adequate termination and separation, and will also stimulate the capacity for self-analysis as one of the important goals of the psychoanalytical process. On the other hand, the failure to work through will bring about a disturbance in the mourning, with a tendency towards a premature termination of the analysis or its indefinite prolongation.

The process of working through, that is absolutely essential in the closing phase of the analysis, is a result of the interaction between progression and regression. In other words, it is a process that takes advantage of the latent capacity for regression in an organized and systematic way, creating a moratorium and allowing the consolidation of the subsequent balancing movement. Pain is always present in every working-through, so we may talk about the 'painful task of working through' (Freud, 1914g, 1917e [1915]) which also includes mourning and reparation for the objects and parts of the self that the patient feels are hurt by his own phantasies (Grinberg, 1963a), and which underlie the reactions that bring about substantial and permanent changes in the attitude of the ego faced with its conflicts. During this working through, the analysand will need the help and support of the analyst, who will offer him his capacity for floating attention, and the understanding and containing of his pain and anxiety. Insight is a fundamental milestone in the process of working through in that it is a consequence of the integrative tendencies of the ego, and it is also the cause of subsequent integration.

The development of the closing phase of the analysis and its termination are closely linked to the acquisition of insight. Insight, besides meaning the conscious understanding of unconscious processes, is the foundation of lasting changes in the personality, through the capacity to discriminate between the internal and external world, consolidate the reality principle, and diminish omnipotence and activities subjected to the pleasure principle.

Segal (1962) pointed out that 'psychoanalytical insight is different from insight in any other situation. . . . It involves conscious knowledge of archaic processes, normally inaccessible to the most intuitive person, through reliving in the transference the very processes that structured one's internal world and conditioned one's perceptions. The insight itself is a constant new factor in the process, and it is always dynamically altering. . . .'

The learning that has been achieved through insight will help us to overcome psychotic anxieties (Klein, 1950) and will produce changes and remodelling of the ego, which will continue spontaneously in the analysand, allowing the application of the acquired understanding to all subsequent experiences. During the closing phase of analysis, a point in time and space will appear in which a 'state of separation' begins (Winnicott, 1971) between the analyst and the analysand, which would also correspond to the state of 'separation–individuation' (Mahler, 1965). The analysand, thanks to acquired insight, begins to develop his greater capacity for discrimination, reality-thinking, and creative potential in an autonomous and separate way, although the transference neurosis is often not entirely resolved; at the same time he will feel able to work through the mourning for his irrecoverable losses.

In my opinion the concept of insight is interwoven with the concept of 'becoming O' as formulated by Bion (1970). The road to the deepest and most genuine understanding would be through the processes of transformation, which have as their starting-point an initial experience or situation that Bion calls 'transformation in O'. This term can be applied by extension to everything that could otherwise be called 'the unknowable ultimate reality', 'absolute truth', 'the unknown', 'infinity'. In psychoanalysis we use the symbol O to represent all that the patient does not know, that is, his psychic reality, which shows itself through his multiple trans-formations. The transformations related to 'knowing about some-thing' correspond with what Bion calls 'transformations in K', which result in a kind of intellectual knowledge. On the other hand, 'transformations in O' are related to experiences of deep change, mental growth, insight, and 'becoming O'. According to Bion, reality, by definition, cannot be known, although it can be 'been'; he says 'there should be a transitive form of the verb to be, expressly for use with the term reality' (Bion, 1962). This is what he calls 'becoming O'. The analyst is concerned with his patient's psychic reality in such a way that he goes beyond 'knowing about it' even though this knowledge (K link) is an important part of the analytic process. The transformation in O is thus something like 'being that which is'. In the same way, this transformation is feared and resisted because of the danger and pain that 'becoming O' implies, in so far as 'becoming O' is the equivalent of 'being oneself, one's own truth', with the responsibility inherent in such a transformation. So, for example, it is not enough that a patient knows he has envy; he should rather feel that he is envious and be able to tolerate it. That is why insight is related to 'becoming O', since this is what enables us to approach the truth about ourselves.

It would of course be very important to be able to distinguish such insight, intimately bound up with coming close to truth, from all other types of intellectual knowledge or 'pseudo-insight, which tend towards the opposite, that is to say the avoidance of truth. [Bion (1962) considers that fundamental emotions exist that are ever present in the relationship between people. He proposed three important links with their corresponding emotions: the love link (L), the hate link (H), and the knowledge link (K).]

Precisely when talking about the goals of psychoanalysis, Freud (1937c) showed us that the business of analysis 'is to secure the best possible psychological conditions for the functions of the ego; with that, it has discharged its task'. He adds ' . . . We must not forget that *the analytic relationship is based on a love of truth*, that is, on a recognition of reality, and that it precludes any kind of shame or deceit' (my italics).

In my opinion, not only the analysand but also the analyst should achieve the best possible psychological conditions in order to carry out 'the psychoanalytical function of the personality' and to be able to help his patient so that the psychoanalytical experience that evolves within the time-space of a continually expanding universe may develop towards insight and the search for 'the love of truth'. This is why analysis should unfold in such a way as to create the conditions that allow the analyst and the analysand to transform an activity that consists of 'talking about psychoanalysis' into another one, which '*is* psychoanalysis (becoming O). Bion also stressed that the search for truth was as essential for mental growth as food is for the growth of the biological organism. Without truth, the mind does not develop; it dies of starvation. But insight, based on the love for truth, and the principal goal of analysis, awakens in the majority of cases, the most powerful resistances. Bion (1978) pointed out that 'we have to alter to a point where we can comprehend the universe in which we live. The trouble is that supposing we reach that point, our feelings of fear or terror might be so great that we could not stand it. So the search for truth can be limited by our lack of intelligence or wisdom and by our emotional inheritance. The fear of knowing the truth can be so powerful that the doses of truth are lethal'. The analyst, during his work of investigation, disclosing the secrets of the patient's mind, often stumbles against not only the barrier raised by the patient's resistance to insight and truth, but also his own barrier, which is determined by the anxiety that this getting closer to insight means. Frequently, therefore, as I have pointed out before, both resistances join together and gain strength to avoid facing up to the psychic pain associated with the acquisition of insight. This collusion can be demonstrated through mutual idealizations and convictions of omnipotence, the use of intellectualization, pseudo-insight, and other defence mechanisms. One of the results will be inhibition of the functioning of the creative part of the personality and stimulation of the psychotic mode of mental functioning, with a tendency towards falsehood and cheating.

When the analysand manages to overcome his fears and resistances and, with the help of the analytical work, achieves insight and is able to approach the truth, he will try to get rid of his 'false self', creating the conditions that will allow his 'true self' to come to the surface (Winnicott, 1955). This will give him the ability to go on with his investigation and self-analysis.

I shall now present some clinical fragments on a patient whose analysis I supervised; they illustrate some of the vicissitudes of the closing phase of the analysis.

The patient is a man of 35, the only son of the family; he has an older married sister and two younger sisters who are single. His parents are still alive; they are farm workers with a humble background. The patient is single and works as an architect, a profession that he studied in response to his father's wishes. He would have preferred to study philosophy. He was in the seventh year of analysis, which he had initiated because of a depressive state and because of difficulties in his object-relations. One of the problems to which special attention was paid during long periods of his analysis was the patient's feeling that his parents had overburdened him with heavy responsibilities since his childhood because of the fact that he was the only son, and that he had had to satisfy the ambitions and aims of his parents most of his life. This relationship of dependence and frustrated rebellion had prevented him from considering his own wishes. The patient had used different defences to counteract these situations; among others, that of a strong conviction of the 'purity' of his moral and ethical values. In this way, by setting up a façade (pseudo-self) of a compensatory self-idealization, he could consider himself as one of the few 'non-contaminated' in this world of 'falsehood and lies'. Part of the material that I shall present of the last period of his analysis will be precisely related to the problems of truth and lies, linked to the oedipal and pre-oedipal conflicts and the corresponding trans-ference phantasies.

In one session during this time, the patient said he felt 'corset-ted' and could not talk naturally. He said he was afraid of acting aggressively towards his analyst, and for this reason he had to control himself very carefully, the greatest risk being, according to him, that the analyst would leave him because of this. Then he associated this with the possibility of the ending of the analysis, and he asked himself what the termination of the analysis would depend on and how and when this could be determined. He had no idea at all about this. The analyst told him that in a way he had implicitly supplied the answer, suggesting that the analysis should go on until the relationship with the analyst was no longer inhibiting and he felt free and autonomous. That is to say, the analyst realized the latent claustrophobic anxiety, interpreting his fear of being trapped within the analysis, and he could see the termination on the horizon once his fear of being 'enclosed' had disappeared or diminished.

In another session, the patient complained bitterly about women and, in particular, an attractive woman whom he had known lately and who was too demanding. (He repeated again the story of his dependence on his parents). Stemming from an affair of a friend of his, who said that he was very much in love with his wife but had managed to make a prostitute his 'exclusive' lover, he said he felt indignation, although he admitted that this situation fasci-nated him. It was interpreted that he was furious at having to depend on women and on his analyst and at not being able to have them at his exclusive command as he would have liked—just as he felt his friend, whom he envied, had done with the prostitute. It was added that he felt like a cheated baby discovering 'Mummy's lies': instead of dedicating all her time to him, she also looked after 'Daddy' and his 'brothers'. The 'Mummy–analyst' appeared as a mother whom he wanted to cheat for vengeance, and at the same time treat as a prostitute whom he wanted to possess exclusively for himself.

In the following session he said he had thought a lot about 'lying', and he had realized that he was obliged not to lie to the analyst but to tell him all the truth, as had happened with his mother who looked him straight in the eyes and intimidated him. Later he related the following dream: 'I was at the session, and you made an interpretation of this kind: "You are trying to tell me your mother is going to have another baby"; it seemed that she was going to have it by my father. I told you that this was impossible, that my mother was 70 years old; and you answered that it was unusual but not impossible. I felt uneasy and anxious in the same way as I feel when I doubt if I am telling you things because I really feel them or because of my loyalty to you. Then I felt very anxious, and I ran away, trying to flee from you, and you were running after me. I got into my parents' house, and I saw some wire netting around the lift shaft. I don't know how I did it, but I took some of the wire netting and wrapped it round me to protect myself from you, but it was very heavy, and because of this, when I got to one of the upper floors, I took it off over my head and threw it down the lift shaft to get rid of it.'

He realized then that he had associated his mother with his analyst, and, as regards the wire netting, it was like saying: 'That's enough of this defensive play and fighting against you: but the funny thing was that I did not feel any relief, nor did I feel free. Rather, I continued to feel oppressed.' There was a long pause, and then he went on: 'In the middle of all this, lately I felt more optimistic . . . but I still felt pain. It is a mixture of feelings . . . a kind of loneliness and helplessness, of hope and despair. I am alone, and I feel as if I have nothing.'

The dream demonstrates, among other things, that the failure of omnipotent control over his parent–analyst—he was trying to prevent his parents from having other children who would separate him from their love and replace him—transformed them into persecutors. He tried to find refuge by covering himself with the 'wire netting pseudo-self', which made him feel again omnipotent and 'pure'. But in so far as he felt he had acquired a maturity in his analysis ('on arriving at the upper floors'), he achieved more insight into his attitude of cheating and lying (wire netting pseudo-self), which, on this occasion, manifested itself in his apparent condemnation and criticism of his friend (into whom he had projected his lying, omnipotent pseudo-self) and whom he envied because he, his friend, could cheat, not giving himself exclusively to others, and exercising 'exclusive' control over the rest. His increase in insight and his perception that he was getting close to the final phase of analysis helped him to understand that he could not continue with this façade of the pseudo-self, which was now becoming a heavy weight that he wanted to get rid of. But though it meant staying with his more authentic self, it also made him feel anxious and alone.

According to M. Klein (1963), with integration and the growing feeling of reality, omnipotence is bound to be lessened; this con-tributes to the pain of integration and brings greater hopelessness, increasing the feeling of loneliness and loss of idealization, as the patient said. The fear of death also plays an important role in loneliness, together with the feeling that some aspects of the self have been split off and put away and can never be recovered. Winnicott (1958) also referred to 'the capacity for being alone', which develops and strengthens when one has been able to go through the infantile experience of peaceful solitude, helped and guaranteed by favourable conditions that allow one to begin the experience of loneliness, though this moment should be of 'loneli-ness with someone'. Similar situations will happen in the closing phase of the analysis.

Returning to the clinical example, some time after the sessions that I have mentioned it could be verified that the patient tried to reinforce his manic defences in order to counteract his depressive feelings; he also had phantasies in which he saw the analyst as a 'mother–baker' who was obliged to feed him and even to feel gratitude for doing so, since, through his very existence, the ana-lyst could develop as a 'mother'. But, gradually, an appreciable change was noted in the transference link. The manic defences gave way to another kind of affective reaction, through which he felt moved on realizing the dedication, stability, and interest with which the analyst had treated him 'continuously, day after day, for so many years'. In one session during this period, near to Christmas, he related the following dream: 'Luz, this married woman with whom I have this good relationship, arrives and tells me that she is on the point of separation from her husband. I was sorry that she was going to separate, and I took her hand to console and protect her. At the same time, I felt that her separation pleased me in a way.' (Luz is a feminine name in Spanish, which also means 'light'). The analyst interpreted this as a reference to his own separation from his analyst because they were very close to the Christmas holidays, but that he was experiencing this as a foretaste of the definite separation that the termination of the analysis would bring. If he felt sorry because of having to separate, he also experienced the need to acquire the 'knowledge–light– mother' (insight) so that he could form a couple with 'Luz/(light)– knowledge' and make the most of her for himself.

It is true that, at a certain level and by other associated sequences, the dream could be understood as the restructuring of an oedipal situation in which he felt he took away the capacity for insight from his 'father–analyst', which was symbolized in the dream for a 'mother–light' with whom his 'father–analyst' formed a couple. But the feeling of triumph partly endangered the positive aspects of his capacity to identify himself with the psychoanalytic function of his analyst in order to take over the responsibility for, and to protect, the knowledge (insight) he had acquired and to be able to make good use of it for his own future self-analysis.

The topic of termination arose, on different occasions, in the manifest and/or latent content of the material in a spontaneous way, as the analysand was gaining greater insight into his omnipotent behaviour, his aggressive phantasies, and his tend- ency to cheat. Increasing understanding of the meaning of his attitudes and cheating behaviour on the one hand, and the dimin- ishing of his omnipotent phantasies on the other, meant that he could get closer to a truth that he had feared and avoided almost all his life. The analyst felt, for his part, that during all this time he had been working with material presented by the patient without having openly thought about the possibility of the termination of the analysis or that it could come about shortly. The analysand commented, on another occasion, that the way his analyst had 'worked like an ant', slowly and surely, was priceless; and he felt easier knowing that the analyst was disposed to be available as long as was necessary, since this prepared him better for his future separation.

Once again, I would like to point out the advantage of considering the terminability of the cycle of interaction between the analyst and the analysand during the psychoanalytic process. This idea of terminability can become more evident and explicit at specific moments during the closing phase of the analysis. It is natural, therefore, that the analyst, *while he is away from the sessions,* thinks about the evolution of his patient, tries to evaluate his progress, and considers the possibility of terminating the analysis if he feels, among other things, that he has been able to awaken the patient's 'longing' or his love for the essential food of the analysis, that is to say the approach to the truth that is what will fundamentally stimulate his mental growth.

But while he is working *within the sessions* with his analysand, I think it would be useful for him not to feel compelled to look at all the material of this phase through the prism of termination. The predominance of the aprioristic and deliberate thought that the analysis is 'on the point of' ending or 'should' end would condition the analytic work in such a way as seriously to obstruct the ability to detect what is authentically new in the material and what is most unknown and feared by the patient, such as getting closer to 'the love of truth'; and it can therefore endanger the achievement of greater insight and psychic growth.

Freud, in one of his letters to Lou Andreas-Salomé (Pfeiffer, 1972), included the following sentence: 'I know I have to blind myself artificially in my work in order to focus all the light on the only dark point.' Eissler (1975) when he quoted this sentence in his book, added that Freud emphasized 'the great advantage of approaching the field of observation without any pre-established or preconceived ideas'.

In recommending the technical attitude of not having aprioristically in mind the idea of 'termination' during the closing phase of the analysis, I am suggesting something similar to what Bion (1970) proposed: working 'without memory or desire', which, in my opinion, constitutes an extension at the same time as a deeper application of the concept postulated by Freud of 'floating attention'. I think that this attitude will in some way be transmitted to analysand and will favour more beneficial and productive analytical work during this period. I also believe that the analyst should offer his *availability* for as long as the patient requires it. The topic of termination will arise spontaneously and on its own at the right moment as a natural consequence of the dynamic interaction that has developed between the analyst and the analysand and the development achieved in the analytic process, giving rise, therefore, to the fact that the material regarding the possibilities of separation may be analysed, with its phantasies and mourning reactions, in a mature and shared way, as long as both parties can be free of all kinds of external and internal pressures. Nevertheless, I am conscious of the fact that there is an area of the pathology of some of our patients that prevents them from thinking about termination as they are unwilling to take on responsibility for themselves.

The experience of the closing phase of analysis, with its inevitable frustrations and uncertainties, will stimulate the analyst to increase his tolerance towards these and face up to the mourning that he will have to work through as well as the analysand. Perhaps one of the most difficult types of mourning to get through for the analyst will be the mourning for his omnipotent belief in his ability to reach a solution to all of the analysand's problems that he has come to face. He will, therefore, accept his own limitations and those of analysis with more humility and modesty. He will try to balance whether dedicating part of his life, attention, and effort to this particular experience, whose results may probably have been less than he had initially expected, has been worthwhile: but on other occasions he will feel the satisfaction of having helped another human being to grow mentally through, as Meltzer (1967) has stressed, 'the most mature segment of the personality beginning to develop its capacities for introspection, analytic thought and responsibility. These accomplishments set the stage for the *work of termination,* on the one hand, and the *interminable work of integration through analysis and self-analysis,* on the other' (my italics).

I would like to add a few words about the post-analytic period. I believe that the consideration of this period is a topic of enormous interest, which deserves continued systematic investigation in the future, following the path already begun by different authors including Pfeffer (1959), Kramer (1959), Rangell (1966) and Guiard (1978). I think that the evaluation of the progress of the analysand in stages subsequent to the termination would be of even more value if it could be completed by a deep and detailed study of the maintenance of insight, 'getting closer to the truth', and the development of self-analysis.

Consideration of the emotional experiences that will move the analyst in the closing phase of his analytical work will be equally important and will influence, in one way or another, the post-analysis and subsequent stages of his professional life.

CHAPTER SIXTEEN

Regressive aspects
of obsessive mechanisms:
omnipotent control
and realistic control

I In this chapter I intend to discuss the nature and aim of some
obsessive mechanisms (particularly that of obsessional control) and the influence they have on the state of the self and
object-relations.

We are all familiar with Abraham's (1924) classical differentiation of two sub-phases at the anal stage. He insisted on the line of
demarcation between the two phases because it shows the point at
which a real object-relationship is established, thus highlighting
one of the main distinctions between neurosis and psychosis. The
second anal stage belongs to obsessional neurosis and relates to
the conservative trends of retention and control of the object.

In my opinion, we can discriminate still further, considering
more regressive as well as more developed aspects of the obsessive
mechanisms. The former correspond to the well-known entity of
obsessional neurosis characterized by a severe symptomatology,
the cruelty of the superego, and a distorted interpretation of reality. On the other hand, the latter preserve reparative elements,
make it possible to establish a better contact with reality, and

endeavour to maintain the relation with the external object. Melanie Klein (1932) pointed out that obsessive mechanisms begin to operate at any early stage in infancy, but, at first, they are not organized into what later, in the course of evolution, would arise as an obsessional neurosis. She added that to overcome anxiety, the ego resorts mainly to a guarantee of the protection of its objects. Abraham placed this reaction at the secondary anal stage. Klein holds that obsessive mechanisms also constitute an attempt to modify the psychotic conditions underlying infantile neuroses.

It is my concern here to deal specifically with the mechanism of obsessive control as it appears at regressive levels as well as in more highly integrated ones following the distinction I made above.

At a more regressive level obsessive control functions together with an acute feeling of omnipotence, leading to the 'omnipotent control' that is closely connected with the 'omnipotence of thought' as described by Freud (1913 [1912–1913]). Abraham (1919) studied some patients he described as the 'narcissistic type', who are very difficult to analyse and whose attitude is one of deceit, selfishness, and anal 'omnipotent control'. Rivière (1936) also referred to narcissistic patients with a negative therapeutic reaction, who, prompted by an unconscious feeling of guilt and a deep depression they cannot cope with, resort to a manic defence of 'omnipotent control' over the analyst and the analytical situation. But she adds that this aspect of defence by control is quite near to the obsessive technique and can be mixed up with it.

We know besides that the feeling of omnipotence as well as 'omnipotent control' have been regarded quite differently in psychoanalytical literature as they were thought to be either schizoid mechanisms, manic defences, or obsessive symptoms. Incidentally, Klein (1940) has shown in several papers the close connection between manic defences and obsessive ones.

It is not relevant here to insist on this point, but I think it would be useful to proceed with the investigation of the relation between those two types of defence with a view to distinguishing the quality of the obsessive and manic elements that are represented, for example, in 'omnipotent control'. I should like to point out the relationship between obsessional control mechanisms and manic reparation, although I cannot discuss this relationship here. Segal (1964) includes 'omnipotent control' among the manic defences, together with feelings of triumph and contempt as a defensive triad at the beginning of the depressive position, which arises at a more developed stage of the ego and is aimed specifically against depressive anxiety and guilt. Then she defines omnipotent control as the means used to deny dependence and yet make the object fulfil the need for dependence. I fully agree with this criterion, but I should like to add, following Klein (1946), that the impulse to control other persons plays a decisive role in obsessional neurosis. She adds: '. . . one root of obsessive mechanisms may thus be found in the particular identification which results from infantile projective processes'. She also says that every relationship based on projective mechanism is of a narcissistic nature because, in this case, the object represents one part of the subject.

It is my aim now to differentiate 'omnipotent control' of an obsessive nature from the kind of obsessive control present at a more mature and integrated level. For the latter, I propose the term 'adaptational control', to stress the fact that it functions with better adaptation to reality and with a stronger tendency to cathect the external object. This mechanism helps to maintain the integration of the self and its connection with reality, through the control of the parts of the self projected on to the object. Projections of parts of the self into the object will be discussed later.

To gain a better understanding of these processes, it would be well to consider how the projective identification mechanism functions and also the way in which re-introjections occur when they can be accomplished. As a result of what has been described so far, we can realize the considerable importance of the functioning of projective identification mechanisms as described by Klein (1946) and her followers.

Under normal conditions, these mechanisms permit empathy with the object, for they allow the subject to put himself in somebody else's place. Every person inevitably provokes certain emotional reactions in another, according to the attitudes he shows, the way he looks at or speaks to him, the content of what he says, his expressions and gestures, and so forth. This is to say that projective identifications—coming from the different sources that awaken the corresponding emotional reactions: sympathy, anger, sorrow, hostility, boredom and so on.—are always in action. This is what usually takes place in any human relationship and represents the core of human communication; the object, in turn, also functions with his own projective identifications; there is thus a mutual exchange. This would correspond to the mechanism described by Freud in *Group Psychology and the Analysis of the Ego* (1921c) through which the replacement of the ego-ideal by an external object occurs. The genetic prototype of this mechanism is represented by the anal expulsive mode, but it may convey the phantasies proceeding from various erogenous levels and zones. It might happen, for instance, that in certain regressive stages projective identification would operate with particular violence, as is the case in schizophrenia and other psychoses. Nevertheless, under more normal conditions, projective identifications work under the influence of the obsessive mechanisms of 'adaptational' control and can be better regulated. In certain cases, these control mechanisms help the subject to maintain contact with reality and to achieve a certain degree of adaptation, even in serious illnesses.

Obsessional control would be adaptational or omnipotent, depending on the quality and intensity with which the mechanisms of projective identification function. In other words, if projective identification is particularly strong and destructive, the aspects projected on to the object and the object itself have suffered the effects of this violence, and re-introjection would be hardly accomplished, as it would be burdened with highly persecutory contents. This will determine the subject's incapacity to maintain a relationship with the external object, and he will then resort regressively to omnipotent control.

When projective identification acts in a milder way, or presents characteristics closer to normality, it will be easier for the subject to accomplish re-introjection and to accept the introjects. In such circumstances adaptational obsessional control will function, thus maintaining the relationship with the external object, with the projected parts and with reality. On this level the logical process prevails, contrasting with the magical thinking that is present at the regressive level of omnipotent control.

It seems that what causes regression from adaptational to omnipotent control is the collapse of the underlying depressive organization. This can be specially observed in those cases of obsessional neurosis in which a schizoid pathology predominates.

In general terms, it might be said that when there is an evolution of the paranoid organization towards the depressive one, the adaptational control mechanisms are likely to be reinforced; on the other hand, when a breakdown of the depressive organization occurs, with the subsequent relapse into schizoid pathology, the functioning of the omnipotent obsessional control is increased.

When, due to different stimuli, the self feels its cohesion is threatened, these mechanisms of adaptational control tend to strengthen. Nevertheless, there are times when the stimulus is sufficiently strong to impair, for a longer or shorter period, the functioning of those mechanisms; it is then that a loss of the control of the projected aspects may occur, precipitating a lessening of the organization of the self, with the ensuing disturbance of the sense of reality, feeling of estrangement, and disturbance of object-relations that characterize the phenomenon of depersonalization.

To sum up, I consider that there is a more integrated adaptational control as opposed to the more regressive omnipotent control. The failure of the former mechanism triggers the 'omnipotent control' as well as states of disturbance of the self such as depersonalization.

'Omnipotent control':
a clinical example

A brief example will illustrate the first type of this well-known 'omnipotent control'.

A young patient, severely traumatized by war experiences when he was a child, developed a serious obsessional neurosis, with acute schizoid and paranoid traits (Grinberg, 1955). The strong persecuting and dramatic elements of the external reality, under the Nazi invasion, had considerably increased his already existing anxieties, resulting from conflictual relations with his parents. He suffered from a series of obsessions that hampered his life, for he exerted an exaggerated control over his thoughts, actions, and words. From the very beginning of his analysis these symptoms were clearly shown in the transference. He adopted a typical paranoid attitude and exercised an omnipotent and massive control, which pervaded the whole atmosphere in his sessions. Thanks to this 'power' of his to 'manage' at will our whole relationship, he thought he was able to foretell the phrases and words I would use, the extent and duration of my interpretations, the tone of voice I would use, and even my emotional reactions.

After dealing with this material for a long while, he came to one of his sessions complaining of being tired and having pains in the precordial area. He fancied he might be having heart trouble and added that he panted when running to catch a vehicle to come to the session. Afterwards he told me the following dreams: In one, he dreamt of the Russian revolution, Cossacks, policemen with machine-guns; the Czar had to run away, and he said it had all happened in order to take him away from his wife, the Czarina. In another dream, someone was driving a car at high speed and crashed against a wall; it might have been himself. In a third dream he was travelling with his mother in the front part of a locomotive when suddenly he fell on the rails and was run down by the train. Right away he saw himself as if he had been another person, asking his mother what was left of himself, to which his mother replied, 'Nothing, just some rubbish and blood'. The mother used the Polish term, which meant dung.

We could analyse that these dreams, like the hypochondriac reaction, were concerned with his mother's present pregnancy and the unusual fact that he knew of her decision to have an abortion. This had been a severe blow to him and to his phantasies of omnipotent control, as he had been an only child for so long. He tried to take an active part in the discussions and in the decision to be taken, talking separately with his mother and father. And he had tried to 'influence' indirectly a doctor, a friend of his mother's, to advise her to have an abortion.

In that session he was very anxious and resorted to his omnipotent mechanisms to maintain his control and obsessive isolation. He carefully timed when he should speak after my interpretations, and he avoided the words I had used in my formulations. He made a point of pronouncing differently the letters 'v' and 'b' (which in Argentine are normally pronounced alike) etc., etc.

I interpreted his need to control in an omnipotent manner the foetus that was in his mother's womb, as a way of controlling his father's penis inside her and, ultimately, of achieving control of the primal scene, and that was the reason why he tried to prevent some of my words–penis–interpretation from turning into a foetus inside him. On the other hand, by controlling, he sought to keep his parents separated outside and inside him ('b' and 'v'), as he was trying to maintain the separation between him (mother) and me (father) during the session. This conflict was expressed in his dreams by the bloody revolution in which the Czar had to leave the Czarina; by someone crashing violently (abortion); by his being thrown away and turned into rubbish or dung–blood (identification with the foetus). I also pointed out that when he was confronted with the failure of his omnipotent control, a conflict arose between his internal objects, parents fighting, by a revolutionary–sadistic coitus that caused a hypochondriacal symptom (heart pains), which appeared when he was running after the vehicle (car, train).

As a response to this interpretative sequence, he remembered that lately he had been worrying about his two profiles. He found the right side of his face quite different and 'inferior' to his left one. He felt they belonged to two different persons. He felt compelled to look at both profiles in the mirror over and over again, till one day he thought the left one was like his father's. From that moment on he was obsessed by the idea of actually separating the two halves of his face, even if it meant splitting it surgically.

'*Adaptational control*'
and its relationship
with some states of depersonalization

I shall now present another clinical example to illustrate the second type of control and how the failure of adaptational control leads to the emergence of symptoms of depersonalization.

Some years ago I had the opportunity to treat a patient who suffered from depersonalization phenomena of a non-schizoid type, associated with acute reactions of anxiety and confusion, only during the course of his psychoanalytical sessions (Grinberg, 1954). He asked for analysis because of sexual impotence as well as phobic and compulsive symptoms, which made him feel extremely anxious and depressed; his behaviour was characterized by typical rituals.

He happened to be a patient who made important progress in his relationships and his work, and there were times when his symptoms virtually disappeared, revealing proper adaptation to his environment and reality. His adaptational control mechanisms would then function successfully, thus allowing the predominance of his good aspects in his object-relationships and in his relations with reality. But confronted with an increase of some of his impulses and of his separation anxiety as shown in the example presented here, he became panic-stricken and his mechanisms of adaptational control regressed to those of omnipotent control.

In one period of treatment, we had been analysing the way he had projected certain aspects of his self into me as well as the control he exerted over all those valuable things he believed I possessed, which he strongly envied. One Monday he came to the session feeling extremely depressed. He talked laboriously and told me that he had recently failed in sexual intercourse. While he was introducing his penis, he had a phantasy that 'it would die inside the vagina'. He added that he had been thinking of what I might have done during the weekend and that he had lived it as if he had been in my place, driving my car, being with my family and enjoying everything I had. In this way he exercised, in his own phantasy, control over the separation anxiety and, at the same time, took possession of all those things he envied. He said his reactions wavered between the feeling of having 'swallowed up all I possessed' and that of being installed like a 'rock' in my belongings.

Due to the exceptional intensity of his oral-sadistic and anal-sadistic phantasies, and to his separation anxiety, it seemed that his usual mechanisms of 'adaptational' control had failed, and that they could no longer provide him with protection. The first consequence was the symptom of sexual impotence. When I interpreted to him the relationship between this symptom and the fear he had experienced during the weekend of what might happen to his penis in the vagina, as well as the fear of what might happen to those parts of his self projected into me, he remembered the following dream: 'I was with M. (his fiancée); suddenly she approached me and tried to kiss me. I was panic-stricken and rejected her with a gesture. I had the impression she wanted to suck me, like a leech . . . that she was going to bite me and suck my blood.' He associated that he had seen his sister-in-law nursing her baby at her breast, and that he had felt sexually excited and strongly impressed by the physical sensation he had experienced in his own mouth. I pointed out to him his own difficulty in his speech during the session and added that this was related to his dream and that part of him wanted to suck and drain me of all my contents, and that he himself felt like a leech. He was silent for a while and then said that he had to make an enormous effort to open his mouth and articulate the words. He added at once that he felt all the objects in the consulting room strange and distant.

His speech became more and more broken; he made long pauses between the different syllables of each word, saying he was unable to connect them. He was obviously undergoing a process of speech depersonalization. In my intepretation I showed him that what he was experiencing with his words was identical to what was happening to those aspects of his self and of his body representations that were projected on to me. As a consequence of the loss of his control, all those parts related to his aggressive phantasies now became isolated and unconnected. At another level, this was a phantasy of cutting into pieces in which his penis–word was used as the sadistic instrument with which he carried out his aggression through his projective identifications. This frequently happens when there are present obsessional symptoms in which the speech is endowed with erotic contents and reflects specifically the fear of castration.

In this period of depersonalization his identity was disturbed due to the feeling of loss of contact with his projected infantile parts because the mechanisms of adaptational control that guaranteed such contact had failed. [The loss of contact between the projected infantile aspects and the adult level of the self is illustrated in Melanie Klein's paper 'On identification' (1955). I have also dealt with his problem in my book *Guilt and Depression* (Grinberg, 1963a) and in my paper 'Two kinds of guilt' (1964), in which I refer to the specific mourning caused by the loss of parts of the self.] This example is, at the same time, a sort of contact taboo in which the syllables could not be connected with each other, since they were considered as 'symbolic equations' (Segal, 1957).

A few days later he repeated the episode of depersonalization. He complained of having had gastric trouble and a hypochondrical phantasy with the sensation of having a hole in his stomach. Then a dream came to his mind in which he saw his dead mother with a hole in her forehead. He associated this hole with the one in his stomach. He felt compelled to stop up that hole with food to calm his hunger; but the food he ate not only failed to calm his hunger, it also made him feel like defaecating again and again, although he could only eliminate 'scybalums' after considerable efforts. In his unconscious phantasy the hole was transformed into a sphincter, which turned the food into excrement. During his sessions, it was very difficult for him to listen to or remember what I said to him. When speaking about the material just described, his difficulty in expressing himself became still more acute. He said: 'I do not know what's wrong with me. I have the feeling that words come out of me as if they were stones . . . it's so difficult for me to pronounce them . . . even the letters look heavy, like pieces of granite, and it seems to me I must put them together to form each word. Again I feel that the pictures and the walls become distant and smaller.'

The image in his dream was the representation of myself as a maternal image, which he was ill-treating with his words– scybala–stones, due to the particular sharpness of his oral and anal aggressive phantasies. The hole was caused by the extreme violence of his projective identification and the hardness of its contents. The failure of his obsessive mechanisms brought about an increase of his persecutory anxieties. He felt that all he could receive from me would attack him with the same violence with which, in his phantasy, he had attacked me. This accounted for the difficulties he experienced in accepting my interpretations–food, which meant for him a retaliation, since he identified himself with the very object he attacked and thus felt exposed to similar attacks and damage. On the transference level, the infantile parts projected on the analyst were experienced as in danger of being trapped in the attacked object, i.e., the analyst's inside. As he could not cope with his separation anxiety he grew scared. This state of panic was replaced by a hypochondriacal identification with the object he needed and attacked by his projected infantile parts: the attacked analyst to whom he could no longer listen.

I should like to emphasize that depersonalization reactions of this kind might be underlying episodes of an increasing compulsive obsessive symptomatology present in some patients (Meltzer, personal communication; 1964). On the other hand, a failure in the functioning of the obsessive mechanisms of adaptational control— that is, the loss of contact with the parts projected on the object— can upset the fragile equilibrium of the self, and this means a breakdown into psychosis or into depersonalization or some other regressive state, with the ensuing loss of adaptation to reality. According to Rosenfeld (1947) depersonalization is a defence not only against impulses from all levels, but it is also a defence against feelings of guilt, depression, and persecution. He points out that there is a definite relationship between the two clinical states. Jacobson (1959) has pointed out that depersonalization implies a disorder in the relationship with the object.

I have tried to emphasize the parallel between depersonalization and obsessive mechanisms, on account of the deep psychological relationship existing between them, a parallel already pointed out by Reik (1927) and Oberndorf (1934). We can observe in many patients slight symptoms of depersonalization that become manifest by dizziness, emptiness, or similar manifestations, particularly towards the end of the analytic sessions. These symptoms

are due, in my opinion, to the peculiar use of projective identifications and to the failure of obsessive control mechanisms. Up to a
certain extent, it is possible to connect the phenomena of ego-
disintegration and restitution that take place during sleep and
waking up, respectively, with some aspects of the depersonalization process and loss of the obsessive control I have described. I
think that in the loss of contact with reality due to the withdrawal
of the libidinal cathexes that takes place when one goes to sleep, as
described by Freud (1917d [1915]), there occurs a switching-off of
the mechanisms of adaptational control. Then we encounter a
gradual disconnection of the ego-functions that re-establish the
contact with reality and the obsessive mechanisms that guarantee
this control.

CHAPTER SEVENTEEN

The Oedipus
as a resistance
against the Oedipus
in psychoanalytical practice

T he 'Oedipus myth' and the theory of the 'Oedipus complex' were treated classically from the point of view of their sexual significance and from that of the emotions of love, hate, jealousy, rivalry, and so forth that occur in that myth.

Bion studied the Oedipus myth from a different point of view from that which put the accent on the links of love (L) and hate (H). He considered it mainly from the point of view of knowledge (K), taking as his basis Oedipus' persistence in carrying out his investigation. In his theory of transformations, Bion postulated two types of knowledge: that corresponding to the K link, which constitutes a more intellectual type of knowledge; and the knowledge of 'becoming O', which is deeper and closer to life and is the one related to change, growth, and insight. The interpretations of the K link correspond mainly to 'knowing about something', while the interpretations of 'becoming O' are nearer to 'being that something'.

On the basis of these concepts, I shall discuss in this chapter the resistances on the part of both the patient and the analyst, sometimes forming an unconscious alliance between them, to avoid the depressive suffering and psychic pain caused by the development of knowledge and the acquisition of insight. That is to say that on certain occasions they may use the 'Oedipus–K–knowledge link' to avoid arriving at the 'Oedipus–becoming-O link'.

I shall go on to describe my transformation of some of Bion's ideas concerning the Oedipus myth, which I am trying to apply to the psychoanalytical process, considering them as much from the analyst's point of view as from that of the patient.

Myths can be compared to a mobile polyhedron, which, according to the angle we see it from, demonstrates different faces, vertices, and edges.

Some myths have deeply influenced psychoanalytical thought, particularly the understanding of early human emotional experiences. One example of this is the Oedipus myth, told with mastery in Greek tragedy, which was elaborated by Freud and his followers in the theory of the Oedipus complex (Freud, 1913 [1912–1913], 1921c, 1923b). Myth, tragedy and theory are, without doubt, important elements in the understanding of a number of repressed situations, repeated and reactualized in an 'undesirably faithful' way in the relationship between the patient and the analyst and allowing its clarification, the lifting of the repression, filling of the 'mnemic lakes' and the modification of symptoms through the analysis of the transference.

It is known that psychoanalysis has placed the Oedipus complex as the central nodule of neurosis and the basis for bringing to light love, hate, jealousy, and rivalry as essential aspects of the sexual development of the individual. Research into the Oedipus myth has become enriched lately by important contributions that have referred, almost all of them predominantly, to the sexual content of the drama and to the active or passive, sadistic or masochistic, libidinal or aggressive links between the individual and the parental couple. There have also been valuable contributions from the linguistic and semiotic fields.

Bion (1962, 1963) tried to approach the Oedipus myth from the perspective of those other elements that were displaced by the emphasis given to the sexual components of the myth, although the essential importance of the latter is not excluded. He points out that its different components are linked in a narrative form, and in such a way that none of them can be understood in isolation. He proposes to study specifically the elements related to the K link, that of knowledge (K), as essential to the human being as those of love (L) and hate (H). The riddle of the Sphinx is an expression of the curiosity of man directed towards himself, but that curiosity is also presented by the determination with which Oedipus pursued his investigation into the crime, against the warnings of Tiresias.

Scientific curiosity is one of the major characteristics of the psychoanalyst's work (R. Grinberg, 1960). Nevertheless, I feel that his eagerness to seek out and unravel the secrets of the patient's mind often stumbles not only against the barrier put up by the patient's anxiety, but also against that erected by his own anxiety, which, in a 'tiresianic' way, warns him of the dangers and the high price that he could pay on coming face to face with the 'catastrophic change' (Bion, 1966) and possibly with psychosis. ['Catastrophic change' is a term under which Bion attempts to combine certain facts characterized by violence, invariance, and subversion of the system, elements that he considers inherent in all situations of change and growth. A new idea or a new situation contains a potentially disruptive force which violates the structures of the field in which it appears.] According to Bion, psychoanalytical research has its background in a respectable antiquity, because curiosity regarding the personality is a central feature in the story of Oedipus. Significantly, that curiosity has the same status of sin in the Oedipus myth as those of Eden and of Babel.

Myths have a richness peculiar to them. They transmit certain ideas in constant conjunction in such a way that on occasions they do it better than technical terms that refer specifically to the idea they are trying to describe. Some myths have broken very strongly into the sphere of psychoanalytical knowledge. The myths of Eden and of Babel make it possible to give new intelligibility to that part of the personality which actively opposes the knowledge and organization of the ego in contact with reality.

The common elements that can be found in the three myths are: an omnipotent and omniscient god who forbids knowledge; a model for mental growth; an attitude of curiosity and challenge; and a punishment related to the curiosity stimulated by the prohibitions existing in the myths. The models for mental growth are represented in the myths by the 'Tree of Knowledge', the 'Riddle of the Sphinx' and the 'Tower of Babel' (Bion, 1963).

For Bion, the Oedipus myth is an essential part of the learning apparatus in the early stages of development. It constitutes an 'oedipal myth preconception', which operates as a precursor of an important function of the ego for the discovery or knowledge of psychic reality. This preconception will lead to investigation into the relationship with the parental couple, the realization of which will appear in contact with the real or substitute parents. Therefore Bion postulates the 'private Oedipus myth', formed by alpha elements, and suggests that it is an important factor in the so-called 'psychoanalytical function of the personality' (Bion, 1963).

This 'private Oedipus myth', a foundation for mental growth, may suffer destructive attacks due to envy, greed, or sadism stemming from the psychotic part of the personality, which opposes knowledge. The consequences of the attack are the fragmentation and dispersal of that preconception, preventing its forming part of a 'learning apparatus', and of the attainment of intuition, and preventing the development of the 'psychoanalytical function of the personality' and its evolution towards the transformation in O.

The primitive repressed material belongs mainly to elements of infantile sexuality. The theories of Melanie Klein (Klein et al., 1952) contribute with concepts about even more primary levels of mental functioning, analogically modelled on the relationship the baby has with the breast. This model has made it possible to understand, in a clearer way, different situations that arise in the analytical link. What interests us now is the approach to another level of mental functioning: that of the 'psychotic personality' (Bion, 1957). The notion of 'psychotic personality' as described by Bion does not involve a psychiatric diagnosis but rather a modality of mental functioning that manifests itself in the individual's behaviour and language and in the effects it produces in the observer. This mental state co-exists with another conceived of as the 'non-psychotic personality' or 'neurotic personality'.

Freud has already confirmed that more primitive levels of functioning than that of desire, or that of the 'pleasure principle' exist;

levels that, for lack of binding together, 'go beyond the pleasure principle' (Freud, 1920g).

At this level, psychotic phenomena are found (not necessarily psychosis), which we understand as Bion explains them, following Freud, as states in which the mind acts as an apparatus to discharge the increase of stimuli (just as the baby does before the first experience of satisfaction). For this level of mental functioning we are probably lacking more models and myths to make them accessible to understanding. The myth of Narcissus (as well as the concept of narcissism) does not respond to this need, since it tries to express libidinally the degree of disorganization, rather than to explain the functioning of the psychotic personality.

I suppose that this level of functioning exists not only in psychotic patients but also in all of us (although in small proportions) in a real or potential way. It is possibly the most primitive level of the mind. It is the most 'surpassed' by the different levels of organization and also the most difficult to detect and interpret.

Part of the Oedipus myth, and that of Babel, offer the possibility of making more intelligible the phenomena of the 'psychotic personality'. We can see it in man's attempt to reach understanding or communication, and an omnipotent god who opposes this, punishing with exile or confusion of tongues the attempt to reach knowledge. Also in the Oedipus myth, separating the elements that form the sexual and incestuous part, it is possible to detect, in the enigmatic and bizarre figure of the Sphinx, in the plague that destroys Thebes, in the arrogance of Oedipus in following through his investigations, in the warnings of Tiresias, in the omnipotence of the oracle, and in the final catastrophe (suicide, blinding, and exile) a 'constant conjunction'.

I should now like to study the Oedipus myth from the vertex of Bion's theory of transformation (Bion, 1965).

Bion points out that the processes of transformation have, as their point of departure, an experience or initial situation categorized as the O of the transformation, as described at the beginning of this chapter. This sign 'O' represents the 'ultimate unknowable reality', the 'absolute truth', 'reality', the 'thing in itself', and 'infinite' or the 'unknown'. In psychoanalysis we may use the sign 'O' for all the unknown in the patient, which shows itself by way of the multiple transformations that are brought about. The transformations that are related to 'knowing about something' correspond to the transformations of the K link (Knowledge). These are opposed by the transformation in O, which is related to change, growth, insight, or 'becoming O'. Bion says that reality cannot, by definition, be known, although it can be 'been'. To this he gives the name 'becoming O'. The analyst deals with the psychic reality of the patient's personality in a way that goes beyond 'knowing something about it', although this 'knowing something about it' (transformation in K) is an important part of the psychoanalytical process. The 'transformation in O' is something like 'being what one is', and that transformation is feared and hence resisted. The resistance phenomena of the analytical process can be understood as the defence against danger, which brings into play 'becoming O', in the way that 'becoming O' is equivalent to 'being one's own truth', with the corresponding responsibility inherent in such a transformation. They are resistances that oppose the transformation K → O. Only the interpretations that manage to change the transformations of 'knowing about something' (K) to 'being that something' (O)—that is, K → O—will have any real effect of change and mental maturation (Bion, 1970).

I have already pointed out the common elements that exist in the three myths. On re-examining the myth of Eden in the light of previously mentioned concepts, it occurred to me that it was possible to find a different interpretation of the importance of the 'Tree of knowledge' and the 'Tree of life'. The first, to which Adam and Eve had access and for which they were punished by being expelled from Paradise for having eaten of its fruit, would correspond to the Tree that provides the type of knowledge of the transformation in K, with a tendency towards the type of knowledge of the transformation in O, albeit without reaching O (K → O). But the true intuitive knowledge corresponding to 'becoming O' is that which is symbolized in the myth by the 'Tree of life', from which one could gain everlasting knowledge O, the 'language of achievement', which lasts through the centuries, and access to which is barred by the 'omnipotent and omniscient god' who punishes the achievement of knowledge K and who strictly prevents all possibility of approaching knowledge 'becoming O'. The Bible says literally that after expelling man from Paradise, Jehovah 'placed at the east of the Garden of Eden cherubim and a flaming sword which turned every way, to keep the way of the tree of life'. It is precisely this form of punishment and obstruction to attaining intuitive knowledge (O) that is repeated in the myths of Babel and Oedipus. These myths provide the messages that help us to understand the difficulties that arise for both the patient and the analyst in bearing the pain of mental growth. If the mental pain of the 'catastrophic change', which leads towards intuitive knowledge (with its characteristics of evolution, immortality, and language of achievement), is not tolerated, one can fall into the psychopathic or psychotic attitude, with its characteristics of omnipotence and omniscience.

In my opinion, each of the myths shows that it can only reach the stage of transformation in K, represented in the Eden myth by the tree of knowledge, by the riddle of the Sphinx in the Oedipus myth, and by the building of the tower in the myth of Babel. But when the possibility arises of approaching the kind of knowledge of the transformation of 'becoming O', then omnipotence, omniscience, and even 'knowledge K' act as a resistance or barrier to prevent the suffering of the 'catastrophic change' that leads towards 'knowledge becoming O'.

Oedipus returns to Thebes in order to find out the truth; on solving the riddle of the Sphinx, he reaches knowledge K. This search for knowledge symbolizes the 'preconception oedipal myth', precursor of the capacity for learning and insight.

It has already been shown that the Sphinx can not only symbolize Jocasta, but, like all mythological monsters, part man, part woman, half human and half animal, it represents the 'bizarre object' image of the parents whose union gives rise to very primitive persecutory phantasies. On defeating the Sphinx, Oedipus feels that he is defeating the combined couple of his parents, from whom, in his phantasies, he snatches knowledge and, on taking possession of this knowledge (transformation in K), fills himself manically with omnipotence and omniscience, which prevent his developing towards knowledge 'becoming O' (transformation in O).

It is here that the negative influence of the psychotic personality over the neurotic one appears. As I pointed out before, we are still lacking mythological models in order to understand the functioning of the psychotic part of the personality and its effects on the neurotic part of the personality and on the analyst, when the psychotic part of the patient produces real effects of projective counteridentification on the analyst, through pathological projective identification. The story of the death of Palinurus, as described by Bion (1970), provides us, in part, with a model for these situations.

In chapter V of the Aeneid of Virgil, we are told how Palinurus captains the fleet of Aeneas, and, while he is at the helm, the god Somnus draws near, disguised as Phorbas, and tries to persuade him to go and rest now that the sea is calm. Palinurus does not let himself be convinced, saying that one cannot let oneself be deceived by the appearance of a calm sea. Then the god sprinkles a 'Lethean forgetfulness' over him, and Palinurus is overcome by an irresistible urge to sleep; then he is thrown into the sea, taking with him part of the prow and the helm. When Aeneas realizes what has happened, he takes charge of the vessel and bewails the excessive confidence of Palinurus, which cost him his life and left him in the sea, unburied.

This myth is striking and suggestive. It is important for its narrative and pictorial quality; it is also important for its language, as is also the myth of Oedipus. I believe it represents also a useful complementary element for the understanding of some of the aspects of the Oedipus myth, especially those that reflect the emergence of the psychotic part in Oedipus' resistance through omnipotence and omniscience and his later melancholia due to 'persecutory guilt' (Grinberg, 1963a) seen in his putting out his eyes and thus blinding himself.

The myth of Palinurus allows one to explain better the direct action of the patient's psychotic personality over the analyst's mind and its violent and clouding effect on the functions that are necessary in order to carry out his task.

We could compare Palinurus with the vicissitudes of an analyst, who is carrying out his psychoanalytical treatment in the peace and quiet of his consulting-room (with the calm that the familiar and comfortable surroundings give him), when suddenly he sees himself in danger of being thrown violently from the analytical situation by the elements that appear as a model in Virgil's story. The effects produced by the 'psychotic personality' affect both members of the analytical couple. It is possible to see in the myth the relationship between the analyst and his patient, or between the psychotic and the non-psychotic parts of the personality, between the ego allied to phantasy and the ego in contact with reality, between dreams and hallucinations, lethargy and psychic death, and so on. We can also see the fate of the analyst if he does not guard himself adequately against the effects of the 'psychotic personality' of his patient and/or his own.

The psychotic part of the personality, be it in the patient or in the analyst, acts as an element of resistance that interferes with and prevents the achievement of insight. In the Oedipus myth one aspect of Oedipus obstructs the determination with which another part of him tries to continue the search. The split aspect of Oedipus, which represents the dissociations and projections that occur frequently in the patient, and even in the analyst, clearly appears represented in the myth. An illustrative example is that of Tiresias, who, significantly, was also blinded for seeing the forbidden primal scene, and it is he who tries to prevent Oedipus from going ahead with his search. But Tiresias, who received from Zeus the gift of prophecy and the privilege of long life (seven human generations), not only acts as a 'superego', but also, up to a certain point, comes near to Knowledge 'becoming O'. Tiresias symbolizes a split aspect of Oedipus, shown by the change of the oracle by which the gods, who had previously brought him down, now extol him and foretell peace and prosperity in the land that receives him, instead of the plague that destroyed Thebes. The dialogue with Ismene represents an interior dialogue between two aspects of Oedipus himself. We wonder if the Oedipus myth could not also be categorized as a dream in which all the characters represent split-off aspects of the dreamer, as Freud pointed out.

Now that I have mentioned the subject of dreams, I should like to add that, according to Erikson, Freud, interpreting Irma's dream, came close to the 'hubris' of creative persons, evincing the strong need to investigate, unmask, and recognize. It was the keystone of Freud's identity, this desire to overcome the 'disdainful fathers and unveil the mystery'. It was a true discovery, a great leap, which enabled him, on the pinnacle of consummation, to identify himself with the power of the father, the fertility of the mother, and the newborn child, all at the same time.

Joseph in the Bible must have had a similar experience when he interpreted Pharaoh's dreams, or Oedipus when he solved the riddle of the Sphinx.

Freud was able to overcome the 'catastrophic change' determined by the hubris of his discovery because he was Freud. But how many analysts have such a capacity? Usually we cannot bear to expose ourselves to the danger represented by the new and unknown that can develop in the analytical process. We immediately take refuge in the stockade of known theories, so that we may stay with what is familiar to us.

E. Liendo and M. C. G. de Liendo have approached the oedipal conflict from the semiological point of view, based on the double-link theory described by Bateson and colleagues. When the narcissistic spaces of the parental couple predominate, the child of this couple may have serious difficulties in defining his identity, as they demand a complementary attitude when they interact separately with him, whereas when they do it simultaneously, as a 'combined couple', they put him into an untenable situation, as they demand from him two mutually exclusive complementary attitudes. The child finds himself in a destructive situation, pulled three ways: if he is like the father, he is punished by him; if he is like the mother, he is punished by her; and if he is like neither, he is punished by both. Significantly, Oedipus was initially condemned to death by the parental couple.

In my opinion, this conflict with no way out, when faced with contradictory instructions, appears in both the Eden myth and in the Babel and Oedipus myths; the gods appear on the one hand to be stimulating knowledge, and on the other hand they prohibit it.

In the analytical couple the 'resistential Oedipus' can be reproduced, because each one of the components takes upon himself the role of an 'omnipotent god' who, on the one hand, stimulates curiosity and the search for knowledge, and on the other hand obstructs or sabotages it.

Defensive operations are brought into play against the emergency of whatever material could release anxiety or psychic pain in either the patient or the analyst. We find among them splitting, pathological projective identification, acting out, omnipotence, omniscience, 'reversal of perspective' (Bion, 1963), psychosomatic symptoms, and the resistential use of psychoanalytical theories.

The first four defensive processes are sufficiently well known, but I think it useful to say a few words about the others. Omniscience is characterized by an accompanying superego typified especially by envy and moral superiority without morals—a 'superego' that tends to oppose all search for contact with truth and reality. Patients who use this phantasy, instead of trying to learn, insist that they 'possess all knowledge' in order to avoid the painful experience of the learning process. The avoidance of psychic pain is at the service of the activity called '−K link' (minus K). In terms of the container–content model, it constitutes a − ($\female$ $\male$), a relationship that is mutually denuding and destructive. Meanings and emotions are actively stripped of vitality and sense; thus no learning, discovery, or development is possible.

The 'reversal of perspective' consists in a silent and constant rejection of the tenets on which the interpretation is based, disguised as an apparent agreement with the analyst. Thus, for example, a patient may say that he has had a dream even though he has not had it, and go on to relate it so as to receive the interpretation from his analyst and obtain the confirmation that what he has had was 'only a dream' and not an anxiety-causing hallucinatory experience; he is not interested in the contents of the interpretation.

There are patients who react to certain interpretations as if they were a countertransferential confession, misrepresenting in this way the objective of the analysis. What the patient is really doing is denying the dynamic character of the interpretation and its investigatory aspect, which are fundamental preconditions by which the analysis can be capable of furthering change and mental growth.

For his part, the analyst can also reverse the perspective, taking the associations of the patient as an antidote for his own anxiety in face of the unknown and unknowable of the material and transforming them into the confirmation of a fixed theory that gives some meaning to what is happening.

Situations of this type in analysis are characterized by a peculiar lack of emotional contact. It will become evident in the long run that there has been no dynamic change to indicate progress in analysis; in short, that there is a lack of mental growth and development of insight.

Another type of defensive operation that tends to counteract the danger of psychic pain consists in the unconscious evacuation of such pain, along with the conflict that originated it, into the body. Generally physical pain appears to be better tolerated than psychic pain. In this way the mental phenomenon is transformed into a sensory feeling that is devoid of the dreaded emotional meaning, or, better still, the intolerable psychic meaning is changed into a sensory experience. I believe that my postulate is comparable with what Bion describes as characteristic of the hallucinatory phenomenon: in the domain of hallucination the mental fact is changed into beta elements that can be evacuated and re-introduced so that the action produces, not a meaning, but pleasure or pain. The meaning, as a psychic fact, can be a prelude to transformation in becoming O, giving rise to an unbearable emotion, which an attempt is made to suppress through sensory experience.

Analyst and patient can also resort to the resistential use of analytical theories because they cannot bear the 'catastrophic change' that would lead them towards having to face psychic pain associated with the discovery of a new idea, a strong emotion, or insight. On confronting it with the possibility of arriving at Knowledge 'becoming O' or with insight, the new idea can provoke in the analyst or the patient a defensive opposition, which increases his tendency to remain with the familiar and already known without presenting himself with new doubts. In this way he is flattening or dogmatizing psychoanalysis and therefore avoiding the 'catastrophic change' and mental growth.

On different occasions I have tried to apply a mathematical model, mentioned by Bion (1965), to different situations of theory and clinical experience. It deals with the model represented by the circle crossed by a line at two points ($\emptyset$), the circle crossed by a line at one point ($\mathrm{O\!\!\!/}$) and the circle and line completely separated without any point of contact ($\mathrm{O}/$). These three variants can represent, for example, the discrimination between the subject and the object, the symbol and that symbolized, reality and phantasy, consciousness and unconsciousness, and so on, for the first case; either the state of confusion or of projective counteridentification in the second case; and that of the psychotic personality, which is in a world completely separated and without any contact with the neurotic personality, the lack of contact between the patient and the analyst, and so forth, in the third case.

I think this model can also be applied to the different types of interaction between the two components of the analytical couple.

If the 'analyst–patient' couple functions in a discerning way, facing up to psychic suffering that will allow the 'transformation in K' to change to 'transformation in becoming O', it would be represented by the secant ($\emptyset$). If the 'analyst–patient' group is allied in resistance, for example through mutual idealization and phantasy of omnipotence in order to oppose the evolution of 'Knowledge becoming O' it would be represented by the tangent ($\mathrm{O\!\!\!/}$); and when the 'analyst–patient' functions with the predominance of 'reversal of perspective' or of strong feelings of envy, the model that would represent this is that of the line that has no contact with the circle ($\mathrm{O}/$).

The relationship between the two members of the group may be symbiotic, commensal, or parasitic. In the first case there is confrontation and development, or there may be disruption, but there is movement. In the 'commensal' relationship the two parties co-exist without either affecting the other; the analytical process can be 'killed by mutual indifference'. In the parasitic relationship, the two members act in a mutually destructive way. The patient may work with the analyst as sometimes institutions work with some of their members—overwhelming them with honours and letting them sink without trace, thus destroying their creative capacity.

The patient, by his pathological use of projective identification, can evoke a response of projective counteridentification in the analyst, which, among other things, leads him to increase the use of his analytical theories (transformation in K) and to utilize them in a resistential way (the Oedipus resistance). In this way the creative part of the analyst can be inhibited, and at the same time an increase of his psychotic personality can be stimulated. This leads him to resort to 'hyper-memory' and omniscience, formulating omnipotent interpretations as if they were the 'only possible truth', without admitting doubts or replicas; he may also resort to episodes of acting out.

One could also use Bion's model of the container–contained relationship (Bion, 1963) to represent the existing link between analyst and patient. In this model each partner of the therapeutic couple can personify, alternately, the 'contained new idea' that requires a group container to allow its evolution. But if in the analytical link anxiety, faced with the achievement of 'knowledge becoming O', becomes predominant, then the 'contained–interpretation–new idea' that could potentially promote the evolution of that knowledge might be obstructed (instead of stimulated) by the 'group container' made up of the patient and another aspect of the analyst to form a resistential alliance K. Inversely, the 'contained new idea' may be provided by the patient by means of his associations, and instead of being stimulated in its evolution, it is attacked by the 'group container' formed by the analyst and another aspect of the patient, resorting to 'resistance K'.

Applying the 'theory of transformations' to the concepts I have illustrated, I can sum them up in the following way: the final product of the transformation in K used by the patient in a resistential context (Oedipus resistance — patient) is added to the final product of the transformation in K that occurs in the analyst at a resistential level (Oedipus resistance — analyst) in order to obstruct the evolution of the analytical link on its way towards intuitive knowledge of the 'transformation in becoming O' ('Oedipus knowledge — patient–analyst').

CHAPTER EIGHTEEN

Drives and affects: models instead of theories

I n this chapter I put forward the idea of using models rather than theories to focus on the concepts of drives and affects. I think that this new approach enables us to investigate and understand with greater flexibility the importance and influence of these concepts, as well as the relationship between the two in the behaviour and links between human beings; in other words, in object-relations.

I believe that affects operate from the very beginning of life as basic constituents of drives, generate meaning, and trigger off the motivations at the basis of the search for the object. One of the fundamental objectives of psychoanalysis, after all, is to reveal the meanings of object-relations that make the behaviour of the individual intelligible to the analyst. 'Emotional experience lies at the very heart of the meaning.'

The meaning or purpose of behaviour implies an 'intentional structure'. This intentionality refers not only to conscious purpose but also to those intentions that arise from the dynamics of aborted desire, conflict, defence and anxiety, guilt, and unconscious phantasy.

That is why I believe that drives, affects, meaning, motivation, and intention are conceptual unities, intimately interrelated, which we must take into account in order to understand any object-relationship.

The ego always seeks to obtain something from the object, or rid itself of something (tension, insecurity, anxiety, depression, etc.) according to the pleasure–unpleasure principle. The meaning contained in the affect and quality of the motivation will determine the different vicissitudes in the relationship with the object. Anxiety and depression are the prototypes of affects, intrinsically linked with the love and hate of the life and death drives, expressed in different ways according to the quality of the object-relations.

Taking this idea as my point of departure, I consider that the 'container–contained' model is one of the most appropriate ones to depict the functioning of affects and whether or not they are capable of being transformed, according to the response of the objects to which they are directed. If the object responds with 'reverie', it may be able to mitigate the persecutory intensity of these affects and thus favour the healthy growth of the mind. The opposite response will return or increase the persecution, giving rise to serious pathological alterations in the personality.

The importance of everything I have pointed out can be particularly appreciated in the analytic session, in the interaction that takes place between the patient and the analyst through the mechanisms of projective identification and 'projective counter-identification'. Because the latter is less well known, I shall summarize the conceptualization and functioning of these mechanisms, as I have been able to observe them in my own clinical experience and in the experience of many colleagues in supervision and clinical presentation.

The theory of drives has constituted one of the basic pillars of psychoanalytical research from its very beginning. At the same time, however, this theory has become one of the subjects that have aroused the greatest controversy, concentrated particularly on Freud's second dualistic theory of life and death drives. The same can be said of the theory of affects, which is no less controversial. Freud was never able to formulate a central theory of affects as a primary phenomenon in the organization and functioning of the psyche.

I believe, therefore, that it is appropriate to discuss both concepts, since they are related to each other.

We know that drives are abstractions that cannot be verified by direct observation, although we are aware of their existence through their consequences in the emotional attitude and behaviour of the individual.

The classic psychoanalytical theory of drives, as described by Freud, has not satisfied many analysts, because it leans particularly on biological speculation and the economic concept of energy.

It is possible that the concept of 'psychic energy' has given rise to many difficulties and misunderstandings in the application of psychoanalytic theory to clinical facts.

George Klein (1976) held that the supposition of psychic energy was basically inadequate in Freudian metapsychology. For Klein, this metapsychology was more a theory of *how* a process operates, searching for the neuro-physiological basis, than a theory of *why*— that is, of its motivations. Moreover, it leaves aside the fundamental idea of the psychoanalytic task, which is to reveal *meanings*. He also pointed out the importance of *intentionality,* contained in all mental activity and behaviour.

In the last symposium organized by the European Federation of Psycho-analysis on 'The Death Instinct', Laplanche (1984), H. Segal (1984), Green (1984), and Rechardt (1984), in spite of their differences, agreed in not ascribing an exclusively biological nature to drives.

Widlöcher (1984) proposes a psychoanalytic theory of association of thoughts instead of the theory of drives. He points out that what we call a 'drive' is merely the hierarchically organized group of actions engaged in the realization of the acts of daily life or the total operation of thought.

Grotstein (1985), influenced by Bion's hypothesis of the inherent pre-conceptions that 'each infant brings as his or her phylogenetic bundle of knowledge', points out that the death instinct has access to inherent pre-conceptions of the 'prey–predator series', which is one of its priorities, so that danger that can extinguish the life of the organism is known and knowable. The breast becomes a terrifying victim of our predatory feelings and is further transformed, via projective identification, into a persecutory predator towards the self, which has then been transformed into a prey.

He suggests that the death instinct represents a portion of a larger inherent instinctual principle, which has been 'programmed' into the DNA of our chromosomes, both literally and figuratively. Its emanations, warnings, impulses, until now called aggressive drives, are merely RNA messengers dispatched from the DNA template to warn the organism of dangers in the external world and the internal milieu, and to institute defensive tactics and strategies against them. Organismic panic is thus the first inchoate response of the organism to danger. Maternal containment allows for the maturation of this panic into specific signal anxiety.

Ogden (1985) says that Grotstein's hypothesis would modify the Kleinian conception of the death instinct by saying that it is not the origin of danger; it is rather the facet of the psyche responsible for generating meaning relating to danger, and the information from generation to generation must be encoded in and transmitted by RNA and DNA; but he does not propose a model for the psychological correlates of these structuring and transmitting processes.

Ogden suggests that instinct might be conceived as analogous to Chomsky's (1957, 1968) notion of linguistic deep structure. Chomsky contends that it is inconceivable that infants could learn any language if they had to deduce the grammar. It is only because infants are equipped with a code, a deep structure that is built into their perceptual and motor apparatuses, that they are able to discriminate between groups of sounds and to organize them into a system that becomes the syntactic and semantic structure of language. The code is, simultaneously, limiting and potentiating.

Instinct could be thought of as constituting a similar deep structure. The death instinct, for example, could be thought of not only as a system of inherited impulses or inherited preformed ideas, but as a code by which meaning is attributed to experience along highly determined lines (for example, as Grotstein proposes in terms of the relationship of prey and predator).

If I have mentioned the hypothesis of some analysts who criticize the classic theory of drives, it is to show that drives can be studied from other perspectives without having to adhere rigidly to the established theory. I would therefore propose the use of models (a term I would apply to the points of view of these colleagues), because of the advantage of their flexibility.

'The model can be considered as the abstraction of an emotional experience or as the concretization of an abstraction. Models are more ephemeral than theories. If the model is not beneficial or advantageous, it can be discarded and eventually replaced by others. If, on the other hand, it proves to be useful on several different occasions, we can contemplate the possibility of transforming it into theory.

The construction of models makes it possible to retain the structure of the psychoanalytic theory without losing the necessary flexibility to face up to the necessities of psychoanalytic practice that appear at each moment' (Bion, 1962).

What has been said of drives can also be applied to the subject of affects.

Some authors considered the affect as specifically an organizing phenomenon. P. Noy (1982) related the affect to the organization of behaviour, perception, and communication. For him, the affect is a kind of programme of a 'computer model' that organizes various systems and psychological and physiological processes. He considers that the 'imagination' is one of the most important components of the affect; imagination adds to the affect the dimension of the past and the future and enables the individual to use memories to try to reconstruct the anticipated action of the internal scene. He also suggests the hypothesis that psychosomatic symptoms are caused by the activation of opposing or contradictory affects that can mutually block each other.

A. Green (1970) presented an exhaustive and well-known report on the evolution of the notion of affect, beginning with Freud's first works. Elsewhere (Green, 1977), Green held that the affect constitutes a real challenge to thought. For the moment, and unlike representations, it is impossible to refer to affects theoretically, leaving aside their relationship with the object.

Freud's final theory of anxiety, that of 'signal anxiety', leads to consideration of the maternal object as a source of semantic stimuli. Green quotes Freud (1913j) when he says that 'the unconscious speaks more than one dialect'. He adds that, since the affect has been accorded a semantic (rather than cognitive) function, the affect must take the place of the *meaning* . . . 'The process of meaning is linked to the existence of the 'chains' of affect, a reformulation of Freud's concept of 'binding', whether this applies to energy or to representations. Affect is understood, like language, as a product of psychic work. Language without affect is a dead language, and affect without language is incommunicable' (Green, 1977).

Bion also placed great importance on *meaning*. In his book on Transformation (Bion, 1965) he points out that 'The infant's experience of the breast as the source of emotional experience (later represented by terms such as love, understanding, meaning) means that disturbances in relation to the breast involve disturbance over a wide range of adult relationships. The function of the breast in supplying meaning is important for the development of a capacity to learn. In an extreme instance, the fear of the total destruction of the breast, not only does it raise fears that he himself is ceasing to exist (since without the breast he is not viable), but also fears that meaning, as though it were material, has ceased to exist. In some contingencies, the breast is not regarded as the source of meaning so much as meaning itself.'

Commenting on Bion's ideas, J. F. Rodriguez Perez (1985) points out that the breast, while providing satisfaction, in turn confers meaning. In other words, when a need or wish has been satisfied, this implies that it has been understood correctly. The subject that receives the satisfaction can then understand, when it is satisfied, *what* it was that it was lacking. In the breast–infant experience, there would be two kinds of superimposed satisfaction: the first and most obvious is the satisfaction of having been understood in its need, and, in this way, discovering the meaning of the need itself.

As we can see, meaning operates fundamentally through the object-relationship. Corresponding to the satisfaction of the infant on being understood, thus discovering the meaning of his need, is the mother's satisfaction at having been able to understand her infant's needs and meaning. The gratification is mutual. Obviously this also occurs between the analyst and his patient.

Bion's work is based on the assumption that emotional experience exists prior to thought and, furthermore, that emotion should be placed at the true centre of meaning. He holds that emotional experience must be thought out and understood in order that the mind may grow and develop.

Both M. Klein and Bion especially brought out the importance of object-relations and affects throughout their work. M. Klein (1933) followed Freud's theory in so far as she placed the accent on the existence of life and death drives. But in her theory she emphasized the prior emergence of anxiety derived from the operation of the death drive. She also studied the primitive defences used by the primitive ego. It is this basic fear, of a persecutory nature, which leads to the projection of the death instinct. According to Klein, the object has split into a 'good object' and a 'bad object'; and it is this splitting that constitutes the first mechanisms of defence against anxiety. The duality of the life and death drives could be seen as the origin of the dialectic between good and bad objects.

The nature of the early dyadic relationship between mother and child will determine the possibility or otherwise of a psychic growth tending to the acquisition of a capacity to discriminate between subject–object, symbol–thing symbolized, phantasy–reality, internal world–external world, and to attain the phase of 'separation–individuation' described by M. Mahler (1963).

I think that the 'container–contained' model, represented by the dynamic relationship between something that is projected (contained) and an object that contains it (container) suggested by Bion (1970), constitutes an extremely useful hypothesis for understanding the vicissitudes that may arise between the infant and his mother, which, in the best cases, would give rise to the formation of the 'apparatus for thinking' and the creation of symbols. The baby needs to evacuate his anxieties and painful emotions into the breast. The normal or 'good enough' mother, in Winnicott's words (1971) with a capacity for 'reverie', would function as an effective container for the suckling's unpleasurable affects and would succeed in transforming hunger into satisfaction, pain into pleasure, loneliness into company, and the anxiety of dying into tranquillity.

Bion (1962) describes three basic emotions as being intrinsic to the link between two objects: Love (L), Hate (H), and Knowledge (K). The sign K is used to refer to the link between a subject that searches for knowledge and an object that lets itself be known. This link represents an emotional experience expressed by the pain inherent in the search for knowledge. It can also represent the individual who tries, through introspection, to know the truth about himself. Bion suggests that Freud implicitly attributed this function to the conscience when he defined it as the 'sense organ for the apprehension of psychic qualities'.

It is necessary to distinguish between the 'acquisition of knowledge' as a result of the *modification* of pain in the K link—in which case the knowledge acquired will be used for further discoveries—and the 'possession of knowledge' used for the *avoidance* of the painful experience. The latter can be found in those personalities in whom omnipotence, envy, and greed predominate and whose destructive activity tends to denude any relationship of its vitality or meaning. This activity is called 'the minus-K link'. It occurs to me that Bion might have wanted to express, in this way, his model of the life and death drives, through the affects contained in the K link (seekers for the life and object-relations) and the minus-K link (tending to destroy and annihilate), respectively.

Moreover, for Bion, a central goal of analysis is to help a patient to increase his capacity to tolerate suffering. This capacity seems to be linked to the ability to recognize emotions in their premonitory state before they become converted into obviously painful emotions. The anxiety would be closely related to that premonitory state of emotion which could be compared with Freud's theory of 'signal anxiety' (Freud, 1926d [1925]).

So far, anxiety has featured as the prototypical affect in analytic theory. I would now like to deal with another affect, depression, which also plays an important role, not only in the patient's pathology but also in the interaction between the two members of the psychoanalytical couple.

In chapter thirteen I referred to 'microdepressions' among the psychopathological phenomena of everyday life. I think that some of these depressive micro-reactions may function as a 'depression signal' in order to allow the ego to be able to use defence mechanisms against the risk of suffering a severe depression or, in some cases, what might be felt as a catastrophic depression. In saying so I am in agreement with others, who have also referred to the depression signal. According to Schur (1969), the signal concept is not restricted to anxiety but is applicable to other affects. P. Heimann (1974) stated that the depression signal differs significantly from the signal of anxiety. The latter is directed towards the ego, the former towards the maternal figure.

I believe that it is very important to take into account the interaction between the analyst and the patient in order to understand the patient's need to use projective identification for the purpose of converting the analyst into a container–repository of his anxiety and of other painful affects that he cannot tolerate. On occasion the analysand's unconscious phantasy in this interaction is of manipulating and controlling the analyst, making him play certain roles and experience certain emotions that he is unable to avoid. I have termed this reaction of the analyst (projective counteridentification', a concept I have developed in several articles and books (Grinberg, 1956, 1962, 1979, 1985). I first coined this term in 1956 to refer to a specific countertransference reaction in the analyst. As a result, he is sometimes unconsciously and passively 'carried along' into playing roles and feeling affects that the patient unconsciously 'forces' on to him through projective identification.

This process occurs much more frequently than is usually believed. The analysand may have the magical and omnipotent feeling of having accomplished his own phantasies by projecting them on to the analyst who will play the roles for him. The analyst will react sometimes as if he had acquired and assimilated the roles projected on to him, in a *concrete way*. In such a case he may resort to different kinds of rationalizations in order to justify his bewilderment.

Some authors have recently dealt with a similar problem. For J. Sandler and A. M. Sandler (1978), the part played by affective experience in the development of object-relations is central. According to them, the object-relation represents the wish-fulfilment of important needs of the child and the adult. They believe that the idea of transference does not have to be restricted to the fact that the patient distorts his perception of the analyst, but that it should be taken to include all those unconscious and subtle attempts to manipulate the analyst in the analytic situation in order to 'evoke' a particular type of affective response in him. The analyst's response is termed 'role-responsiveness'. When this happens, 'the analyst has in fact responded to the patient in that particular way, because the patient has, in a sense, "pressed the right buttons" in him'.

Hanna Segal (1977) also admits that the projections of some patients are so powerful that they affect the countertransference: 'There is a whole area of the patient's pathology which specifically aims at disrupting this situation of containment, such as: invasion of the analyst's mind in a seductive or aggressive way, creating confusion and anxiety and attacking links in the analyst's mind.'

Betty Joseph (1978a) stated that 'the more the patient is using primarily primitive mechanisms and defences against anxieties, the more the analyst is likely to feel that he is being involved and used by the patient unconsciously, and the more the analysis is a scene for action rather than understanding . . . Such patients will actively try to get the analyst to collude with them in the use of these various defences.'

Joyce McDougall (1979) suggests that when the communication is primitive, it would be a means not only of remaining in intimate connection with someone, but also 'a way of conveying and discharging emotion in direct fashion, with the intent to affect and arouse reactions in the other'. J. Bergeret (1970) mentions the case of patients who are incapable of tolerating certain affects, but who make an effort to awaken those very affects in their listener and even provoke reactions in him. This process might be called the 'anti-effect' or 'the affect and how to liberate oneself from it'. The purpose of this projection is not only to transfer the affect on to the other, but also to make this affect live within the other and incite him to action.

I think that in the use of projective identifications as well as in the reaction of projective counteridentification—which, in my opinion, were contained in the comments of the colleagues I have mentioned—there was a meaning: that of affect (anxiety or envy, for example), which impelled the patients to attack and destroy the analyst's capacity for thought and his analytic function. This attitude would correspond to the predominance of the death drive, but, at other times, the massive projections of patients can be determined by the need to make the analyst feel the affects whose meaning they may not have been able to detect or tolerate. In these cases, the search for understanding or tolerance of the meaning would correspond to the predominance of the life drive.

My present view is that projective counteridentification is not merely a pathological reaction of the analyst who feels obliged to act out the roles projected on to him by the manipulative tendency of the patient. On the contrary—I think that it can also serve as a point of departure for experiencing a spectrum of emotions that, well understood and sublimated, can be converted into very useful technical tools for entering into contact with the analysands' most regressive levels and their most profound affects (Grinberg, 1985). In order to achieve this, the analyst would need to be especially disposed to receive and contain the patient's projections for as long as possible. This does not always happen. On many occasions, we feel fear of being invaded ourselves by the psychotic contents of these projections because they can threaten our own psychic balance. It is above all at these moments that our degree of tolerance and capacity to receive and contain these phantasies and emotions is put to the test. Carried to its most extreme expression, this willingness on the part of the analyst reveals itself in *consenting* to be invaded by the projection of anxieties and, perhaps, by the psychotic phantasies of the analysand, in containing them until their final consequences, in order to be able to share, and *feel,* and *think* with him and, at the same time, to be able to achieve *consubstantiation* with the affects contained in those projections, no matter what their nature (murderous hate, death-anxiety, catastrophic terror, etc.) as if they were a part of his very self. This is to offer every availability, time, and mental space for the space and mental time that the patient requires, with its different affective contents.

The transition to 'convergence', understanding and mental growth should, perhaps inevitably, pass through projective counteridentification, but in this transition should attempt to go *beyond* projective counteridentification, avoiding the risk of becoming stagnant. [Translator's note: The word 'convergence' was suggested by a patient of the author—the occasion is described in chapter eight.] As Freud (1911b) pointed out, the important thing is to be able to return later to reality, in the same way as the artist who wanders through the world of phantasy but then finds the road back to reality.

To sum up, I have suggested the idea of focusing on the concept of drives and affects from the point of view of the use of models rather than theories. I think that this new focus will enable us to investigate and understand with greater flexibility the importance and influence of these concepts, as well as the relationship between the two, in the behaviour and links between human beings, in other words, in object relationships.

I believe that affects operate from the very beginning of life as basic constituents of drives, and function as generators of meanings and triggers of the motivations found at the basis of the search for the object. One of the fundamental objectives of psychoanalysis, after all, is to reveal the meanings and significances of object relationships that make the behaviour of the individual intelligible to the analyst. 'Emotional experience lies at the very heart of meaning.'

The meaning or purpose of behaviour implies an 'intentional' structure. This intentionality refers not only to conscious purpose but also to those intentions that arise from the dynamic of aborted desire, conflict, defense and anxiety, guilt, and unconscious fantasy.

This is why I believe that drives, affects, meaning, motivation, and intentionality are conceptual unities, intimately inter-related to each other, which we must take into account in order to understand any object relationship.

The ego always seeks to obtain something from the object or to rid itself of something (tension, insecurity, anxiety, depression, etc.) according to the principle of pleasure–unpleasure. The meaning contained in the affect and the quality of the motivation will determine the different vicissitudes in the relationship with the object.

Anxiety and depression are the prototypes of affects, intrinsically linked to love and hate of the life and death drives, which will be expressed in different ways according to the quality of the relationship with the object.

Taking this proposal as my point of departure, I have considered that Bion's 'container–contained' model is one of the most appropriate to depict the functioning of affects and the possibility of being transformed or not, according to the response of the object to which they are directed. If the object responds with 'reverie', it may be able to mitigate the persecutory intensity of said affects and thus favour a healthy growth of the mind. The opposite response will return or increase the persecution, giving rise to serious pathological alterations in the personality.

The importance of everything I have pointed out can be particularly appreciated in the analytic session, in the interaction that takes place between the patient and the analyst through the mechanisms of projective identification and 'projective counter-identification'. Because the latter are less well known, I have presented a synthesis of the conceptualization and functioning of these mechanisms, as I have been able to observe them in my clinical experience and in the experience of many colleagues in supervisions and clinical presentations.

CHAPTER NINETEEN

Psychoanalytical observations on creativity

I should like to begin by quoting Freud's well-known words from *Creative Writers and Day-dreaming* (1908e [1907], which seem to me to be very appropriate and significant as an introduction to the subject of creativity: 'We laymen have always been intensely curious to know—like the Cardinal who put a similar question to Ariosto—from what sources that strange being, the creative writer, draws his material, and how he manages to make such an impression on us with it and to arouse in us emotions of which, perhaps, we had not even thought ourselves capable. Our interest is only heightened the more by the fact that, if we ask him, the writer himself gives no explanation, or none that is satisfactory; and it is not at all weakened by our knowledge that not even the clearest insight into the determinants of his choice of material and into the nature of the art of creating imaginative form will ever help to make creative writers of us.'

On the other hand, we cannot fail to mention some of the classic works, such as those by Rank and Sachs, on art and the artist. Rank (1932) asserted that only the artist can achieve 'creative re-integration', in contrast to the ordinary man and the neurotic,

271

adding that the creative impulse derives from the artist's need to immortalize himself, due to his 'fear of death'. Hans Sachs (1951) stressed in his work that poetry is a social phenomenon in its widest sense; it is the product of *one* mind but can move thousands of other minds and link in a common emotion the most divergent personalities, most separate in space, time, and culture. For him, both life and death are present in the beauty of a work of art. It is the presence of death that produces the feeling of sadness in contemplating the beauty of a work of art; the difficulty does not lie in understanding beauty, but in bearing it in all its plenitude. It suggests movement, but it can also impress by its eternal immutability. Without a minimum of beauty the burden of life could not be borne.

Another valuable contribution to the understanding of the creative process is that of Hartmann, especially in his concepts of neutralization and sublimation. To Freud's theory of desexualized libido, Hartmann (1955) added that of energy deprived of its aggression to form the basis of the neutralization of both kinds of impulse, a process carried out through the ego and an essential element of sublimation.

M. Klein (1940) especially related the capacity to form symbols to the development of the ego, sublimation, and creative activity. For her, the symbol is not only the foundation of sublimation, but also the point linking it with reality. Both sublimation and the creative impulse are bound up with the re-creation of objects felt to be damaged or lost.

Kris (1955) carried out one of the most systematic studies with the aim of clarifying the different moments of the creative process, especially those related to the phases of inspiration and elaboration; he also studied the difference between the artistic expression of the normal personality and that of the psychotic. He finally presented to us his concept (which has become a classic) that there is in creation a 'regression in the service of the ego', a concept to which we shall return.

Of course we also have authors like Greenacre and many others who have made valuable contributions to the concept of creativity, but whom we cannot discuss in detail here.

The creative capacity exists in every individual; symbolization and the formation of dreams, phantasies, and daydreams would be examples illustrating this capacity. We should therefore consider the existence of at least two types of creative capacity: (1) the common denominator of all development and mental ripening, which, with certain qualitiative and quantitative variations, constitutes a patrimony of the human condition; and (2) the exceptional capacity that raises certain individuals above the common herd and enables them to conceive original ideas.

It is precisely in relation to this second category of creative capacity that doubts and polemics have arisen. Some authors establish a close relationship between genius and madness, creative faculty and abnormality. There are some who stress the existence of pseudo-hallucinatory states during the act of creation, with the use of idealizing mechanisms and omnipotence, but regulated by the secondary process. [For Weissmann, creative phantasies have a hallucinatory and delirious character; their way of operating would go *beyond the reality principle* in the service of the ego-ideal. Giovacchini also maintains that the creator's mind may sometimes rest on a certain psychopathology (hallucinations) that helps him to create. His ego-spectrum has a wider range of reactions and more elasticity and flexibility. He supposes that creative skills are facilitated and even characterized by particular ways in which the ego operates. The ego has the ability to bind the cathectic impulses emerging from the unconscious and fuse them with external reality. There would, moreover, be a megalomanic basis to its fervent idealization and creativity. I would say that psychopathic megalomania is irreversible; on the other hand, 'creative' megalomania, so to speak, is reversible and does not lose contact with reality; it allows the maintenance of the appropriate limits and of reality.] Others reject this supposition and in the same way refuse to consider the unconscious as the source of the whole creative faculty, attributing it to the preconscious (Kubie, 1958a).

I should like to enter this controversy and explain my point of view.

In the first place, I wish to postulate the existence of 'creative potential' in all human beings. The ultimate fate of this potential and the possibility of it developing to form the basis of a creative personality or of genius would depend, among other things, on certain specific capacities of the ego and on the quality of internal and external object-relations, so that such potential can be contained and its development favoured.

I believe, on the other hand, that the creative act can be thought of as the result of a process during which the individual must inevitably pass through stages of temporary 'disorganization' and the breaking of the established structures and then be re-integrated *in a different way*. Both the moments of 'disorganization' and those of later re-integration are part of the creative process and are reproduced and condensed in the act of creation.

In other words, the creative act is the final link in a series of stages (process) characterized by fluctuations, generally unconscious and transitory, between reality and phantasy, states of 'disorganization' and reorganization, hallucinatory phantasies and objective perceptions, abstractions and concretizations, and so forth. [Sleep and dreams also produce phenomena of a certain 'disintegration' and restitution of the ego, as pointed out by Federn (1952) and others.] The act of creation is the achievement of a dialectic synthesis of the phases previously described, which will give rise to the product of creation. [Hartmann (1964) refers to a 'co-ordinating tendency' of the different parts of the organism and its functions, which develops gradually in the course of evolution, replacing more primitive controls. He adds that within the process of synthesis there is an important element of differentiation, which he calls 'division of labour'. He suggests for this the term 'organizing function' (instead of synthetic function), which includes elements of both differentiation and integration.]

The creative idea usually appears as a sudden 'illumination': like an 'evolution' corresponding to integration—by a *sudden precipitating intuition*—of a series of apparently incoherent and unconnected phenomena, which acquire coherence at that moment through an idea that surfaces in the mind 'unexpectedly and as a whole' (Bion, 1967). Bion mentions a state that Freud described in a letter to Lou Andreas-Salomé, in which he said: 'I know that in writing I have to blind myself artificially, in order to focus all the light on one dark spot'. For Bion, this procedure of 'blinding oneself' temporarily so that the individual can become free, ceasing to be a 'creature of circumstance', allows him to know by intuition a present 'evolution' and lay the foundations of future 'evolutions'. Einstein also asserted that a new idea appears 'suddenly and intuitively'; in general it is not reached through conscious logical conclusions, even when the reasons that unconsciously led to its emergence can be discovered. In his view, intuition is nothing more or less than the *sudden result* of an experience previously stored up.

It will be useful to quote as an illustration the famous experience of Poincaré, which has already become a classic in the field of mathematical invention. He described the circumstances in which he made his discovery of the functions of Fuchs. Poincaré's testimony (1967) was as follows: 'Since a fortnight ago, I was trying hard to show that there could be no function analogous to that which I then called Fuchsian functions; I was then very ignorant. Every day I sat at my desk, remaining there for one or two hours trying numerous combinations and getting no results. One night when, contrary to my custom, I had had a cup of coffee, I could not sleep; ideas came one on top of the other; I noticed how they pushed and shoved each other . . . I then walked to Caen. The walk made me forget my mathematical work; on arriving at Coutance we got on to a bus to go I know not where. The moment I put my foot on the step *the idea struck me,* though none of my earlier meditations appeared to have prepared me for it, that the transformations I had used to define the Fuchsian functions were identical to those of non-Euclidean geometry. . . . It came into my mind with *brevity, spontaneity and immediate certainty; suddenly, the decisive idea appeared.'*

This description sums up the nature of the creative act as the synthesis of a more complex and longer process.

Progression through the phases of 'disorganization' and the essential participation, even though in a peculiar way, of certain elements of the primary process, has generally been the reason for relating the creative process to psychosis. But although they have more elements in common than is usually admitted, they must not be confused.

When we speak of the transitory phases of 'disorganization' and the use of elements of the primary process, we are really referring, not to a state of true degeneration of the ego of the creative individual, but to different organizational forms, with modification of the functions of the ego and its relationship with other psychic instances and the external world, which enable reality to be grasped in another way or from new perspectives. It is precisely in this that lies the creativity that, breaking the old classical moulds, determines a real revolutionary change and encourages the search for new structures and systems. Naturally its value does not rest only on novelty, but on its character of repercussion, transcendence, and progress for others, by possessing the quality of the 'language of achievement' (Forman, 1931). [In one of his letters, Keats said that the 'language of achievement' is characterized by its penetration through time and space, and that it depends on what he called 'negative capacity'—that is, the ability to 'bear uncertainties, mysteries and doubts without experiencing the irritating search for facts and reason'.] I consider that the creative imagination effectively uses mechanisms from the primary process, but that they function in a different way in the personalities of the creator, the normal person, and the psychotic.

It is possible that all three develop along a common path, but on arriving at a 'crossroads' the road forks into three branches going in different directions. This 'crossroads' would be represented by the absence of the object or the experience of losing the object, which would give rise to different responses in the normal, creative, and psychotic individuals, respectively. [Beres defined the imagination as the capacity to form a mental picture of the absent object. Rosen established the role of the imagination as a function of the ego designated to fill the void of ambiguity.]

The hallucinatory satisfaction of desire would be the first organizing function of the ego faced with the absence of the object. According to the nature and permanence of this hallucinatory process and its relationship with reality, and the specific quality of the functions of the ego, a psychotic, normal, or creative mind will develop.

The mind of the psychotic, dominated by intolerance to frustration, cannot bear the absence of the object, or abstractions. His

PSYCHOANALYTICAL OBSERVATIONS ON CREATIVITY   277

thought will be concrete and will have recourse to hallucinatory images or to the delirium characterized by confusion with the object and the blurring of limits between reality and phantasy and between symbols and that which is symbolized. For those personalities, words, hallucinatory images, and thoughts are not representations of objects or their qualities, but constitute concrete objects ('things in themselves'). The psychotic mind tends predominantly towards a type of stereotyped hallucination, totally alien to reality, with the concrete characteristics of the symbolic equation in which the hallucinated object is considered as the 'thing in itself'. The predominant sentiments are intolerance of frustration, hate rather than love, excessive envy, and destructive tendencies.

The normal mind can accept the absence of the object, and in consequence make the corresponding abstractions. It has the power to work through mourning caused by the experience of object-loss, and is able to discriminate adequately between the self and the object, the symbol and what is symbolized, phantasy and reality. Its thoughts and words are representations of objects that are not considered as 'things in themselves'. Nevertheless, its tolerance of moments of 'disorganization' is not great, and it lacks the capacity to 'surrender' to idealized objects and to 'submerge itself' in the mechanisms of the primary process for fear of succumbing and being unable to turn back. The hallucinatory gratification of the normal baby, more connected with any aspect of reality, though it may let him tolerate for a moment the absence of the object (the breast), rapidly exhausts its substitutive and protective function and demands the return of the object. If this happens while the hallucination is still functioning, since his tolerance of pain and frustration is limited, the child will not hesitate to abandon it and immediately grasp at the relationship with the external object.

The creative mind is close to normal development in its tolerance of abstraction and of the absence of the object, but creative persons bring with them certain elements of the primary process that lead them to recreate objects in order to combat frustration and the absence of the object; they have phantasies of the hallucinatory type and use their creative imagination to go 'beyond the reality principle' without separating completely from reality.

Their creations do not claim to be objects or aspects of the self as 'things in themselves', but neither are they mere representations of them. They share with the psychotic a certain quality of concretization of a phantasy or hallucination, but at the same time they maintain the characteristics of the secondary process relative to the possibility of abstraction and differentiation. In those who possess a creative mind, the hallucinatory type of phantasy is richer and original in content, is capable of development and has greater permanence, but without being stereotyped. [I would like to put forward the opinion that the hallucinatory phenomenon appears in creative personalities as well as in the normal and psychotic, though treated in different ways. Flournoy (1933) said: 'By hallucination we mean only a point in a series extending from imagination to perception'. Freud, besides describing the hallucinatory satisfaction of desire in the suckling, distinguished hysterical from psychotic hallucination. The former would be related to total objects and associated with an increase in the individual's capacity to tolerate depression; the latter contains elements analogous to partial objects (quoted by Bion). In addition, in his article on 'Constructions in analysis', Freud (1937d) suggested that hallucinations could be equivalent to constructions, 'genuine attempts at explanation and cure'. Bion (1967) also mentioned experiences with psychotic patients who used the 'bizarre objects' of their hallucinations in the service of therapeutic intuition.] Such people are capable of maintaining a relationship with the external world but can tolerate non-gratification, even in the presence of the object—that is, they can resist the temptation. This may be due to a pressing need of authenticity, which leads them to be faithful to the idealized internal image, making them capable of resisting both frustration because of the absence of the object, and the temptation caused by the stimulus of the presence of the object. They are able to bear 'revelation' without becoming totally disorganized or destructively disorganizing their environment. They can better manipulate their primary process mechanisms by submitting to them, and to the internal objects, without succumbing. There is therefore a greater capacity to tolerate the moments of 'disorganization' and later fusion, so as to become again in touch with reality and to work through the mourning for the absence of the object, through attempts at re-creation by means of hallucinatory-type phantasies. [Freud (1911b) says that 'art brings about a reconciliation between the two principles (of pleasure and of reality) in a peculiar way. The artist is originally a man who turns away from reality because he cannot come to terms with the renunciation of instinctual satisfaction that it at first demands, and who allows his erotic and ambitious wishes full play in the life of phantasy. He *finds the way back to reality*, however, *from this world of phantasy*, by making use of *special gifts to mould his phantasies into truths of a new kind*, which are valued by men as precious reflections of reality' (my italics).]

Naturally the description we have given of the creative mind must be understood as a conceptual model, subject to different variations. This is a purely schematic illustration, which does not exclude the co-existence in the same individual of the other two types of 'mind' or of possible fluctuations and changes from one type to another.

In one of the first phases of the creative process, the creator feels 'consubstantial' with the work he is creating. But in order to arrive at that point he has to be able to bear the preceding phases of 'disorganization' (with consequent anxiety), which will enable him to detach himself from his established structures and bonds, accept the transient blurring of the limits of the ego, and submerge himself, by projective identification, in a *fusion* with idealized internal objects from which the creative product will be emerging. He will experience this as though it were a part of himself, and at the same time he will feel that he is a part of his work.

Within this category of creative personalities or geniuses, we must of necessity mention those who have not been able satisfactorily to control or regulate the elements of the primary process and consequently fall into an obvious pathology (psychotic), which is occasionally irreversible. Nevertheless there may arise a very particular type of functioning of the mechanism of dissociation, which, abetted by the obsessional mechanisms of realistic control, enables the creative sector of the personality to operate in parallel with the psychotic sector. [The functioning of this splitting mechanism recalls that described by Freud in his works on 'The splitting of the ego' (1940e [1938]) and 'Fetishism' (1927e) and by Bion in

'Differentiation of the psychotic from the non-psychotic personalities (1957). Weissmann (1967) describes a 'dissociative function' (or desynthesizing) at the service of the synthesizing or integrating function. It enables the ego to dissociate itself from its
established object-relations and its habitual responses to the
demands of the id and the superego; it breaks the patterns that
originate in the pleasure principle and allows the reality principle
new modifications. It plays an especially important part in the
creative process, although it also comes into action in normal
persons when they begin new enterprises in their life and prepare
for revolutionary changes in their usual way of living. For his part,
Arieti (1967) gives the name 'tertiary process' to a special combination of mechanisms of the primary and secondary processes
which occurs in the creative process. In it, primitive forms of
knowledge, generally confined to pathological conditions, join
together with innovative ideas.] Such individuals succeed in
developing their creative capacity to its full value at the same time
as, and in open contrast with, the remaining psychotic aspects of
their personality. Dostoievsky and Van Gogh are examples.

According to Kris (1955), some psychotic artists have a 'sudden
explosion' of creative activity, which bears no relation to previous
aptitudes or learning. The dynamic significance of anxiety and
outbursts of creation may lie in an attempt at restitution or
recuperation. [The term 'restitution' was introduced by Freud in
the 'Schreber case'. It is supposed that in the schizophrenic the
hallucinatory system is intended to reconstruct the world
destroyed in his phantasies, recathecting external objects.
Recently the concept of restitution has been linked with that of
reparation.]

The distinction that Kris suggests as essential is that in normal
persons there is a 'controlled regression in the service of the ego',
contrasting with the way in which the primary process over-
whelms and incapacitates the ego, as happens with psychotics. I
think that in addition to the regression I have mentioned, in the
creative personality the primary process also functions with a
progressive quality, which expands and enriches the ego.

Kris also distinguishes the creativity of the psychotic from that
of the normal artist, contrasting the compulsions of the former

with the liberty of the artist. I feel nevertheless that this argument is not consistent if we consider that non-psychotic creative personalities quite often show a compulsive tendency in their creative activity.

I shall go on to give a few brief clinical examples to illustrate my opinions on the relationship of creative activity with psychotic mechanisms and fluctuations in the state of the ego.

A patient of one of my colleagues became creatively active after going through a serious depressive-melancholic crisis (in which he began, among other things, to work through the loss of his idealizations, and which marked the attenuation of a series of acting out episodes that had started in the previous period). [J. Granel (1970), 'Acting out, Idealisation and Creativity. Study of their development in psychoanalytical treatment.'] This was a modification in the structure, form and style of a product with a system of technical improvements that he had invented.

During the sessions in his creative phase it was possible to observe the beginnings of his 'capacity to think'; his tendency towards action and motor discharge was replaced by states of 'ecstasy' in which he achieved inspiration. It could also be observed that he abandoned omniscient control for the method of trial and error. The product he created appeared as a consequence of his greater ability to symbolize and sublimate. It was in addition a sign that his internal objects were less persecutory and were beginning to be metabolized in the ego and the ego-ideal.

A significant dream marked the change from his melancholic crisis to the beginning of the creative phase.

'Yesterday I was reading poems by Alfonsina Storni and Amado Nervo. Afterwards I dreamt of death. There were enormous horrible tortoises; they came out of their shells and were like lizards stretching themselves out, showing a soft part. A tortoise that had been hibernating began to soften up and turned into an octopus with suckers and eyes like jelly. I explained to my children that tortoises hibernated in those gourds; now it was only a shell. I did not feel bad, it was not a nightmare. Now I feel anxiety telling you about it.'

Through reading those poets, the patient came into contact with his melancholic, suicidal, 'idealistic' parts, linked with death, which were in process of being worked through. He was acquiring a capacity for emotion, he could bear to feel without at once ejecting the affect.

During the night following his reading, and stimulated by it, he had a dream expressing his development. The dream showed that his primary contents were being transformed. His ideal objects, which had come out of their lethargy and whose psychotic contents had been set in motion, were being integrated into the nucleus of the ego, enriching it: they could be symbolized in this dream.

Another patient, a well-known and talented authoress, used to have asthma attacks in her periods of greatest creativity; she saw them as crushing attacks on the integrity of her ego. They were accompanied by an increase in her persecutory anxiety, horrific nightmares peopled with images of dangerous animals, and a deep-seated feeling of 'reaching rock-bottom'. But on those same days she worked with feverish activity and managed, through her creativity, to transform the persecutory images into human characters, which saved her from the 'pit'. A clinical fragment will serve as illustration:

'I dreamed about spiders again; it was a dream full of creepy-crawlies. I was in a big house, the country kind; I saw an enormous spider, but it was something between a crab and a lobster. I panicked and shut the doors, but I saw that a skylight was open. I heard voices saying that it had escaped into the fields; it was dangerous, and I had to chase it. Then I saw vipers and crocodiles in a cellar, but my real fear was of the spider.'

'. . . I was touching rock-bottom. The asthma was like a warning. . . .'

'. . . One has to learn to live with chaos. . . .'

'. . . With my writing plan I felt rejection, fear, and more asthma. . . . I thought in more terrifying images. . . . I imagined concentration camps and six-year-old children working in factories. . . .'

'. . . I knew people in the Resistance. I should like to know to what point one can live with horror. I imagine myself as a territory occupied by asthma; I think what it would be like to swallow poison gas, for example; it's like breathing thick dirty air that cannot be digested. . . .'

'Suddenly I think how horrible it must be to go to war. . . . It never enters the soldier's mind that the war he is fighting is useless. . . . Now with Vietnam, people are refusing to go to war; poor kids who do go! Many go convinced.'

'Yesterday I read of a novel idea: exorcism. What I read consists of calling demons to come out. . . .'

'I am afraid of delirium, of imagination.'

'People are more permeable to poetry than one thinks. They feel the need of poetry.'

'If I want to create something, it comes out better. . . . It's like a workshop in which I work things out in rough. . . .'

It can be appreciated how the patient struggles in her moments of 'chaos' and 'disorganization' to emerge after 'touching rock bottom'; the 'poison gas', which she cannot digest, and the horrendous images of the dreams are persecutory objects that threaten destruction and war, trying to convince her to submit to them. But it is creativity and poetry that in the last analysis will enable her to free herself from her demons, exorcizing them by means of creative activity developed and worked out in the workshop of her mind.

In so far as the creative process gives rise to a situation of change, it inevitably implies a reaction of mourning for the loss of the old structures and aspects of the self and objects (with the corresponding link between them), which are necessarily replaced by new structures and links contained in the creative process. All work of creation takes as its specific base the working through of depressive phantasies tending to restore and recreate the lost object, which feels destroyed, and which represents the earliest objects, the parents, as pointed out by M. Klein (1940), H. Segal (1925), and L. Grinberg (1963a). [We must also consider the guilt the creative person feels because he possesses creative capacity and sometimes feels that he is 'chosen'. Sometimes the depression that follows creation is also due to the loss of expectations and the urge to create, which are temporarily exhausted in the act of creation.] [The fertilizing sexual relationship of the internal parents, the primal scene, has an influence on the creative phantasies that are experienced like the conception of a child.]

M. Milner (1969) points out that some patients seek to break their false internal organizations through a temporary chaos or 'creative fury', which destroys a compliant and conformist adaptation to allow the emergence of a more authentic organization. [M. Milner gave the name 'illusion of one-ness' not only to the attempt to recover the memory of gratification by the mother's breast, but to one extreme of a constantly alternating polarity that constitutes the basis of psychic creativity, the formation of symbols and psychic growth. The alternation is between the feeling of 'one-ness' and the state of 'two-ness', or differentiation between the self and the object. In my opinion this alternation occurs in the creative personality, but not in the psychotic, who usually falls into indifferentiation and confusion with the object. This fusion with the internal object is equivalent to the 'oceanic feeling' described by Freud (1930a).] This recalls Winnicott's (1955) theory of the necessity to replace the false self, which serves as defensive armour, by the true self. [Greenacre (1957) points out that divisions in the feeling of identity of some creative people may result. This division into two or more egos is experienced in infancy and is accompanied by anxiety and the desire to deny the creative ego and favour the ego that is a social stereotype. The child feels that the creative ego can be monstrous and abnormal and that he has to fight against it.] It also comes close to the idea of 'catastrophic change' maintained by Bion (1966), which can be applied to the creative process in so far as it implies the breaking of established and well-known canons and their replacement by the new or 'Messianic' idea which may appear in a disruptive or creative form.

It is precisely by using Bion's 'container–contained' model for the different forms of object-relations that we come to agree with his opinion that the 'genius' needs a group (container) to enable him to develop and grow. But I would add that at the same time he must be able to contain his own work, because as the genius is potentially destructive or creative, he may use his mind, or the representation of the self, or a co-ordinating function of the ego, as the first container of the creative idea, and he must have the capacity to contain it without letting himself be destroyed by his potentially disruptive character; this will favour his growth. The second container will be an idealized internal object, and finally he will seek as container an external object (mother, father, master), which represents the idealized projected object.

The creative person represents in his work, as in his dreams, the continual process of relationship with his internal object, including all the vicissitudes comprised in his aggressive phantasies and his phantasies of reparation.

In my opinion, when the artist is faced with the persecutory and depressive phantasies inherent in the course of his relations with internal objects, he may feel impelled to seek relief, and he does this through the mechanism of projective identification; his projection may then have an aggressive connotation. But he also uses this mechanism to express his desire to be understood by the objects of the external world, especially when these objects correspond to good internal objects.

We could postulate in the creative personality the existence of an innate capacity or 'creative potential', which would endow the mechanisms of the primary process with their capacity for development and for being deployed while keeping their contact with reality; the co-existence of concrete and abstract in a harmonious synthesis and the specific use of projective identification mechanisms permitting the fusion and synthesis of aspects of the self with aspects and representations of idealized internal objects; the creation of phantasies of a hallucinatory type, which remain beyond the reality principle, without losing contact with reality; the capacity to 'forget' what is known (Bion, 1970), without trying to cling obstinately to logical and ordered structures, feelings, and concepts. The creative personality will tolerate frustration and the anxiety of remaining temporarily in the 'void', in 'disorder', and in 'chaos'; he will have an urge to seek for truth and will be able to let himself be overcome by intuition and carried along by it. In such cases we would speak mainly of a progressive process in which the mechanisms of the primary process meet the 'creative potential', which, manipulating them in a special way, begins the series of transformations characteristic of the creative process. This latter, whatever its nature, lacks meaning in the initial stage; it produces only pleasure and pain (Bion, 1970). Meaning will be acquired only at a later stage, when the act of creation has been transformed into a product of creation. [H. Reichenbach (1938) gives the name of 'context of discovery' to the here and now, including the psychological event, and 'context of justification' to the rational reconstruction subsequent to this event for purposes of communication.]

We could consider the different phases of the creative process not only as a 'regression at the service of the ego' (Kris, 1955), but also as a 'progression of the primary process towards the ego'. The benefits of the creative process, for both the ego and the object, are great, through the transcendence of the creative product and its impact on the external world, an impact that, through its quality of 'language of achievement', will be able to survive through the centuries.

PART FOUR

Theoretical
and clinical aspects
of supervision

CHAPTER TWENTY

Theoretical aspects
of supervision

Before entering into a thorough discussion of this subject, I am tempted to quote Freud's well-known remark upon the three 'impossible' professions: analysing, educating, and governing (1926d [1925]). As supervision implies a process of education, and the training analyst usually holds a post within the institute, it follows that he is, *ipso facto*, engaged in the three demanding and 'painful' tasks. Concerning the first of these, the task of analysing, Freud asked himself: 'But where and how is the poor wretch to acquire the ideal qualifications which he will need in this profession?' (1926d [1925]). I would like to apply Freud's words to educating and put still another question: How can the training analyst cope with the heavy burden imposed by the practice of these 'impossible' activities while trying to do his work well? Naturally, the first answer is to be found in the analyst's own analysis, which, as Freud pointed out, still stands as the most reliable guarantee. The deeper and the more successful this analysis is, the more confident and resourceful will the analyst feel in his work. Apart from this, the analyst should have other qualities:

knowledge, intuition, talent, teaching capacity, empathy, and so on.

We are now confronted with the first serious problem in the context of supervision, which, as far as I know, has not yet been faced or solved in the majority of psychoanalytical institutes. I refer to the lack of concern for teaching graduate analysts in their turn, so that they acquire a capacity for teaching. This deficiency glaringly contrasts with the thorough psychoanalytical training (which also includes supervision itself) that qualifies the candidate to psychoanalyse patients. Frequently the new seminar teacher or the young supervisor is obliged to improvise or simply to repeat what he has gained from his student experience. Although this assimilation or identification with his teachers is very useful, he has not been given the specific, organic, and systematized programme, both theoretical and technical, that might have provided him with conceptual information and trained him to accomplish his teaching tasks satisfactorily.

I shall later deal with a certain approach to this problem that offers a possible solution by means of special courses for teachers in our Institute, and the experience of a 'supervision of supervisions' carried out in our clinic. [I refer to the Institute of Psycho-analysis of the Argentinian Psycho-Analytical Association, as at the time when this chapter was first published, I was living in Buenos Aires.]

One of the most important aims of supervision is the integration of theory with clinical practice. It is equally essential to pass on the procedures used by the analyst to adapt his theoretical knowledge to the clinical material and to understand the analytical process. The process of supervision seeks to increase the student's 'analytical instrument'.

It is difficult to say how this passing-on is done, as it depends on the particular case and on the link between supervisor and student.

It is not an easy task to decide which are the essential problems among those that arise in the process of supervision. Moreover, these difficulties can be approached from various angles. One viewpoint regards them as integral to the very nature of all learning processes and constitutes the relatively constant factors that

are present in the development of all of them, and that are determined by the complexity of the object of study. Another viewpoint
stresses those problems elicited by the personalities involved in
the process and the dynamic field produced by the interplay of
mutual relations. A third approach is centred on the kind of
supervision (individual, group, etc.) and the quality of the specific
problems in each case. Other authors stress the problems arising
from responsibility for the patient's future or any emergency situations that may occur (psychotic breakdown, etc.). Ekstein and
Wallerstein (1958) consider separately 'problems about learning'
(arising between supervisor and student) and 'learning problems'
(arising between therapist and patient). There are, of course,
many other possibilities that lie beyond the scope of this work.

In order to be as clear as possible, I shall group supervision
problems according to different categories. This does not mean
that I believe that such problems appear separately; on the contrary, they usually come together, thus increasing the number of
pitfalls that hinder the normal development of the process and
sometimes lead to its interruption.

One of the most important starting points for the understanding
of the problems that may arise in any supervision can be found in
its philosophy. I refer among other things to the body of aims,
frameworks, techniques, and expectations of each supervisor in
his specific task. The institute to which he belongs has an established philosophy as regards supervision, which he may or may not
share. When views differ, conflicts may arise in the supervisor–
institute relationship.

Accordingly, as we follow the concepts of different authors, we
shall find different definitions of the concept of supervision, based
on the emphasis given to particular elements. For instance, it is
described as: 'a special type of learning process based upon the
joint examination of the record of a therapeutic interaction
between a patient and his therapist' (Arlow, 1963), or 'a highly
complex function performed by an experienced psychotherapist
whose aim is to enable a less experienced psychotherapist to
become effective in his task of benefitting his patient' (Hora, 1957),
or 'a learning experience in which one is sharing with a colleague

the fruits of one's clinical knowledge as well as clarifying one's thinking and technique' (Anderson & McLaughlin, 1963).

In fact, each supervision is made up of several important elements and a series of variables. Fleming and Benedek (1966) state that the supervision situation consists of a triadic system of subsystems in a complex process of inter-communication between the three elements that take part: supervisor, analyst, and patient (S $\leftrightarrow$ A $\leftrightarrow$ P). Each person in the triadic system is a member of a dyadic system that, in certain circumstances, acts independently of the third component.

Ekstein and Wallerstein (1958), on the other hand, postulate what they call the 'clinical rhombus' of the supervision, in which the interrelation between the four vertical entities is outlined: S (supervisor), T (therapist), P (patient), and A (administrator or institute).

To my mind, other elements could be added to these systems of relationships, such as the latent presence of the student's training analyst, which may weigh on the interplay of relationships both as regards the student or the supervisor; or perhaps another supervisor or supervisors by whom the student may be supervised at the time, and so on. Emch (1955) points out that the elements present in a supervisory situation can be multiplied so far that they form combinations of positive and negative feelings that might reach an extraordinarily high number of possible conflicts.

In the early days of psychoanalytical institutes, training analysts were clinicians rather than educators. Consequently, their main concern was with the patient, but at the same time their demands on the student were very high. Balint (1948) objected to such a training system and called it 'superego training'. One can easily imagine the troubles it must have engendered.

To continue this brief historical view of supervision, mainly as regards its problems, it is worth while to remember the controversy resulting from the 'Hungarian system' supported by Kovacs (1936) and presented at the Four Countries Conference in 1935 (Glover, 1935). The philosophy of this system was based on the advisability of having the training analyst himself working simultaneously as supervisor. This was objected to by those who pointed out the serious complications that would arise.

Another controversial aspect within the philosophy of the educational process of supervision is the double role of therapist and teacher assigned to the supervisor. Either of these roles excludes the other. This double function constituted a dilemma for the supervisor–analyst. Lewis and Ross (1960) refer to it as the 'syncretistic' function of the training analyst. Sometimes, as we shall see further on, it can cause confusion between therapeutic and educational aims.

There are supervisors whose main concern is with the student (Wagner, 1957). They focus their attention primarily on the student's work, assessing how and when he interpreted, his understanding of the material, and so forth. Carried too far, this approach seems more like an examination than a process of training.

If the supervisor's philosophy goes further and tries to see what happens in the student's unconscious, and to deal with his blind spots and his countertransference, supervision is in danger of becoming a sort of therapy.

The opposite phenomenon can also occur—i.e., if the supervisor believes he must concentrate on the patient at the expense of the candidate. This will obviously harm the teaching and foster learning by imitation. It may also happen that when the supervisor devotes himself excessively to the candidate, he is actually trying to convey his own *Weltanschauung*. On the other hand, if his attention is mostly focussed on the patient, he may be trying to apply his own reparatory phantasies and the curative capacity he attributes to his analytical technique.

I want now to refer briefly to my own philosophy. I try to start a candidate's supervision by establishing a sort of contract stating explicitly the way in which our common experience will be realized. I prefer the candidate himself to choose the case to be submitted to supervision. If he shows doubts, or requests my opinion, I offer to help him in the selection, once the cause for his doubts is clearly established. It is always my purpose to focus attention chiefly upon the teaching–learning relationship. I think the particular case under supervision should be taken as the basis for general and clinical teaching, including theoretical and technical concepts, but by no means leaving aside the consideration of the specific features of the case. I advise the student to prepare a clinical record for each patient, besides the one under supervision, and to keep them up to date. I also consider it useful to revise the other cases periodically, during the supervisory hours with the same candidate.

Finally, in order to present a panoramic idea of the supervision process, I shall describe briefly the opinions of Fleming and Benedek (1966); they postulate three periods: initial, intermediate, and final. This does not mean that I agree with the elements they put forward as characteristic of each period.

They suggest the following aspects of the experience of the candidate being supervised:

In the first period, or initial phase:

1. listening with floating attention (the self acts as an instrument of reception and perception, with a synthetical function);

2. learning to infer interpretations from the latent meaning, but without formulating them yet;

3. learning to estimate the degree of resistance and anxiety in the patient, and developing empathy with the patient's regressive state (function of sensitivity).

In the second period or intermediate phase:

4. judging the moment and distribution of responses and interventions;

5. grasping, at the greatest possible depth, reactions of transference and countertransference.

In the third period or final phase:

6. recognizing the dynamic trends and changes from session to session;

7. recognizing *insight,* working through, and the possibility of termination.

A. Aberastury (1958) gives the criterion of a gradual transmission of knowledge, stimulating the development of capacities. She also points out three periods in the process of supervision. In the first period she prefers that teaching should be centred on dealing with transference and countertransference. In the second period she stresses the basic concepts in the analysis of one session taken in detail and as a whole, placing the emphasis on the development of the capacity for observation and the formulation of interpretations. In the third period she includes the session with the total development of the case and the direction to be taken in working out the case history.

CHAPTER TWENTY-ONE

Practical and technical aspects of supervision

As we have seen, supervision is one of the pillars of psycho-analytical training. It implies a confrontation rather than a course of teaching—a confrontation that takes place between a young analyst beginning his professional experience and an analyst who is generally senior to him and more experienced. In addition, the task of supervision implies a teacher–pupil relationship and the evaluation of the student's capacity as an analyst. But perhaps the most important purpose of supervision is 'the transmission of the psychoanalytical knowledge of one generation to another by means of information and confrontation', as Lebovici (1970) says, through a true 'work alliance', to use Frijling-Schreuder's happy expression.

The supervision session generally takes place once a week, and lasts fifty minutes, like the psychoanalytic session. The student presents the clinical material that should preferably have been reworked after the session. I shall discuss later on the reasons why I suggest that this is the best procedure for recollecting the material. The supervisor comments in as much detail as possible on the different aspects of the session: beginning, greetings, development of the associative process, evolution of unconscious phantasies, transference–countertransference link, principal anxieties and defensive processes, state of the functions of the ego, projective–introjective interplay of the analytical couple, formulation and appropriateness of interpretations, the patient's attitude and response to them, dreams, verbal and non-verbal language, end of the session, and so on. He will have to make clear his own method of analytical work, but must take care not to exert too much influence or impose extreme identification with it on the student. It will be as well to go into the different practical aspects of analytical training such as the contract, fees, holidays, absences, late arrivals, *acting out* problems, and so forth. Another aspect to which great attention must be paid is the termination of the analysis. Usually this is left aside because the period of supervision is relatively short (two years in general) compared with the duration of analytical treatment. But it is advisable to include some experience of the ending of an analysis and to discuss it thoroughly.

The choice of supervisor and student

In many institutes the students can choose the training analyst to supervise their cases. In others the rules lay down that it is the institute itself that nominates the supervisor.

In either case the choice of a supervisor may raise some problems if we take into account certain manifest or latent ideologies that sometimes split an institute into rival subgroups. In that case the candidate whose training analyst belongs to a certain group will try to be supervised by someone from the same group. He will sometimes be prompted to do so by his own training analyst. Another will apparently act on his own initiative, but will in fact be under the influence of a strong transference dependence that has not yet been overcome. In extreme cases this kind of supervision will be vitiated by an *a priori* approach by both parties (Grinberg, 1963c).

On the other hand, if the institute chooses the supervisor, the student may be uncomfortable because of the ideological influence upon the supervision, if the supervisor belongs to a different group from that of his analyst. He may fear a conflict of loyalties.

At times, selection criteria may depend on purely unconscious motives. So, for example, a candidate would choose a woman analyst as supervisor to find a benevolent maternal image that counteracts the 'strict' paternal image of his own analyst, and so forth (Anderson & McLoughlin, 1963).

The supervisor may have a similar experience when he has to accept a student sent by the institute. He may find it difficult to handle the situation if he thinks the student belongs to another ideological subgroup. Or he may dislike the candidate's personality because it clashes with his own.

The choice of the moment to begin

On this point there are opposite criteria, depending basically on whether or not the student is required to be in analysis when the supervision begins. Everybody agrees that he should be psychologically mature and have a satisfactory theoretical and technical level. Some authors insist that supervision should not start until the student's own analysis is in its final stage or has already been satisfactorily brought to an end. They argue that countertransference invariably hampers not only the candidate's capacity to analyse, but also his capacity to learn academic material, since this capacity is diminished by transference neurosis. Although this seems to be a sound way of reasoning, those who hold the opposite view stress the suitability of having the candidate in analysis, as this may enable him to analyse the reactivation of the problems or conflicts reawakened by the stress of supervision.

I am in favour of the second criterion, because I believe that, apart from the reasons mentioned above, it is essential for the candidate to have the possibility of analysing his countertransference reactions and blind spots, since their resolution is beyond the aim of supervision. Besides, the opportunity is thus granted for analysing thoroughly and from different angles the working instrument that is being studied and perfected within the specific field of supervision.

Other authors stress the advisability of having personal analysis and supervision simultaneously, as they believe students can make the most of the learning process if they can bring to the analysis everything that appears in the course of supervision, as regards both the patient and the supervisor. That is why they advise institutes to have both experiences at the same time (Anderson & McLoughlin, 1963).

Although I am in favour of this simultaneous experience, I disagree with Blitzten and Fleming (1953) and Ackerman (1953) about the supposed usefulness of having consultations between the training analyst and the supervisor. I believe it threatens the necessary privacy and isolation personal analysis calls for and also renders supervision still more entangled and persecutory. Instead of solving problems, it would add difficulties, because the student would feel excluded from the dual relationship between his analyst and his supervisor, who would in fact meet to talk about him.

The choice of the case

In my experience this has also been a controversial issue. Some institutes are markedly interested in finding suitable cases for beginners to start analysing, and also suitable for supervision. They make a point of discerning whether a case of hysteria would be more appropriate than an obsessional neurosis or agoraphobia. It has been recommended that the first case should be previously interviewed by the analyst who will be in charge of the supervision (DeBell, 1963). I agree with those who object to this criterion (Grotjahn, 1955). They consider it excessive, as it would inhibit the candidate. I think that the patients chosen by the student himself are more successfully analysed, and so there is greater advantage in the supervisory training.

Students belonging to most Latin-American institutes have already had some years' experience in the psychotherapeutic treatment of patients before they start supervision officially. In general they are free to choose the case for supervision.

Even though it is true that both ways of thinking have their pros and cons, to my mind it is preferable to allow the student to choose his case freely (even if it happens to be a severe neurosis or borderline). In the first place, he will feel that he is more respected and understood. Besides, he may be allowed to deal with the case with which he has the greatest difficulties, and this is one of the aims of supervision. On the other hand, he will find learning more challenging as he has the chance of discussing precisely what he does not know, does not understand, or cannot cope with in his work.

The choice of the method of recording material

I am not going to deal with the technical reasons underlying the advantages and disadvantages of using one way of recording or another; I shall simply mention the difficulties arising during the learning process involved in supervision. Briefly summarized, there are three methods: use of the tape-recorder, taking notes during the session, and the reconstruction of the session afterwards. I am leaving out those analysts who report just what they remember without having taken any notes.

Some candidates prefer to tape-record the session, on the grounds that this procedure is absolutely reliable. Kubie (1958b), among others, emphasized the fact that the recording of sessions is most helpful in avoiding distortion in the report submitted by the student. He also pointed out the advantage of the candidate being able to listen to his own interventions. For better research, he advised studying the combined recordings of both the analytic session and the supervisory hour. Other authors have stressed the significance of listening to the inflections of the patient's voice. Despite the fact that Kubie's remarks deserve to be taken into account, there may be occasions when this method is used unconsciously to keep at a distance from the patient, the tape-recorder being a third element in the analytical situation, in charge of recording and registering the patient's associative sequence, thus relieving the student of the implied responsibility. Some students have the session typed, and when they read it again, during supervision, react to the material as if they were hearing it for the first time. They have become mere links between 'patient–tape-recorder–memory' on the one hand, and 'supervisor–understanding–analytical function' on the other. In such circumstances, learning will obviously be seriously impaired, apart from the logical harm this can do to the patient. In such cases it is advisable to ask the candidate to change his way of gathering material and give up the tape-recorder for a while, pointing out how harmful this may be for the therapeutic relationship.

Some candidates insist on the need to take notes during the session, because they do not trust their memory and feel it is important for them to register all the data as they come up. But this is inevitably done at the cost of a marked detachment from continuous communication from the patient. Such students are unable to maintain the free-floating attention strongly recommended by Freud and work with only half their potential capacities.

In general, I think it is more productive to ask the candidate to write up the notes immediately after the session. If this is not possible, it can be done in the evening, when the working day is over, or on the following day. The candidate should be told that the notes need not be absolutely faithful, and no attempt needs to be made to achieve perfect chronological reference to all that has occurred throughout the session. It is useful to write down what he remembers first and then try to fill in the gaps. This works as an extremely useful kind of initial self-supervision. Many candidates have told me that as they were writing up the sessions, they thought them over and realized the mistakes they had made, or something they had not been aware of during the session, which they could later verify and elaborate during supervision. Besides, it is a very stimulating training which helps to improve memory and capacity for observation.

Another possibility is to dictate into a tape recorder, after the session, a summary of its development, or at least its most salient points.

Lewin and Ross (1960) point out that in some institutes young supervisors sit in on supervisions directed by senior supervisors, so that they can learn how to supervise. There are then meetings between supervisors to discuss the experience. Tape recordings of supervision periods have been used for the same purpose, and there have even been plans to do it with videotape. J. Fleming, quoted by Lewin and Ross, carried out a pilot study in Chicago in 1954, on the basis of a tape recording of supervision time. It proved advantageous not only for the students but also for the supervisors, who could discuss the recorded supervisions among themselves.

Exchange of recorded supervisions

Some years ago I was invited (Grinberg, 1972b) to discuss the article by John A. Lindon: 'Recorded supervision: a new method of case-supervision', published in the *Psycho-analytic Forum* (1972). In this work Dr Lindon describes more than ten years' experience of a method of supervision consisting in the exchange by post of recorded supervisions (cassettes) with colleagues in the same town or living in areas further away. He asserts that in his opinion this experience strengthens the 'learning alliance' between therapist and supervisor, on the principle that good supervision stimulates later working-through and self-analysis in an analyst with a certain amount of experience.

Listening to the recording several times increases the understanding of the material, overcomes resistance, and makes it possible to return to obscure points. From the point of view of the technique of this type of supervision, he recommends that the recording should comprise three successive sessions, the middle one in as great a detail as possible, with a summary of the preceding and following sessions. The therapist describes and explains the patient's associations and his own interventions. The supervisor, after listening to the recording sent by the therapist, records his comments on the material and the interpretations and may ask for explanations of some aspects that give rise to doubts. He may also point out the therapist's blind spots and scotomas, due to 'countertransferential identifications' as the result of transference projections. Using an expression of Searles, he maintains that this method helps to increase the 'supervisory instrument', approximating it to the 'analytical instrument'.

I should like briefly to mention some of the observations made by other people taking part in the discussion, before going on to my own contribution.

For example, Bertram Lewin (Lewin & Ross, 1960) evinced doubts on the appropriateness of using this method in supervision in common with the student; in his view we cannot expect magic from a machine, nor could it successfully replace human intelligence.

Michael Balint (1948) also stressed this last point. He pointed out that the human mind is without a doubt the best recording equipment known; it works admirably when used selectively, providing that powerful emotional forces do not interfere with its normal function of registering and preserving the original material observed in the conduct of another human being. For him, the method proposed by Lindon would have the advantage of reducing the differences between supervisor and therapist, placing them in more egalitarian conditions, without the inhibitory effect that might be produced by face-to-face supervision, but with the disadvantage of preventing immediate interaction between the two parties.

Joan Fleming (1966) brings out the usefulness of this method for supervision between equals—that is, between analysts of the same level of knowledge and experience. According to her, recorded supervision adds dimensions that do not exist in ordinary supervision, provides more information on the para-linguistic messages sent, and can be repeated and listened to many times by different participants, which, moreover, widens its range of action in the learning context. But she admits as a disadvantage the suppression of the immediate dynamic interrelation between supervisor and student, which stimulates and increases insight.

For some authors, the main advantages of recorded supervision are the following: (1) it constitutes the record of the original exchange without any degree of distortion; (2) it is a permanent record, which can be listened to and studied as many times as required; (3) it can be listened to in a less emotionally charged atmosphere than the original record.

Harold F. Searles (1955) suggests that the comparison between recorded supervision and conventional face-to-face supervision should be gone into more thoroughly. He compares it in a way with the psychoanalytical method of the couch and the face-to-face psychotherapeutic technique. He adds that both the tape recorder and the cassette have their own constellation of transference and projected meanings for each of the participants. He also refers to the meaning and influence of the 'non-human' aspects (the tape recorder and the recorded sessions) that take part in the experience.

In my own contribution I emphasized, among other things, that Dr Lindon's article was especially interesting to me because it went deeply into certain aspects related to the therapist's countertransference. I also included some relevant remarks about the problems of rivalry, jealousy, paternalism, subjection, and so on, which must often arise in the practice of supervision.

I made clear that the 'exchange of supervision between equals' at different levels and also in groups, is frequently practised in our circles. This experience, generally taking place face-to-face, has been as positive and beneficial as Dr Lindon says.

After pointing out my reservations regarding the use of the tape recorder in the analytical session, I added that the recording could be useful in learning situations. On their own initiative, some of my students would record the supervision hour; they maintain that this practice is extremely beneficial because it helps them to perfect their learning skills by listening a second time with more care and attention to the recorded supervision. For my part, when listening to these recordings I had an opportunity to confirm their usefulness, since it was then possible to grasp certain details that had escaped me in the original experience. But I never used the tape recorder systematically as Dr Lindon recommended, nor did I follow the series of successive recordings with commentaries made by each of the participants.

The author maintained that recorded supervision offered, among other advantages, the possibility of detecting countertransference reactions in the therapist, provoked by the patient's projections in the transference, which coincides with my own discoveries regarding a special aspect of the therapist's countertransference, which I called 'projective counteridentification'. This is the reaction caused in the analyst by the patient who, unconsciously and through his projective identification, makes the analyst take on certain attitudes, play certain roles, or experience certain emotions.

Other authors, including Arlow (1963) and Searles (1955), concerned themselves with similar problems but approached them from a different starting point and in consequence used a different terminology for the conceptualization and description of the phenomenon. But I think that my views coincide more perfectly with those of Lindon, since he refers to this problem as 'a countertransferential reaction to a special form of transferential projection.'

Dr Lindon also mentions some disadvantages of his method. In fact, from the practical point of view it may be somewhat inadequate, because it takes more time and is more expensive. Nevertheless, these disadvantages are set off to a sufficient extent by its greater productivity.

In my opinion there is another possible disadvantage, which is that the reiteration of the same material does not always make it easier to understand. The freshness and the stimulating effect of the first impact are sometimes lost. Stereotyped ideas may then arise, which will probably be reinforced by the same factors that produce the countertransference reaction in the therapist.

Anyway, this objection does not diminish the usefulness of the method of recorded supervision, especially with respect to supervision among equals, investigation and supervision by correspondence, carried out as a form of fruitful exchange between colleagues in different countries.

J. Fleming and T. Benedek, in their book on *Psycho-Analytic Supervision* (1966), describe the investigation they are carrying out on the basis of the experiences of recorded supervisions of two supervisors with two students at different periods of their professional development. The principal objective was the separate evaluation and identification of the problems of learning and the teaching techniques used; on the other hand it was also possible to evaluate the evidence of progress experienced by the students. In conclusion they presented their theory of supervision and their philosophy of psychoanalytical teaching in the following terms: (1)

the analyst's education is necessarily more experimental than cognitive; (2) the fundamental objective of his educational experience is the development of himself as an analytical instrument; (3) every phase in his training contributes in different ways to this basic objective.

CHAPTER TWENTY-TWO

The specific setting of supervision

Supervisory situations, like psychoanalytical treatment, call for an appropriate setting. By setting I here mean adherence to a body of given patterns of behaviour so that the task can be accomplished under optimum conditions, without being threatened by attitudes or drives of either party, which could put the aim of the task at risk. In the first place, the supervisor should respect the time and frequency of supervisory hours, as he does with his patients. As he must set an example to the student, any breach on his part will amount to a serious contradiction of his teaching, and he will find it hard to be convincing when he explains the basic need to comply with such discipline in clinical work. A supervisor, for example, was often late for the supervisory session and frequently failed to keep appointments, while he constantly told the candidate that he should interpret his patient's late arrival or non-appearance as an expression of a severe type of acting out.

Supervision must have a setting that expresses quite clearly the difference between this educating situation and that of a therapeutic experience. In this sense another problem that may arise in the supervisor–student relationship is the student's unconscious attempt, for different motives, to make the supervisor behave as his therapist. This wish sometimes springs from the need to fulfil a phantasy of splitting, which converts the supervisor into an idealized analyst and projects the persecutory image on to his training analyst, or vice versa. Langer (1963) has also pointed out the need the candidate may feel to have an ally, 'a good object', in the supervisor, through the splitting that turns his own training analyst into a bad object. The supervisor should take the necessary steps to avoid this situation through a firm adherence to the established setting. The candidate should be treated as a colleague and not as a patient—for instance, he could be offered a cup of coffee, so as to create an atmosphere that contrasts with that accorded to a patient. Of course, this must be done within certain limits, so that the real purpose of the meeting, the supervision, is kept clearly in view.

The analyst's work forces him to be isolated in his consulting-room most of the day, and therefore he has very few possibilities of communication with the outside world. Furthermore, the regression that takes place during the analytical situation affects not only the patient, but also to a certain extent the analyst himself. Moreover, he has to restrict himself to interpreting only the material contributed by the patient. In this way, isolation, regression, and a lack of communication with the outside world will occasionally give rise to a strong longing for outside stimulus. This may account for a particular reaction supervisors may experience towards candidates under supervision, as they are a sort of escape valve that provides the supervisor with longed-for social contact and free dialogue. It is then important to bear this risk in mind, so that the supervisor's open and friendly attitude does not exceed reasonable limits that might endanger the supervisory setting (Grinberg, 1963c).

It is also important that the supervisor should not treat the student as a patient and enquire about his problems or attempt to interpret his countertransference if it is manifested during the supervision. He should also be alert to avoid any inclination to turn the candidate into an ardent follower of his theories, thus fostering his idealization (Greenacre, 1965). In this respect he should be careful not to use supervision for his own benefit—for example, by looking into the material for proof of an idea he is interested in at a given moment. Pichon-Rivière (1958) has pointed out that what is a serious problem if the candidate happens to be a beginner may become a fruitful exchange of ideas with an advanced student.

The aim of supervision

We are all aware that one of the main goals of supervision is to help the student to acquire the necessary knowledge and skill to perform his therapeutic work as well as possible. The supervisor should try hard to make the student learn through a stimulating assimilation of the concepts he is teaching him and not through imitation. In the first place, the student must learn to listen to his patient, to have the capacity for observing what is happening in the session, to understand, and use his own devices to draw conclusions and give his interpretations.

Isakower (1963), referring to what any supervisor must teach his students, stressed the importance of what he called the 'analytic instrument', having in mind a similar image used by Freud (1912e). He says that the student should be taught to become aware of the functioning and practical significance of this instrument. Isakower holds this to be an entity of the highest degree of psychic reality that grasps and communicates what happens in the analytical session. In describing the 'analytic instrument', he suggests that it is useful not to think of it as a permanently integrated, unitary system within the psychic structure of one person, the analyst. It seems more adequate to regard it, in its activated state, as being in rapport with its counterpart in the patient; or better, perhaps, to see it as a composite consisting of two complementary halves. Its nature is transient. Besides, when it works at its highest degree of expression, it cannot be simultaneously observed. It can only be distinguished when looked back upon after the session.

The problem of how to formulate interpretations worries almost all students, especially during the early stages of supervision. They often ask the supervisor how he would have worded an interpretation that he feels is unsatisfactory because of its ambiguity, complexity, or inclusion of technical terms that render the meaning obscure. The supervisor would be wrong to lend himself to being copied or imitated in his personal style. In my experience it has often been fruitful in such a situation to ask the student to explain to me what he really meant. As a rule, this explanation turns out to be the best way of formulating the interpretation, because, as I point out to him, the language is now plain, straightforward, and coherent. At the same time, it may prove useful to remind the candidate that the supervisor does not by any means have the magic interpretation.

I should like to mention something I have come across quite often and consider significant. The student who comes for supervision occasionally starts with a trivial remark about the weather, the state of the traffic, something that has occurred during the seminar or has happened to his children, and so forth. Experience has taught me that very frequently these incidental comments are a kind of free association indirectly connected with the main theme of the material he brings. This proves that unconsciously he has been able to take in fundamental latent aspects that he had failed to make manifest. If the supervisor discusses this situation every time it happens, it will help the candidate to be more confident and to be bolder in handling more directly the discovered content.

As might be expected, the supervisor will contribute through his suggestions and teachings to increasing the elements that will give shape to the candidate's own equipment.

Bion (1963) put forward a method for considering the problems that appear in the course of psychoanalytical practice. He called it 'the grid' and it consists of two axes: a vertical one that is marked from A to H and spans the genetic growth of the mind from a primitive situation (A), in which there is no thought yet, up to the highest possible degree of abstraction (H). The other axis is horizontal and is numbered from 1, 2, 3 . . . up to N. This axis shows the 'uses' given to the genetic elements in the vertical axis. In other words, the vertical axis is meant to denote a phase in the development, while the horizontal axis denotes the use to which those elements or phases are put.

Every event that is part of the communication between analyst and analysand, a word, a sentence, a gesture, or interpretation itself, can be placed under one category of the grid. It is, then, an instrument for classifying statements. Bion considers any phenomenon of psychoanalysis as a possible statement that can be evaluated by referring it to one or another of the grid categories. The grid should never be used during the session but after it, and as a method to help to think about and categorize what has happened during the analytical session.

Problems arising
from the supervisor's personality

It is not an easy task to accomplish the aims of supervision on account of the problems arising from factors inherent in the respective personalities, and from the sometimes almost inevitable interference of transference and countertransference.

I shall deal first with the psychopathology of the supervisor's personality. It should not be forgotten that although he has finished his own analysis, he has not always overcome his neurotic conflicts. On the contrary, they may often be reactivated and even aggravated in certain circumstances, including the supervisory situation.

A supervisor with paranoid characteristics may have to face serious problems in the performance of his function. As he fears the candidate may try to deprive him of his original ideas, he will be very cautious in his teaching, giving as little of himself as possible and restricting his work to general concepts. He will avoid exposing himself to what he experiences as a theft of his concepts and ideas. Needless to say, a supervision that develops in this atmosphere is bound to be vitiated; it lacks an essential in teaching, the teacher's capacity to transmit his experience openly and deeply. It may happen that this paranoid tendency is found among those analysts who, for various reasons, have difficulties in writing, developing their concepts, and publishing their work. They are often intelligent and potentially capable of thought-provoking teaching, but, as a result of their problem, they accuse others of taking possession of their ideas and presenting them as their own. This phenomenon appears to a certain extent in any teaching process and is part and parcel of the teacher–pupil relationship. As he communicates his knowledge, the teacher cannot help feeling he is giving it away. The pupil will receive this knowledge and use it as if it were his own, because he has assimilated it. Naturally I am not referring to well-developed theories whose authors are widely known, but to general concepts: those shades and details that constitute the personal style present in the work of the scientist and the artist.

Any teacher, and consequently any supervisor, should be fully aware of this problem and work it through. It has to be accepted that in this specific relationship the teacher gives and the pupil receives. It is what Erikson called 'generativity'—that is, 'concern to establish and guide the next generation' (1950). The supervisor who has a paranoid personality and does not give himself would suffer a regression of his 'generativity', thus impoverishing and sterilizing his communication with the pupil.

There also exists the opposite case—that of a supervisor who has a depressive personality and a masochistic tendency in his work. Owing to his conflictual phantasies related to guilt feelings, this supervisor will try to pour out compulsively all he knows and possesses. He will find it hard to draw the line, and the student will be overwhelmed by the avalanche of knowledge he receives.

I could, of course, describe other manifestations and clinical types of supervisor psychopathology, but for the sake of brevity I have mentioned only two. Nor have I wanted to go too far into the wide field of the supervisor's 'countertransference' and the different emotional reactions when confronted with the candidate's neurotic traits or the clinical material he reports. Nobody is free of such reactions, and it is important to be alert to detect them and avoid the counterproductive effects they may have on the process of supervision.

Problems arising from the student's personality

I have found the experience of supervision intensely gratifying because of the mutual benefit implied by a task of investigation in common, and because of the interest, receptivity, and constant stimulus that I have always received from my younger colleagues. However, in a very few cases I have had to face certain problems arising from the type of personality of some students and their particular attitude to supervision. My own experience, and similar experiences of my supervisor colleagues, have led me to deal with this topic, which adds to the difficulties inherent in the personality of the supervisor.

Confronted with the persecutory anxiety that supervision usually awakens, some students resort to manic attitudes and behave as though they have understood all the patient said. Others react with intense inhibitions, which prevent them from fulfilling even the minimum that is expected from them as therapists.

When dealing with 'manic' candidates, who tend to make up for their inexperience or lack of capacity with too many interpretations, it would be useful to show them systematically the mistakes they have made as regards comprehension and interpretation, due to their denial of the complexities involved in the material. Those students who are more inhibited tend to repress what they have understood of the material, and as a rule their interpretations are scanty and ambiguous.

These are, of course, two extremes, but there is a whole gamut of intermediate attitudes. To give just a few: there is the 'confused' student, who fails to discriminate between what is important and what is trivial and confuses form and content; the 'anxious' student, who, impelled by his 'anxiety', resorts to any interpretation, even if it has no connection with the material; and the 'obsessional' student, characterized by his long interpretations, full of rationalizations, in which 'everything has to go in'.

As regards this kind of problem, I remember Gitelson once relating that, on a certain occasion when his attitude to one of his earliest patients had been very active, his supervisor remarked: 'Doctor, when there are two people in the same room and one of them is anxious or in despair, it helps a great deal if the other is not' (1963a).

The examples mentioned above refer to reactions that may be regarded as normal and are relatively frequent in the experience of supervision.

I shall deal now with problems engendered by candidates whose personalities present a more acute pathology, impairing the relationship with the supervisor and the development of the process.

It may happen that some exceedingly greedy personalities go to supervision not to learn but to grasp and store up, without discrimination, whatever knowledge they may receive. They admire and envy the supervisor's capacity, experience, and cleverness, but do not attempt to assimilate his teachings; they try instead to 'swallow' him, so that they may become the absolute owners of what he possesses. On other occasions envy can be so regressive that they cannot stand the fact that anyone should have the knowledge they have not, so their aim is to destroy the other through cunning attacks. Their attitude is critical; they object to all suggestions and attempt to prove that they cannot be applied to their patient, and systematically sterilize the supervisor's work and castrate his mental powers. This situation can become even worse if competitiveness and rivalry reach such a peak that the student tries to dazzle his supervisor, in an omnipotent and manic way, with his 'intelligence' and show of superiority. Whenever the supervisor attempts to introduce a technical suggestion, they react by saying: 'Of course I have already done what you said'. Sometimes they improvise, or invent interpretations that were not really given during the session. They usually base them on something the supervisor has said and bring them out as though they were their own, or try to explain them by saying, 'What a coincidence! In the next part of the session I interpreted in almost the same words as you have just used.'

It is important to take into account not only the seriousness and frequency of this symptom, but also the various motivations involved. It is possible that deceit may be conditioned by a persecutory feeling in the face of supervision, which is felt as an examination situation. When this happens, there is a distortion of the supervisor–student relationship and also of its aims. The candidate does not try to make the most of his learning experience, but is only after a high mark. He brings the best material he has, or the material with which he hopes to show how well he works, in order to placate the supervisor. Sometimes his anxiety may be so intense that he has recourse to distortion of the clinical material, which he reconstructs to agree with his phantasy of what the supervisor might prefer. Deceit is at other times shown by his choice of case; he chooses the patient who fulfils all the theoretical norms and recognized techniques, when this is to be the 'case under supervision'. But it may happen that with his other patients he works in quite a different way.

The opposite phenomenon is found in those candidates who choose precisely the worst cases, those with the greatest difficulties, and those that they obviously analyse badly. But I am not referring to the need to bring a problem case to supervision with the specific aim of getting help and avoiding the pitfalls of such analyses, which would be justified and would respond to one of the main objectives of supervision. On the contrary, I am thinking of students with a marked masochistic tendency who 'need' to show their mistakes and the most negative side of their work. Sometimes they exaggerate their faults and they may even go so far as to distort the material. They 'lie', not to look good, but, paradoxically, to make themselves look worse than they are. This may be due, among other reasons, to guilt and a need for punishment for feelings of rivalry and competitiveness, not only towards the supervisor but towards their friends and colleagues as well.

There are students in whom persecution feelings in the face of supervision take a different form. They fear being invaded by the supervisor's teaching or being compelled to use his style, way of working, and approach, which might differ from their own. They experience supervision as a possible threat to their identity and defend themselves by 'withdrawing', talking all the time, or reading out endless sessions so that the supervisor will intervene as little as possible. They come to supervision as a formal requirement for the institute.

Problems arising from countertransference
and projective counteridentification

I shall now deal with one of the most important problems the supervisor has to tackle in the course of his work: the student's difficulties due to his countertransference. This topic has already been discussed in a large number of papers, conferences, and meetings on supervision. Naturally the most controversial issue is that of the attitude the supervisor has to assume towards the student's countertransference. Lately general agreement has been reached that the candidate's countertransference problems should not be interpreted by the supervisor; nevertheless, owing to the frequency and intensity with which they recur in the student's work, discussion still goes on as to what the supervisor's criterion should be in such cases. For my part, I should like to distinguish two main categories of countertransference problems: One is related to the problems of countertransference properly speaking; the other concerns what I have called projective counteridentification (Grinberg, 1963b). This is a specific aspect of countertransference, but one that is precipitated by the patient and determined by the quality and intensity of his projective identification mechanisms. I believe it is fundamental for the supervisor to be able to discriminate between these two categories each time he encounters such a problem during supervision, since countertransference has to be dealt with on the analyst's couch and projective counteridentification during supervision. If the student has difficulties or blind spots that are mainly due to conflict situations within the field of countertransference properly speaking, the supervisor may refrain from making a direct remark but point out that there was a difficulty and show how to approach the dynamics of what is happening to the patient. Some authors think it is better to make the situation explicit and advise that the student should try to see in his analysis what has happened. But his procedure is questioned by others, as it may have an unnecessarily disturbing effect on the candidate.

But now I should like to return in greater detail to the second category—namely, the problems of projective counteridentification—because they constitute the motive force of supervision; the supervisor must apply himself to the difficulties arising from this situation, since it is here that he must help the student to realize the conflict or misunderstanding, that may not always be a conscious one.

Such situations are generally determined by something the patient has induced in the analyst by using the projective identification mechanism, sometimes causing him to play a fixed role, take on attitudes, experience certain emotions, or function in the way that the patient unconsciously needs. In the analytic situation the analyst can be either an active subject of introjections and projections or a passive object of the analysand's projections. On the other hand his emotional reactions may be due to the reawakening of his own conflicts (countertransference) or his affective resonance can be the result of what the patient has projected into him (projective counteridentification). The patient unconsciously stimulates—through the projective identification mechanism—the analyst's unconscious identification with a given aspect of an internal object or with certain parts of the patient's self, thus leading him to feel certain emotions or act in a particular manner. To explain the difference, I would say that different analysts, because of their countertransference, would react in different ways to the same material of a hypothetical patient if they treated him consecutively. On the other hand this same patient would arouse the same emotional response (projective counteridentification) in different analysts, due to the use and specific type of their projective identification mechanisms. In the latter case, and when the student is passing through a disturbance of this kind, the supervisor has the advantage of having at hand the material that will indicate the source of the disturbance, and it is essential that the supervisor should be able to prove from the available clinical material where, how, and why this projective counteridentification reaction has been caused.

The student can make the supervisor feel an emotional reaction of the same quality as the patient has aroused in him. If the supervisor has a full understanding of the genesis of his own affective repercussions, he can, with his greater ability, objectivity, and experience, show the candidate the origin of the emotional reaction he experienced during the session with his patient.

I mentioned earlier that similar problems have been discussed by other authors, though starting from a different frame of reference and consequently using a different terminology to describe the phenomenon. I think many of the disagreements between analysts of different trends of thought are due to semantic rather than conceptual reasons. J. A. Arlow (1963) says, in reference to this kind of phenomenon, that the therapist shifts from the role of reporting the experience he has had with his patient to 'experiencing' his patient's experience; that is to say the supervisor may find evidence that the candidate 'acts' an identification with his patient. Among the examples he mentions is one of a student who, contrary to his usual manner, began to speak rapidly and breathlessly. Dr Arlow thought he had become hypomanic and drew his attention to this way of speaking. The student's response was immediate: he pointed out that his patient had behaved in this hypomanic way during the session. As he had not recorded the situation and could not reproduce it in words, he did so through action.

Harold F. Searles (1955) says that the relationship between patient and therapist is often revealed by the relationship between therapist and supervisor. He adds that the supervisor has his range of emotional phenomena, as the therapist and the patient have theirs: often these phenomena not only betray classic countertransference reactions, but are also highly informative reflections of the therapist–patient relationship. He calls them *reflection process* to emphasize their source and points out that they can be a decisive clue to obscure difficulties that emerge in the therapist–patient relationship. This author suggests that unconscious identification is one of the processes involved in the genesis of the phenomenon. When discussing the case at a supervision, the supervisor may have the feeling that the anxiety and defences shown by the therapist are an unconscious way of communicating something happening to the patient, which his own anxiety prevents him from describing to the supervisor. The latter can grasp the nature of the problem much more easily, not only because he has more knowledge and experience, but also because he is emotionally more detached.

Hora (1957) explains this type of phenomenon in the following way: 'The supervisee unconsciously identifies with the patient and involuntarily behaves in such a manner as to elicit in the supervisor those very emotions which he himself experienced while working with the patient but was unable to convey verbally'. Further on he adds that 'the therapist orally incorporates or introjects his patient in his endeavour to understand him empathically. While on the conscious level the supervisee proceeds with the presentation of the factual data about the patient, unconsciously on a non-verbal level he communicates the affective aspects of his experience with the patient. This carries the dynamic aspects of the patient's personality make-up.'

Illustrative examples

I shall now give a few examples to illustrate these concepts:

1. A student began his supervision session by saying that he felt depressed and bad-tempered. As this was unusual for him, and thinking that it was a personal matter, I preferred not to remark on it and suggested that we should go on to consider the material relating to the case. He added that on this occasion he had had difficulty in recording the last session and that he was afraid he had forgotten some sequences. He complained of being short of time to fulfil all his obligations and said that for that reason he had not been able to make notes on all the week's sessions, as he had intended to do. He then said he felt hot and asked me if he could open the window (it was a cool autumn day). Surprised and amused by his attitude, I insisted that we should look at the material, suspecting that there was some connection. The patient in question was in fact claustrophobic, habitually depressed, and querulous, with serious matrimonial conflicts. She accused her husband, who was a manic, active type, of having aggressive tendencies. Significantly, the patient had arrived for her session that day completely 'changed', according to the candidate's expression; he had never

seen her so manic and verbose, and he had also felt 'attacked' by her. It was not difficult to show him that the patient had 'identified with the aggressive husband' and behaved as manically and aggressively as he, but at the same time she had projected into the therapist her own depressive, querulous and claustrophobic part, which he needed to act out during supervision.

2. A supervisor, listening to material from the session of a borderline patient read to him by a fairly experienced student, began to feel more and more sleepy as the reading proceeded. He knew no personal reason for this somnolence, since he had not felt tired before the supervision began. His relationship with the student was very cordial, and he respected him for his good work and the receptivity with which he responded to his suggestions. Nor could he attribute it to the voice in which the material was being read, as it did not appear monotonous, nor to the content, as it was an interesting session with a new patient who had begun treatment a short time before. In view of his good relations with the student, he decided to tell him what was happening. He reacted with lively interest and replied that something similar had happened to him with this patient during various sessions in which he had had to struggle against sleep, and halfway through the session he was reading, the patient had fallen deeply asleep. It appeared that the student, through projective identification, needed to provoke in the supervisor what the patient had projected into him, as a means of transmitting to him this specific technical problem, so that the supervisor could help him to solve it. Sometimes it is a sort of 'chain reaction'.

3. On one occasion, when a student came to his supervision session, I noticed that when he greeted me he did not offer his hand, as he usually did. He looked rather anxious and preoccupied and explained that he wanted to tell me something that had happened in one of the sessions with his patient. He told me that he had been deeply affected by the state of anxiety of his patient, because of a serious surgical operation that her small son had to undergo: the amputation of an arm as a result of an

accident. At one moment the patient burst into tears and stretched her hand backwards towards the analyst. He, finding that he had not been able to give her any relief with his interpretations, felt compelled to respond to the woman's gesture, which seemed to him a desperate plea for help; and he took her hand and pressed it. He then felt troubled and guilty at what had happened. He admitted that he felt uncomfortable with me because of the technical transgression he had committed. I then pointed out to him that he had not offered me his hand on arriving. He was extremely surprised, as he had not consciously realized this, and then he remembered that the patient had not given him her hand either when she came for her session. He had wondered whether he should include this in any interpretation, but then he suppressed it. Studying the material from the session, we could show that the woman's gesture was not only a plea for help, but that having projected on to the therapist the image of her son, she was trying to cancel the painful reality by magic, through the unconscious phantasy that her son–analyst had his arm intact and was capable of pressing her hand. The therapist unconsciously counteridentified with her phantasy and played the part she had given him. When he came for supervision, the student unconsciously attempted to cancel out his action in the session by not offering me his hand, but he also reproduced, with further acting out, his counteridentification with the patient, who had not given him her hand on arrival at the session.

CHAPTER TWENTY-THREE

Clinical illustration
of a supervision meeting

W hat follows is the transcription of one of the supervision meetings with a young colleague who was accustomed to record these experiences because she found it very useful to listen to them again in her learning process. For reasons of discretion and in order to keep her patient's anonymity, we unanimously decided not to mention the name of my colleague, to whom I am profoundly grateful for the use of this material.

DR T: On the basis of what we talked about in one of the past supervision sessions, and what you explained to me, I changed the system of going on without pauses, and now I leave five minutes between one patient and another. But I could not properly arrange the interval between the session of the patient we are supervising and that of the patient before her. They sometimes meet. At the session I have brought you today she began by saying:

'Downstairs I passed the patient who comes before me, and I was thinking that I would like to tell him that I have seen him several times outside here. I think he is a photographer because

326 ASPECTS OF SUPERVISION

I saw him in a place in the Calle Cordoba. I have always thought him pleasant. Today I saw him in the distance and he seems a wonderful person. I would like to be his friend, although I do not know who he is. I was not thinking of him as a man, only as a friend. It's extraordinary what I feel about him; I also see him as determined, active, easily moved. I thought he reminded me of N (an assistant in a department of the Faculty where she was studying).'

GRINBERG: What sort of connection has she with N?

DR T: She knows him quite well because he was the assistant in charge of her practical work last year. The patient went on to say:

'I remember that yesterday I said to Horacio (her husband) that N is a special person and good to know. He seems to know a lot about new subjects. And I think he is marvellous. I would like to leave X, the assistant with the other group, and work with N. . . . X does not teach all that well; N does it better. I was also thinking of a friend of mine who does not feel well; she's changed a lot, and I advised her to consult a psychiatrist who would give her some medication, because her present therapist does not give her any'.

GRINBERG: At what moment do you intervene?

DR T: At this precise moment. But before reading you the interpretation, I should like to tell you that I do not know what line to take. I have had quite a lot of doubts. For example, it was her reference to the patient she passed on the way to the session that seemed important to me. But afterwards, I do not know why, I decided on another line. I thought she was complaining of my work and had lost confidence in me. Then I interpreted to her that she was questioning my way of working and did not agree with the fact that I was not giving her medication when she felt anxious, and that she could have phantasies about consulting another analyst whom she would consider better or more capable.

GRINBERG: I understand your approach, from the point of view of the patient's paranoid mistrust of you. In that sense the interpretation seems correct to me. But for some reason I have doubts of the line you were thinking of taking. I was interested that you pay attention to the patient's reference to her meeting with the patient who precedes her. In what way did that reference seem important to you? I would like to know what repercussions it had on you and why you prefer to leave that material to one side. For my part, I think this is the most urgent point.

DR T: Well, I do not really know why I rejected it. The other patient is physically very attractive. He is a good-looking type, though a bit untidy. What caught my attention, besides, is that she said he was a photographer. I connected that with everything we have seen here with regard to the patient's exhibitionistic phantasies.

GRINBERG: I believe that now we can get nearer to understanding this material. Let us try to get it clearer. I think the patient really did propose a change, but she was not talking about a change of analyst so much as—implicitly—about a change that she would like to happen within herself. So, for example, we could express the patient's unconscious phantasy in the following terms: 'I was impressed by that patient who came out of here, I liked him very much, I think he is a photographer; I would like to approach him, not as a woman seeking a man, but as a friend; I would like to approach him . . . to transform myself into him'. In other words, she is not saying that she wants to pair off with him, but that she feels attracted by his personality, by his type, and, more especially, because he is a *photographer*. That is the key. For this patient, to be a 'photographer' means to have a 'special eye', the 'visual equipment' for spying. That is, behind her tendency to exhibitionism, which we have seen in earlier sessions, today we can see her voyeuristic phantasy. The two phantasies complement each other, since she tends to show off the things she has spied out and envied, such as for example the relationship with the 'primal scene' that we were analysing; in that material we could see how much it meant to her to get married in white with plenty of pomp and circumstance, and make other people envious of her. Her specific phantasy today is to be able to transform herself into a man, the photographer, by using projective identification with manic characteristics. Her wish would then be to put herself inside the photographer and take on his qualities, especially those that can attract and seduce a woman.

Here we come across various condensed phantasies, which I shall try to explain. For the present she is seeking to satisfy her exhibitionism by attempting to turn herself into the attractive man who can have a visual impact on the analyst–woman. But there the phantasy is not maintained; she wants to go much further. The aim is to exert an erotic fascination from within the object–man, so as to be able to dominate and control you.

DR T: I understand what you are saying, and now I see more clearly that the patient wants to turn herself into the handsome man to seduce and control me. But what would be the ultimate aim of this control?

GRINBERG: Your question, precisely, is connected with the second part of the phantasy, or with its deeper level. And this relates to the voyeuristic and most regressive aspect of this patient. You have things within you that she envies deeply, which arouse in her curiosity, admiration, and the wish to possess or to destroy; these things have to do with your capacity to formulate interpretations or to have children; in the last analysis with your creative capacity. As you know, voyeurism does not imply simple curiosity or the wish to know, but corresponds to very intense envy, which looks or spies in order to strip the envied object of the value it possesses. So the patient, identifying herself projectively with the man–photographer, specifically because of his occupation of photographer, in her phantasy automatically takes possession of a 'photographic penis–camera' with which she can seduce you erotically, penetrate inside you, spy out and take over all your contents. This would be the foundation and the main motive of her wish to change, which, in the manifest material, appears as 'to leave X and change to N'. She would like to give up her female identity, even though only temporarily, and take over the male identity of N, whom she considered more capable.

DR T: And this identity—would it follow her through manic projective identification?

GRINBERG: To be more exact, I would have to say that she was playing a double game of projective identification. In the first place she projected into you her own female part, which can enjoy a man like that patient, admire him, or excite herself erotically with him. Then, by means of another projective identification, she transforms herself into the photographer–lover who will try to put himself inside you to 'photograph' your hidden parts.

I would suggest that now you go on reading the material from the session.

DR T: Yes, I think so. The patient went on associating as follows:

'With regard to the medication, I wondered what would have happened if I had really needed medication. I shit myself with fright just thinking about it. Although, in periods of anxiety and depression, I think I would have done well to take some anti-depressant, as I heard they suspected about a girl living near me; they had to put her in hospital. Poor thing! They said she was psychotic. But if you did come round to giving me drugs I should think you were doing it because I am psychotic. I do not want even to think of it. . . .'

GRINBERG: In this fragment we can see that she is beginning to admit the possibility of her psychotic phantasy, but at the same time she rejects it because it makes her very anxious.

DR T: Well, I interpreted that the reference to medication was not really genuine, but revenge or reprisal against me, because she supposed that I was treating the other patient better and giving him things that I do not give her.

GRINBERG: Nevertheless, I believe you are also approaching the problem of envy, but tackling it from another point of view. Perhaps—as an illustration—you could attempt to integrate the two approaches like this: 'You would like to turn yourself into the other patient so as to be able to receive everything that you suppose I am giving to him'. In any case it would correspond to the first part of the phantasy, because I already explained that the primal aim was to put herself inside you because it is you she really envies. The wish to penetrate by force with the intention of possessing and destroying by envy your idealized contents corresponds with a phantasy that, at a deeper level, is of a perverse and psychotic nature, and that is what frightens her so much.

DR T: Is that why she attempted to deny it? Notice what she says after my interpretation:

'Of course, he has this nice business, but I'm not attracted. It's certain that he is a photographer, he is creative and can do very pretty things, but I have things of my own as well. . . .'

GRINBERG: She is apparently trying to deny her wish to transform herself into that patient or to 'get into his business', for fear of the psychotic content of that phantasy. That is why she has to reinforce the negation in a very significant way, repeating that she has no reason to envy 'that nice creative business' because she has nice things of her own. If her phantasy had been more polymorphic and less psychotic-perverse, she would probably not have needed to deny it so strongly.

DR T: Will you explain to me the difference between polymorphic and perverse?

GRINBERG: Perversity involves a more regressive and destructive quality; it is nearer to sadism, and the feeling of primary envy predominates. On the other hand, in a polymorphic phantasy there may be confusion of erotic zones, jealousy, feelings of exclusion, but there is no destructiveness of the object. With regard to looking or spying, I would say that in perverse phantasy it is the voyeuristic aspect that seeks to look in order to despoil or destroy. In 'polymorphic' looking what may stand out is curiosity to know and imitate what is admired, but in the final analysis it can be a form of learning. With regard to this session of the patient, I was more inclined to attribute it to a perverse–voyeuristic phantasy (which, incidentally, I consider as a manifestation of the psychotic personality), because on two occasions she spoke of a friend who was 'very much changed' and of a neighbour of whom 'they said she was psychotic'. Of course this does not mean that this patient is clinically psychotic, nor even a great deal less than that. On the contrary, I think she has a rich personality that could develop very well, but with many conflicts and phantasies that function at both the neurotic and the psychotic level. In today's session the latter type of phantasy is more evident, as we have just seen.

DR T: I will continue with the interpretation I gave after she talked about the business, and with the material she produced after that:

INTERPRETATION: 'Then if he is so marvellous, your phantasy is that he might have a special charm for me, and that, through his profession of photographer, he could have more access to me, and know more about me.'

PATIENT: 'I don't know. I don't know whether it's true that he is a photographer. When I passed by his place, I never made up my mind to go in and make contact with him.'

GRINBERG: This seems interesting, and corroborative at the same time. If we took this material as though it were the manifest content of a dream (which I very often do), the expression 'I did not make up my mind to go into a place' would suggest that she is referring to her doubts about whether or not to 'go into' an object–container, by using projective identification. In addition, we can observe afresh her need to deny her phantasy of 'putting herself' into the object.

DR T: The patient went on to say:

'I never made up my mind to go in and make contact with him. Last time I went I saw photographs of children. It was something absolutely lovely, a most beautiful photograph. I thought he must be a very creative person. When I have a child I should like to take it to him.'

I interpreted that she supposed that I too sent him my children to have their photographs taken. And that she wanted to get into contact with him to find out things about me.

GRINBERG: I think your interpretation has now come much nearer to the deep level of the patient's phantasy, because although you did not explain to her all the content of this phantasy, since it was not very clear to you, you gave her implicitly to understand that she supposed that you have sexual relations with this patient, that you are fascinated by him, that he puts himself inside you and with his 'photographic penis' takes beautiful photographs of the children that are inside you. These internal children or babies also represent your knowledge, your interpretations, your creations (which she envies so much), and to want to 'photograph' those children of yours means to her, deep down, acting with her voyeuristic tendency and stealing or destroying all the envied contents inside your mind and body.

Well, today we are devoting the supervision to studying in detail the development of an unconscious phantasy in which perverse-psychotic elements predominate.

CHAPTER TWENTY-FOUR

Group supervision;
supervision between equals;
training supervisors

There is a particular sort of supervision represented by the group supervisions developed in seminars. In such cases the candidate who presents the material may become the target of his colleagues' criticism. They sometimes gloat over his troubles and make him the depository of their own mistakes and difficulties. The opposite situation may occur when the candidate is over-praised by his colleagues, who identify themselves with him. The competitive situation is the most frequent alternative among participants with a clear tendency to show off. Obviously, since this chapter deals with the problems of supervision, I shall not mention the undeniably positive aspects of collective teaching and learning, stemming from the possibility of comparing and integrating different approaches.

There is a type of supervision the aim of which is not to teach the candidate the work of analysis. It is therefore outside the context of an institute's official supervisions, and perhaps also outside the general purpose of this work. Nevertheless, I feel the subject is worth referring to briefly. The type of supervision under discussion here is that carried out with experienced analysts, who ask for supervision because of some critical situation developing in the course of the treatment of one of their patients, or because they are interested in some specific clinical feature that they wish to investigate. These are not the only reasons. In our circles it is common for analysts who are associate or full members of our Association, and even training analysts, to take up supervisions with experienced colleagues with the aim of exchanging ideas and keeping their clinical concepts and approaches up to date. That is, they apply Freud's advice on analysis: to start it again periodically (1937c). These 're-supervisions', as we may call them, have the same advantages as the analyses carried out by students who have already graduated and whose training analyses have been satisfactorily completed. This second analysis, or re-analysis, is the really therapeutic one. Greenacre (1965) says that in the opinion of many analysts, individual analysis within a training framework is so hindered and even distorted as to deprive it of therapeutic validity. Therapeutic analysis could be carried out at a later stage. These re-supervisions are free from problems of qualification and judgement and take place in a much more pleasant environment, with greater authenticity and mutual gain for the participants. I was once asked by a group of recently appointed training analysts to supervise some of their candidates' analyses, in view of their complexity and the specific problems arising from the fact of their being training analyses instead of the usual therapeutic analyses. I was, and still am, most gratified by the feeling of mutual profit derived from this experience. Of course one should not expect these supervisions to be free from problems; conflicts of rivalry and competitiveness may well arise, but with far less intensity than in the case of ordinary supervisions.

Throughout this account I have tried to present the principal problems that may emerge in the course of supervision, as well as the different ways of tackling them. It is my belief that for the sake of better prophylaxis and solution of such problems, the supervisor's work should be constantly revised as regards the frames of reference and the teaching methods applied. This will also help to avoid two risks that seriously threaten efficiency and progress in supervision. I refer in the first place to the danger of routine, which makes relationships automatic and stiff, and in the second place to the omnipotent attitude, which makes people claim to know and do everything perfectly. By being alert to these risks, not only will the emergence of such problems be more easily detected, but a better and more fruitful communication between supervisor and student will also be achieved.

Description of an experiment in teaching supervisors and of a qualifying course for teachers

I would like briefly to describe two experiments started several years ago in the Argentine Psycho-Analytic Association, consisting of an attempt to organize on a systematic basis the instruction of supervisors and teachers in the theoretical and technical aspects of the supervisory process and the teaching process in seminars, respectively. In order to reduce the problems commonly arising during the teaching process, it is essential that the recently graduated analyst should become qualified in teaching and in solving such difficulties.

The first experiment was based on a plan organized by the Racker Clinic, which put every candidate for a given period in charge of the treatment of the patients admitted to the Clinic. At the same time the case could be brought to supervision. These supervisions were carried out by associate and full members of the Association, selected from a list of names of analysts interested in participating. Since its foundation the Clinica de Orientación e Investigación Enrique Racker has been successively under the direction of Drs D. Liberman, M. Langer, J. Bleger, and F. Ulloa.

The aim was not only to help the candidate with his patient's treatment, but also to make supervision training available to analysts who desired it. Courses and joint meetings were organized, together with what might be called 'supervisions of supervisions', whether individual or collective, under the direction of training analysts.

It is worth pointing out that the Clinic chose the team of supervisor and candidate and did its best to make it as harmonious as possible, mainly taking into account common schemes of reference. Occasionally teams were chosen with opposing characteristics and different ideological criteria, in order to investigate the problems arising from such a confrontation or to see whether, on the contrary, it could be shown to be useful.

Apart from the courses, each of the supervisors was assigned a training analyst whom he visited periodically so that the work done during the period could be checked; this analyst was consulted when an emergency arose.

On the other hand, 'group supervisions of supervisions' were organized, at which one of the supervisors would submit material from his supervisions, either written or recorded, to be discussed by all the supervisors in a meeting co-ordinated by a training analyst. In these joint meetings the participants considered not only the specific aspects of the material submitted, but also general problems of supervisory practice: the geography of the analyst's consulting room; the formulation of interpretations in such a way as to help the candidate to find his own technique and personal style; whether it was better to supervise the beginning of a session, the whole session, or a series of sessions, or to alternate these methods so that they were complementary to each other; the way of recording the material; the setting of the situation of supervision, and so forth.

M. Langer and colleagues (1964) considered the complexities of the situation of seminar teaching. They attribute them to the multipersonal dynamics arising from displaced transference acting out, idealizations, pseudo-identifications, rivalry, and so forth. Finally they emphasize and explain the fact that the seminars of the Argentine Psycho-analytic Association have been directed during the past years by a team headed by a titular professor and two assistant professors who collaborate with the titular professor and at the same time learn how to teach. Experience has shown that this co-operation between teachers and students helps develop closer communication, enables the presentation of different approaches, and reduces the student's tensions.

This is a suitable point to pass on to the second experiment on which I wished to comment: the qualifying course for teachers. The course lasts for one year, divided into two terms. The first term is occupied with general and special training. The second term consists of a series of lectures on the practice of teaching psycho-analysis and the different tasks involved in this teaching.

Each class is divided into two parts: the first is the usual type of lecture, according to the established pattern in the Institute's seminars; each participant is successively assigned a different role (including that of professor), so that learning can take place from different points of view. The second part consists of discussion and evaluation of the preceding seminar, with the participation of all the students and teachers under the direction of a moderator–reporter. In order to achieve continuous communication between its members, the teaching team is composed of two groups, one fixed and the other rotating.

The principal aim of the course is to provide information on the methodology of class development, to investigate and increase the applicant's knowledge, and to develop their skill in dealing with group situations. Throughout the year there is an assessment of the applicants, so that a choice can be made and some can possibly be directed to other departments of the institution.

At the end of each term the students are expected to answer a set of questions in order to assess their progress and to obtain feed-back. This has also proved helpful in evaluating the experiment as a whole.

The development of the course so far, the level of the applicants, and the wholehearted collaboration of the teachers lead us to hope that a basis for the methodology and teaching of psychoanalysis may be established as a result of this pilot experiment.

CHAPTER TWENTY-FIVE

Dialogue
with a group of psychoanalysts
on the theory and technique
of supervision

First meeting

The following chapter is the transcription of two recorded meetings with a group of analysts in the Argentine Psychoanalytical Association, in which it was arranged that I would answer questions on the subject of supervision, explain my specific method of supervisory work, and bring some clinical material that I had supervised.

Due to difficulties in recording these meetings, it was unfortunately not possible to mention by name, individually, each of the contributions of the participants, who included Drs. S. Aizenberg, I. Berenstein, H. Cassinelli, N. Cvik, A. Dellarossa, E. Evelson, S. Lustig de Ferrer, J. Mom, M. L. Pelento, J. C. Suárez, M. Tractenberg, S. B. de Vainer, L. Wender, and J. Winocur. My apologies if I have omitted any names.

I am grateful to Dr J. C. Suárez for kindly allowing me to use the recorded version of these meetings.

I shall begin with the first of the two meetings, at which various colleagues present began by asking questions on different theoretical and technical aspects of supervision, to which I am attempting to reply.

GRINBERG: I understand that the object of this meeting is to deal with the experience of supervision and its problems from all possible angles, from the point of view of both theory and technique. We could begin with some general questions on supervision. I should like first of all to hear what occurs to you in this respect.

CONTRIBUTION: I am rather uneasy, and I believe my feeling is shared by other colleagues, that there are many different techniques of supervision that are not explained, nor have we any explanation of the variations that arise or can arise in supervision according to which technique is used. Generally, when someone is going to be supervised, he asks the supervisor how he usually works. An agreement is thus reached, but it is not always made clear what distortions or variations could be caused by whatever technique is used. I realize that it is a different thing to have a session freely noted down afterwards, from having it recorded and then written down. I think both of these methods have their advantages and disadvantages. But I believe that the greatest disadvantage is apparent when the results from one technique or another are not explained. It happens then that we get material in which nuances leading to blind spots are not taken into account, or perhaps other points are emphasized, depending on the technique used. I should be interested in your opinion on this, so that all of us here can clarify our own experiences.

GRINBERG: I should be glad to know how you normally work, how the material brought to you by the candidate is metabolized.

CONTRIBUTION: The clinical material is an element on which we can work in very different ways. One thing we prefer to avoid is to see from the material what the therapist can say to his patient in the future better than what he actually said. The context at that point should rather correspond to the relation between supervisor and student, the strategy, how and why to tackle certain aspects and not others. As for the form in which the material is recorded, I think the written form helps us more to focus on what was said; tape-recorded material might possibly be preferable when we want to work with the general climate, how something was said, and the rhythm of it. I believe that written notes force us to concentrate on *what* and not *how*. Tape-recording, on the contrary, gets us into the consulting-room climate at the moment when the session was taking place—the climate of inter-relationships.

CONTRIBUTION: I should like to see, through this example of supervision, what is taught, how it is taught, how it is learned, and the direction that learning takes.

CONTRIBUTION: The way of recording the material is a specific technical problem with a series of implications that can lead us to collateral problems. I think the basic interest here is to be present for the first time, directly and *in vivo*, at a process that is actually taking place with the student in supervision. There are various types of supervision. In our subject supervision is basically of interest as an opportunity to learn; it is there that we learn to psychoanalyse. For that reason isolated cases and consultations serve only to distinguish technical or immediately practical problems, and that is not the point of our meeting. Sometimes we would need to follow the development and the different possibilities and study the process of learning that is going on and that will continue through time; in this way a case is used to draw inferences in order to learn the technique of psychoanalysis and how to deal with the problems that may arise.

CONTRIBUTION: I am interested in something that I do not think will come up today: it is the way the supervisor deals with other kinds of things that appear in supervision and have nothing to do with the case under consideration. This is when there is an attempt, through supervision, to turn the supervisor into an analyst, or when the supervisor becomes aware of things about the candidate. It is a matter of dealing with something that is not the relation of supervisor to student, but goes beyond it. Often with

people who have begun recently you can see that they are bringing
up problems they do not understand or cannot interpret because
something personal is involved; or they want you to help them
with something that is not strictly interpreting, but understanding what is going on inside themselves. There is a very short
distance between supervising and interpreting.

CONTRIBUTION: I am going to add something that I think is
interesting. It is the choice of the patient whose sessions are going
to be supervised. It is interesting how supervisor and student
arrive at the choice of a certain patient. I believe there are two
ways of doing this. A series of patients may be reviewed, or one
problem brought out, or it may also depend on the supervisor's
opinion. Another factor of choice has to do with diagnosis. The
interview is to some extent our problem—the problem of the
Argentine school—because of its place in psychiatric nosography
and general diagnostics, and so forth, and because it decides
whether a certain patient will be chosen. How does this come up in
the experience of each of the students and supervisors?

CONTRIBUTION: As far as 'this side' and 'beyond' are concerned,
I am interested not only in what happens between the student, his
analyst, and his supervisor, but also what happens between the
supervisor and the student's analyst—that is, all existing relationships that can have a beneficial or prejudicial effect on the progress
of training and on the patient whose case is being supervised.

CONTRIBUTION: I am especially interested in clinical comprehension and how we are going to carry out group supervision,
supposing that the same material can be clinically understood
from the different schemes of reference. Perhaps the only point of
view to take would be the supervisor's method, with whatever
peculiarities it has, his theoretical baggage, and his way of seeing
and communicating the material.

CONTRIBUTION: I should like to bring up something that has
not come up and that I consider important—something related to
previous history and to the supervision problem, which does not

come up in seminars; I am referring to the names given to this procedure: supervision or control. It is a more serious aspect than you might think. Supervision suggests something coming from above, with a much greater tendency to bring out the educative aspect, while control suggests something more related to the therapist's countertransference. I think it is worth re-evaluating this aspect, because it tends to see the process as something persecutory. What connotations has this from the institutional point of view, and to what defences does it lead? Why do we use the term candidate and not student, and what importance does it have for a patient to know he is being analysed by someone who aspires to become a psychoanalyst?

GRINBERG: All the questions and comments I have heard are very interesting, and from a practical point of view we are already well into the subject. It will not be easy for me to answer all your questions in one or two meetings. Before going on to the material, I want to say a few words about how I carry out supervision, what I base it on, what my method is, the reason for my interventions, and the reason for my philosophy.

In my opinion supervision is a triadic system consisting of the supervisor, the therapist and the patient. There is then an interrelation between the therapist and the patient. Others have spoken of what they call the clinical rhombus of supervision, describing it in terms of the important figures functioning in the process: the therapist, the supervisor, the patient, and the institution. I would transform this into what I would call the clinical hexagon: supervisor, therapist, patient, institute, the therapist's training analyst, and the second supervisor. It could also be a many-angled geometrical figure, since there are latent images that undoubtedly gravitate into every supervision.

Generally, each student has two supervisors and is also in training analysis. It has been pointed out that if one tries to deal with everything that can happen in the context of a supervision, there are so many images and so many contingencies that there can be an infinite combination of possibilities, involving both the direct participants—that is, the supervisor and the student—and latent images, the training analyst, the institute, and so forth.

There are various types of supervision: we might mention 'learning' supervisions, which are the usual ones; 'consultant' or specialized supervisions, about which little is said in the literature, and in which an experienced colleague meets one at the same level to deal with a specific problem. In this case there is no question of one of them having greater capacity or experience; it is simply that someone from outside may be in a better position to understand the problem. In 'investigative' supervision, one of the participants who is following a given line of investigation is interested in the approach of another investigator as a complement to his own work. There are also 'therapeutic' supervisions, which are carried out in some places. Of what do they consist? They are for people who have already had an analysis and have experience, but who, at a given moment, are facing a certain problem or conflict. They then go to a more experienced colleague and ask him to supervise some material because it, or the patient whose material it is, has triggered off or reawakened in him certain conflicts of which he is perfectly conscious. He realizes what is happening to him and knows his countertransference, but it is useful for him to discuss the material with a more experienced colleague who can help him at two levels: that of his work with the patient and that of his own conflict. I do not think there is an established technique, but the supervisor, knowing, in this case, some of the problems through his own student, helps him to discriminate or correlate so that he can continue his work without the interference of his personal conflicts. It appears that these supervisions have been very successful.

There exist other supervisions of the investigative type, which are carried out by exchange through the post of recorded supervisions. An analyst sends the material to another living in another town, so that the latter colleague, separated from him geographically—and probably also ideologically, or with a different frame of reference—can study it. The colleague consulted studies the recording and sends his comments. The exchange of recorded tapes or cassettes may go on for a certain length of time and sometimes includes a third or a fourth participant.

I shall now go on to a more personal aspect of supervision, which at the same time answers a few of the questions. In reply, I should like first to give a summary and then to consider each of the items separately. Supervising is one of the activities I enjoy most; I find it very stimulating because it takes me into a new field, with material that I do not know; whoever is working with this material stimulates me to think, work out schemes, and rectify. I believe I have changed greatly in the experience of supervision; I do not supervise now as I did some years ago. I might add that no one analyses now as he did years ago. Though it is more obvious in some analysts than in others. I believe that all, to a greater or lesser degree, have passed through a process of change. But I think it is specifically in supervision that I have noticed the greatest changes, some of them very important.

For my part, I try to be fully conscious of the peculiar features of every supervision, in order to differentiate and discriminate between them. In supervision with someone who has recently begun to be supervised, the accent has basically to be placed on the elementary stages of teaching, such as the understanding of unconscious phantasies, the main defence mechanisms, or diagnosis. This is quite different from supervision with a more experienced person, who has been supervised for some time, since in the latter case more attention can be paid to investigation arising from the material, although I always try to combine it with teaching.

When beginning a supervision, I try to get to know thoroughly all the data relating to the case to be supervised and the environment in which the analysis is developing. I ask the student to describe to me his surroundings, what his consulting-room is like, what furniture he has, whether he works in his own house or elsewhere, who answers the door, what this person is like. I lay stress on the geographical description of the work environment, what distance there is between the door and the couch, what objects (tables, chairs, desk etc.) there are between the entrance and the couch.

I do this because the transference is established not only between patient and analyst, but it also includes the atmosphere surrounding the analyst. If at a given moment a patient speaks of a book or an armchair in the consulting-room, I have to know whether that book or that armchair are really there, how he saw them, with what degree of distortion, how they appear in his dreams, since in the manifest content of dreams material often appears which corresponds to the analyst's environment.

The physical description of the patient is also very important—how the therapist sees him, what has attracted his attention and why. Often in this first description there is already a foretaste of what then emerges during the treatment. It is important to discover the patient's attitude, how he comes in, how he moves towards the couch, how he lies down, if he does it with rituals or not, his tone of voice and way of speaking; that is to say, all the details, large and small, which every analyst must notice.

When supervising inexperienced therapists, I insist that they ask me about everything I say to them, and I try to make clear from whence it arises and on what I am basing it. The object of this is to teach the student to make the same demands upon himself, and not to take countertransference alone as a basis. I believe that countertransference is very useful, and I have had very good results from taking it into account, provided that it can be corroborated in the clinical material.

As for the choice of patient, my criterion is perhaps different from the clinically recommended one. There are institutes that allot the patient to be taken for the supervision. They prefer a hysteric or an obsessional neurosis, and not a psychotic personality or a borderline case. Personally I think it is very important that the student should choose his patient. If he attempts to leave the choice in my hands, I try to find out why he wants me to decide and why he does not choose, himself, the case that is giving him most difficulty. I try to discover the reason for his doubts. If the student is hesitating between two or three cases, I ask him to talk about them so that we can decide between them together.

I recommend that the case giving the most difficulty should be chosen, so that the candidate can profit as much as possible from the experience of supervision, and not be limited to the material of the official patient. I usually ask him occasionally to bring me material from other patients, so that, besides helping the student with the problems he may have with them, I can see how he works with his other analysands.

Whether we like it or not, we are not the same analysts with all the patients. There are always certain nuances and variables that have to do with the quality of the specific functioning of the projective identification of each patient, his level of regression, and so on.

It can happen, for example, that a student says that all is well with the case under supervision, while there is another patient who worries him more. We then devote several meetings to this latter case, until we arrive at an understanding of the problem.

Since we cannot look at all the patients in one supervision, I advise that index cards should be made out for the remaining patients, who are not supervised. These cards are made out weekly or for short periods, giving four or five basic data: for example, what happened during this period, whether there was mainly co-operation or resistance on the part of the patient, whether there was acting out, dreams, or any event that played a definite part in the transference.

As for the recording of the material, I prefer that it should not be tape-recorded—though I do not insist—nor written during the session, but that the hour should be reconstructed later. If someone tells me that he cannot do it that way and brings a tape-recording of the session, I accept it, because I prefer that the change should be made as a result of training. I think tape-recording is very useful, but I do not think it reproduces the climate of the session. It gives us a faithful reproduction of the material and provides useful elements for the task of investigation, in addition to helping the therapist to correct his own errors, but the disadvantage I see is that it lends itself in many cases to an unconscious delegation of the analyst's functions to the tape-recorder. The analyst fails to penetrate to a deeper level because he imagines that the tape-recorder reproduces everything, including what lies beyond words. Of late I have worked very much on clinical observation, and if the opportunity presents itself later I shall talk about what I understand by the theory of the technique of clinical observation.

As regards taking notes during the session, I ask the therapist not to do it, because that leads to a harmful dissociation. However skilled he is in listening and writing at the same time, many important things are lost; I would say that he loses fifty per cent of what he could gain by recording the material in another way. I advise him to do nothing more than observe the patient attentively, with a capacity for *reverie,* and with the 'non-memory and non-desire' that Bion suggests, even though it is very difficult to do.

With respect to diagnosis, after a period in which I insisted strongly on the need to make a good initial diagnosis, I went on to one in which I almost left it to one side. The diagnosis is very relative and sometimes counterproductive. The establishment of a diagnosis from the very beginning limits the capacity to detect other possibilities. I prefer that the student, in the preliminary information, should give an approximate diagnosis and arrive at a more definite diagnosis only after some months of work in common. At any rate I am not unaware of the enormous importance of having a good capacity for diagnosis, for example during an interview, so that the patient can be given adequate treatment.

We have, on the other hand, mentioned the context of supervision, which belongs to the type of knowledge that we take as read, but that has probably not been sufficiently developed. Much has been said about the setting in analysis, but not in supervision. By context I mean a particular attitude on the part of the supervisor, considering all the factors that enable the work to be located in the best conditions in order to carry out the specific task of supervision. I try to enter into the task in full consciousness that there is a learning relationship between a person with more knowledge who teaches, and another person who tries to profit from the other's experience so as to understand a patient's material. To understand what the setting of a supervision is, it could also be defined by opposition to what it is not: supervision is not, and must not be, treatment. This is very important when we consider things 'this side' and 'beyond' about which we have spoken, so that the student will not look for something that the supervision cannot give him, and the supervisor will not act consciously or unconsciously as a substitute analyst, or as an imago, idealized or persecutory, according to the problem that the student may be having with his own analyst. If the student is in a period of negative transference, he uses dissociation and projects his idealization on to the supervisor and vice versa. For all these reasons I think it is a good thing that every meeting between supervisor and student should begin with a brief chat, without, of course, excessive familiarity that might interfere with the work.

As in this meeting, which could be compared with a supervision, we have begun by raising doubts and asking how each one can play his part, in supervision also it is useful to devote some time to explaining the context and the development of the co-operative activity.

In conclusion, I would say that what I consider most important is to teach people to think; I lay great stress on the reason behind everything, to help the student to think for himself. As one of the objects of analysis is for the analyst to help the patient to think, one of the aims of supervision is to stimulate the student to think and discriminate.

I should like to add something that I have seen confirmed many times in my experience. When someone I am supervising begins the meeting with a comment that has apparently nothing to do with the material he has brought, telling me about some incident on the way to my consulting-room or some film he has seen, I have very often found that this short chat has a direct or indirect connection with the session he has brought for supervision. It is equivalent to an association that generally corresponds with something he has repressed during his work with the patient, but that has registered with him in some way. He then expresses it in the form of an incidental comment, which I, on my part, take in the same way as other comments with which he asks my help, for example, in formulating an interpretation.

If a student mentions to me his difficulty in formulating interpretations and in fact I can see that he does it in a sophisticated, complex and elaborate way, I ask him to explain to me what he is trying to tell the patient by this interpretation. Generally he does it clearly and in simple words. I then point out to him that the explanation he has just given me is the best formulation. This expedient, apparently so simple, has given me excellent results in the majority of cases.

We can now go on to the clinical material. I should like to ask Doctor X to give us some of the case-history, and if we do not finish today we shall continue at the next meeting.

Second meeting

GRINBERG: At today's meeting we shall consider the clinical material brought by Dr X. I should be glad if she would begin reading out the session.

DR X: The session took place on a Tuesday at half past two in the afternoon. My consulting-room looks out on to the street and is very light. The patient arrived smiling. I noticed that her eyes were half-shut. She was wearing trousers, a pink jersey and a nylon jacket with a nautical motif. The jacket was closely zipped up, and she was wearing very summery shoes. The patient was smiling broadly, with half-closed eyes. When she lay down she put her hand under her head and began to speak rapidly and more softly than usual. I noticed the rapid rhythm contrasting with the lower tone; on the other hand, when she lay down, I had the feeling that she was plunging into the couch. In addition, with this patient, putting her hand beneath her head had happened up to this point when I felt she was more closely linked with me than with reality. At that moment I noticed that she was plunging down into the couch, and also that she 'plunged' her hand under her head and kept it in that position for quite a long time.

GRINBERG: When I saw how this session began, I considered that the fact that the analyst gave so detailed a description was because something different from usual had attracted her attention. I also noticed the contrast in the patient's dress, to which was added the contrast between her smile and the half-closed eyes. It occurred to me that this patient was putting into action a very particular mode of projective identification, trying to compel the analyst into a contradictory and dissociated response that might lead to confusion. On the other hand, speaking softly and in a rapid rhythm was again a contradiction, so that the analyst would not know what to pay more attention to: the manic rhythm or the depressive tone; so there was an attitude, an intention—unconscious, of course—to cause a certain confusion in the analyst. But why? We have always to ask ourselves, not only about the mechanism that a patient is using, but why he uses it and to what end. In this case there is naturally a defensive aim: that is, the intention of putting into the analyst something the patient cannot bear. What she cannot bear at this moment is, in my opinion, confusional anxiety. We said last time that there are many ways of defending oneself against confusional anxiety; she could use a type of splitting in which she kept one part and projected the other; that is, she could have projected the manic part and remained with the depressive part, or vice versa, all this with the aim of escaping from confusional anxiety. But another form of defence is to project all the confusional nucleus *en masse*. Then the analyst is left with the confusion, not knowing whether to interpret one aspect or the other. In situations like that I explain to the student that it is important to be able to understand the material without transforming it immediately into an interpretation, because it is one thing to understand what is happening and another thing to choose the moment, the opportunity and the formulation of the interpretation, in order to be able to see afterwards whether we were mistaken or not. It is very important to accept the possibility of rectification, not only for the analyst but for the supervisor also, because the worst that can happen is that one can be 'carried away' by a certain idea. If I have a certain impression, the material will either confirm it or not; it will enable me to say whether in fact this initial presumption was correct or whether I have to change my mind because new deciding elements have appeared.

QUESTION: Do you first ask the student what she has understood and then add your contribution, or do you explain directly what you have understood by the material?

GRINBERG: It depends on who the student is and what point the supervision has reached. Dr X has had several years' experience; I know her way of working, and she knows mine; the supervision is at an investigative level. If the supervision is just beginning, I would prefer to wait, not as though I were putting the student through an examination, but because I like to observe what he has seen so that I can see it in the same way. I ask him to explain his grounds for a statement, to tell me the origin of what he has seen; if I think the same, I tell him so, and if I do not, we make a comparison. I then say to him, 'You think this and I think something else; let us see what the material says'. The clinical material has to be the guide. Sometimes the student is right because he knows the patient much better. You know that the supervisor has an advantage and a disadvantage. The advantage is that he is more detached, less emotionally involved; he can see from a better perspective, with more discrimination. In this case I went on to give my impression that the patient was trying to make a massive deposit of her confusional anxiety.

DR X: I agree, in theoretical terms, that my difficulty consisted in seeing at that moment whether there was a confusional defence against confusional anxiety, or a confusional defence against extreme persecutory anxiety with certain manic elements. I felt confused.

GRINBERG: What Dr X is explaining is very important, because with this patient we had this uncertainty at many points in the analysis. It is not always easy to distinguish what confusional anxiety is. The line of interpretation varies absolutely, and the techniques used in dealing with one case and with another are different. The problem is that the patient in both cases may try to confuse. When, for example, he is facing a very intense depressive anxiety, he does not want to know who is the victim and who the torturer, so he uses the confusional defence in an attempt to escape the guilt. He may try to project the confusion into the analyst to prevent the latter from realizing that the patient is the aggressor in a given situation. But if the patient falls into confusional anxiety due to premature integration or the failure of a dissociation, he also projects the confusion because he cannot bear it. In both cases the analyst receives the projection of the confusion, but with different intentions.

CONTRIBUTION: I should like to comment on an aspect linked with the technique of supervision with regard to this type of initial intervention of yours. At this moment I am not going into the contents or what it is that is being sought, but I want to go deeper into what you have done, with which I am very much in agreement: always starting from the fact that supervision is a learning process, the supervising analyst can transmit at a given moment to the student, in a direct and vivid way, what is happening, what phenomena, reactions, theoretical foundations, and previous experience with the patient have brought into being a certain working hypothesis. In this case it is not so interesting to see who is right and who is not, or whether an interpretation is adequate or not, though of course this will all come into it; what is important is a direct application to the problems of the case: the student must be able to confront what it is that happens inside the analyst which generates a location, a response, and finally an interpretative hypothesis. I believe it may be useful from a learning point of view for the supervisor to say to the student at a given moment: 'I am going to tell you what I started with at the beginning when listening to this material'. Generally what happens is that the student can also gain insight, put into words the sources of his own experience, and compare it here to shed light on a lot of things. I think this is a specific part of the technique of supervision, and I find that it works very well.

GRINBERG: I agree. I have systematized that technical method in the last few years. It is a type of dialogue in which what is basically interesting is not so much whether a certain interpretation was correct or not, but rather the all-embracing view, the context. The student is going to learn step by step, learning to make mistakes and to get out of them. We do it together; and so I say it is a stimulus for the work of investigation to our mutual profit. Altogether, in the second part of today's meeting it would be useful to speak of a rather different technique with someone who is beginning supervision. We have to take various risks into account; one of them is that sometimes he takes literally what the supervisor says and becomes completely detached from what is happening to the patient.

QUESTION: Faced with an interpretation by the analyst, do you ask him why he made this interpretation, what he was thinking, what feelings he had? If the analyst gives you his interpretations and they are different from yours, what do you do? Do you take the line that the analyst took, or do you start him on yours?

DR X: I could answer that before Dr Grinberg, to tell you about my experiences and because I think that for me it was a particularly difficult session; now I have a wider view, because some time has passed; it was as though there had been a moment of sudden change in defences and anxieties; afterwards it was dispelled, and I understood better. At one moment of this session I made interpretations that for this point in the analysis are incorrect. What I did was to ask Dr Grinberg two or three times why I found it difficult to understand, since I saw only that the patient was absorbing me. I needed to see not only the attack, but what was happening to her. I asked him two or three times before I could understand. Dr Grinberg does not give answers that are entirely saturated and total. He stimulates one to ask again, and that helps to throw light on the question one was asking and to formulate it better. That is what I felt in my experience of supervision with him.

GRINBERG: I do this often because by helping the student to formulate the question again, I teach him to find the beginning of a reply in his own question. Often they do not really know what the problem is: the re-formulation of the question helps them better to locate the different elements constituting the problem, and then they manage to put it more clearly. Once they have found their location, or rather their centre point, there is already the germ of a reply. That is one of the reasons why I advise that they should not tape-record the session but reconstruct it; I think that the reconstruction of the session is in itself a kind of self-supervision. On the other hand, I consider that in the course of a session or an analysis a saturated reply can never be given. There is always development in the problems and in the patient's unconscious phantasy. And that is what we shall try to show now. I would ask you to listen to a little more of the material.

DR X: I shall read you the patient's first associations, when she had scarcely lain down on the couch.

PATIENT: 'I feel sort of dull (her words are clipped). Last night I took a tablet and at ten I went to sleep. Ernesto told me that as soon as I put my head on to his shoulder I was fast asleep, and I did not move all night. At seven o'clock, as I had a class at the Faculty, Ernesto told me that he put my head on to the pillow and woke me up.'

My attention was drawn, as I said, to the fact that she snuggled down on the couch very easily, too easily. But on the other hand, when she began to speak, with the first three words I noticed her enormous difficulty in verbalizing. Or, rather, there were again two opposed stimuli working within her: like someone doing something with the greatest ease and at the same time with the greatest difficulty. Another thing that attracted my attention was that she went on smiling, still with her eyes half-closed, and it seemed to me that at that moment she was guiding my perception. For example, when she told me she 'put her head on the pillow', I caught myself looking at the pillow on the couch; that is, somehow or other she was directing my gaze, and that what she said was a repetition of an almost identical situation. Later on I shall have something else to say about this.

GRINBERG: Listening to these remarks I felt that part of what I had seen in the patient's attitude at the beginning of the session was confirmed; but I still do not completely understand why she does it. For example, the first words, 'I feel sort of dull', bring out an element the confusion in which appears clearly. Here a doubt arose, because if I think the patient made a massive deposit on entering, before she even spoke, why did she say, 'I feel sort of dull'? To try to clear up this doubt, I think that at that moment the last stage of the deposit of projective identification was coming into play, and that it is very probable that the patient is saying those words from within the analyst. It is as though she needs confirmation of what she did, and by saying, 'I feel sort of dull', she is dramatizing and putting into words what, according to her, the object must be feeling. When I listen to the patient, I have to 'listen' to where she is speaking from. In a case I have brought up in seminars it was very clear that the patient was reproducing, through tones of voice and manner of speaking, his dialogue with his internal objects; it was a really impressive session. I do not know whether you remember Anthony Perkins' film 'Psycho'; the phenomenon of the unconscious is very richly expressed; the actor dramatizes the roles. He was, at one moment, the mother, and he spoke with her and from out of her. The patient to whom I refer reproduced a dialogue with his internal objects and spoke as though from out of the internal object. In a psychotic personality, in whom dissociation can be clearly seen, there is no problem in detecting this phenomenon; it is immediately obvious. But in a 'borderline' personality, or in a neurotic patient's moment of regression, the same phenomenon may occur and is not always easy to grasp.

It is as though the patient said to the analyst, 'If you told me how you felt at this moment, you would say you felt dull'. That would be the patient's explanation; so that when she says 'I feel sort of dull', she receives—according to her—full confirmation that she 'placed' confusion in the analyst, who did become dull, and, moreover, was saying so. After that she spoke fluently; that is, once the deposit was made and confirmed, she could continue in her own way. What does that show us? She describes how she put her head on her husband's shoulder; in other words, how she 'deposited' her head on him. I want to emphasize the importance of the manifest content of material. A few years ago I was working with a study group on the re-evaluation of the manifest content of dreams; we plunge too deeply into the latent content and leave aside the manifest content, which is incredibly rich. I am referring not only to verbalization, the importance of style and linguistic construction, for example, but also to the elements that appear, and why they appear, in the manifest content. When the patient says that she rested her head on her husband's shoulder and went right off to sleep, we have to take this not only as a purely descriptive picture of how she rested her head on her husband, but as a very clear dramatization of the functioning of her projective identification: she 'placed' her head on part of the object, and from then on the object was transformed into an extension of her self, which was going to do the things that needed to be done by her and for her. While describing this situation, she is already telling us that she has done the same thing with the analyst. At what moment did she do it? When the analyst looked at the pillow. This is an assumption that we shall have to confirm with the rest of the material.

CONTRIBUTION: There's something else that attracted my attention. In the morning the husband places her head on the pillow and says it is seven o'clock; that is, he takes the active role of contact with reality.

GRINBERG: At another level it is probable that she is asking the same thing of the analyst: that she should stay awake in order to watch her and look after all the activities one has to carry on when awake, while she goes on sleeping. That would be another possible way of interpreting it.

As she needed before to project confusion so that the analyst would take responsibility for her, now—in a second phase—she needs to place the 'wide-awake' part in the analyst. Patients often attempt to project—either successively or simultaneously—contradictory aspects of their unconscious phantasies or of their feelings. Sometimes these processes take place so rapidly that the analyst does not succeed in detecting them with sufficient discrimination and finds himself, to his surprise, suffering the consequences of a 'confusing' or 'dissociating' projective identification. In the best cases the patient wants the analyst to receive and contain, at different levels and for as long as necessary, both types of projection.

We begin then with the first link of a chain of interpretations. No interpretation is completely saturated, and no interpretation can reply to all the questions. But we can throw out, like an experimental balloon, a first attempt at interpretation in order to see what happens. But it is useful, before formulating the interpretation, to think about what it is based on. If I say to the patient that she wants to load her 'waking' part on to me, I should have to add the reasons: for example, that she needs to, so that I can keep awake in her place and control the danger that could be caused by possible enemies.

DR X: I shall read all the contents again.

PATIENT: 'Last night I took a tablet, and at ten I went to sleep; Ernesto told me that as soon as I put my head on to his shoulder I was fast asleep, and I did not move all night. At seven o'clock, as I had a class at the Faculty, Ernesto told me that he put my head on to the pillow and woke me up. He went for a shower and I went on sleeping. Then I dressed completely, put on my trousers and jersey, and went for breakfast; I remember that I had breakfast and told him that I was not going to the Faculty because I could not stay on my feet. He put me to bed, not in our room but in the other one; at ten he came for a while to see how I was, and I went on sleeping; at just half past one I woke up. I slept for fourteen consecutive hours. . . . I'm pleased that I slept. My mouth feels clammy. . . .'

DR X: Another thing that caught my attention was when she said 'He put me to bed, not in our room but in the other one'. When she said 'the other one', I got the message. Moreover, when she said 'I am pleased that I slept. My mouth feels clammy' the word she used, *pastosa*, drew my attention; perhaps because of a previous code with this girl; at earlier points in her analysis she had spoken of 'pastitos'. ['Pastoso' like the French 'bouche pâteuse'—'paste-y, clammy.] The 'pastito' was an experience or a moment in the day when she went to bed, which, phenomenologically, appeared as a moment in which she made contact with herself. She had a kind of memory of the past: she went to a park when she was a child: her family did not allow friends from the street to come in, so her governess had the idea of letting her have a picnic in the park; she brought a tablecloth and invited all the children in the park; she associated it with this 'pastito' of her childhood: it was a place of freedom, of contact with her peers. Later the 'pastito' had another connotation: the condensation of her masturbatory phantasies.

To come back to the session:

PATIENT: 'I think that if at this moment the light goes out, I will go back to sleep; and I will if it does not go out, too.' At that moment I thought that the only light that could go out was that of the sun, because it was day. It was possible to reconstruct, during the analysis, a time—at the age of six-teen—of very severe autistic defence; the patient's activity con-sisted of sunbathing from six to eight hours a day, not in the garden of the house, because the trees blocked the sun, but on the balcony. It was a time that coincided with mutism and negativism: she would not speak to her mother at all. The only person with whom she would enter into contact was her father, who was to some extent the intermediary between her and the world. She brought this up at another session: 'I think I spent many months in a kind of sun-madness: I had third-degree burns and an associated allergy problem, but in addition I was physically ill because of the burns'. While she was talking about all this, the smile she had worn when she arrived was fading. She was silent for a while. Then she said: 'I feel uneasy, being half asleep like this, especially because this afternoon I invited Mummy and two friends of Mummy to coffee; one of these friends is one of those ladies who did not come to the wedding; do you remember that lady in the story I told you?' I interpreted here, saying: 'Now you have asked me a question, so that when you hear my reply you will know for certain that I am awake, and that I can receive all the fear that you have, as an adult, of losing contact with yourself and with me in today's session. You need me to contain for the moment another more intense uneasiness that you feel inside yourself, like being exposed to something very powerful that will not let you be either properly asleep or properly awake.'

GRINBERG: In this fragment of the session there is a very interesting situation. I like the interpretation, but I will make clear to Dr X that in my opinion that interpretation was directed more to the neurotic part of the patient's personality than to the psychotic sector. That is, although they function together, it is important to move towards the part that predominates in the 'here and now' of the session. Dr X took up the patient's implicit plea that she would take upon herself the waking part of her so that she could come together with the analyst and with herself. But she added that the patient asked her to be ready to defend her from someone, from a very powerful internal object which, from within her, would not let her be either properly asleep or properly awake. I think this is a very happy expression. She can be asleep but not properly, and she can be awake but not properly, because of the increase in her anxieties. If she had taken that more into account, probably the interpretation would have been different; she would have directed it more towards the aspect of confusion, the functioning of projective identification, the detail of the head, her husband's shoulder, the pillow, the hand under the head, and so on. I was sure of the way in which that mechanism was used, and it was confirmed practically in everything the patient said, especially when she said that her husband put her to bed, not in her own room but in the other room, which was equivalent to describing how she submerged herself in the interior of another object, which could be the other room, the consulting-room, but could also be the analyst. I am interested in the sequence of the invitation to 'Mummy' and Mummy's two friends to coffee, and above all when she addressed the analyst directly. Generally it has to be taken into account when a patient speaks directly to the analyst, because often this attitude can contain the key of the predominant phantasy. The analyst took 'do you remember, doctor?' more as a deposit of memory—that is, 'you have to remember, because I cannot', which would be very correct in another context. In my view, in this context, it seemed rather to have a very subtle psychopathic and inoculatory nuance.

DR X: That is certainly so. I was thinking that my approach was 'what shall I do to wake her up', and not 'how shall I understand what is happening'. I think the inoculation was from earlier.

GRINBERG: What the patient wanted was, in fact, to project the confusion outside. But in addition what she was putting into the analyst was an excluded part that could not be present at the primal scene—the wedding—so that the analyst had to take upon herself everything that this exclusion meant, with all the corresponding phantasies and their consequences. That is, she split Dr X into two friends; the friends are split-off parts of 'Mummy', but one of them is the one who did not come to the wedding. To what wedding? This girl had just got married; then she had to project the condensation of a whole history of exclusions, especially her exclusion from the 'wedding–primal scene' of her parents. We shall have to see whether the content of the phantasy is polymorphic or perverse in type. Today I am inclined to take the perverse type as a psychotic manifestation of the personality. Perversion is not only a defence against psychosis, or the negative of psychosis; it is in itself a psychotic expression by the content and the violence of its destructive impulses. Incidentally, I should like to comment briefly on the typical phantasy of the child as regards the primal scene. As Meltzer points out, it includes five characters: the father, the mother, the female part of the child, the male part of the child, and a fifth character, which is the baby inside. This is the case in polymorphic phantasies. Then the child, faced with the exclusion and frustration he experiences at not taking part in the relationship of the parental couple, reproduces a primal scene with these characters, who do all the things that he imagines or phantasizes as part of his parents' primal scene. In order not to be excluded, he invents the fifth character, the baby who, from inside the mother, looks on at everything. I think, therefore, that when the patient put her hand under her head, it was not only to separate herself from the pillow, but also to look; she was trying to do this from a situation of being 'fast asleep', which is like being inside the mother, from whence she can spy. To end the explanation, I would say that in perverse phantasies there is a sixth character, who looks on from outside, because the baby who looks on from inside is a harmless baby who does not attack the couple directly; while the sixth character of the perverse phantasy, the 'stranger', attacks with destructive and voyeuristic impulses, based on envy and intolerance of the couple in coitus. Unlike what happens in the polymorphic phase, in which there is not this destructiveness and envy, only an effort to overcome exclusion and frustration, the main motivation of perverse phantasy is destruction, because the union of the parents cannot be borne. In the case of the patient, we see that she projected into the analyst 'the lady who did not come to the wedding', who could not take part in the primal scene, and who therefore will look voyeuristically and aggressively at what the parental couple are doing. In the same way the relative attack on objects is also explained. The first clinical element that I take to support the interpretation I am suggesting is the 'clammy mouth' (*boca pastosa*). Manifestly it is from having slept a lot, but it happens that the *boca pastosa* has a history (as Dr X explained) of all her masturbatory phantasies. The *boca pastosa* is the synthesis of the confusion of zones (mouth, vagina, eyes) which take part in the phantasy of the primal scene.

QUESTION: I should like to repeat my question: What would be the strategy? Would it be aimed more at the confusional anxieties or at dealing with them?

CONTRIBUTION: I believe that the supervisor's first hypothesis about whether this is a massive projection of confusion or a projection of the confused defence is losing its primacy as a question. I think it would be a good thing to see how this is developing in the supervisor. I do not think it is a total projection of her confusional anxiety, because there is an expectation of 'sharpening', a plea to be 'sharpened'. The patient dramatizes it when she asks for light. I'm coming to the second point: I agree that there are two levels, one neurotic and the other psychotic; the psychotic level is very clearly seen. Now, the two lines may also be connected in a way that is perhaps more operative, beginning with the neurotic level, as Dr X did, gradually leading the patient to face certain psychotic perspectives, then suddenly changing to this point and working rather, in a second interpretative phase, with the more psychotic and destructive aspects.

GRINBERG: In another, less psychotic, patient I would direct the interpretation more towards the neurotic part. In this case I think it is better to direct it towards the psychotic personality in order to clear the functioning of regressive mechanisms as quickly as possible.

CONTRIBUTION: The question I should like to bring up concerns not so much the material as the supervisor–student interaction, so that I do not know whether I should do it now or later. When you two were interacting, Dr X replied to something that Dr Grinberg had said by saying, 'Ah, well, what you told me was useful because I went on to think. . . .' What do you do when the student (not as in this case) replies to what the supervisor says with 'Ah yes, but what you are saying to me is what I interpreted later'? This sort of response establishes a type of interaction that, for me at least, causes difficulties, because perhaps the student does not realize that an attitude of competition with the supervisor has begun to form, which to a certain extent cancels out the type of intervention that the supervisor can make. I suppose that at best this does not happen in a supervisor–student relationship of long duration, but it may be the kind of problem found at the beginning of supervision. I should like to know how it is solved, how it is explained and by what type of intervention.

CONTRIBUTION: There is a type of student who may begin to speak of the patient in exclusively theoretical terms; he says, for example, 'this patient is in the middle of the paranoid–schizoid phase'. This may well be the case, but it keeps the supervisor apart from the contact between the student and his patient, so that it is much more useful to have the type of account that Dr X gives, more narrative, less 'in quotation marks', less scientific.

GRINBERG: There exists a pathology in both the supervisor and the student. It is very important to distinguish situations, sometimes inevitable, of competition and rivalry, and to try to sweep the field of work clear of such contaminations. In general I do not say to the student that his attitude is due to competition or rivalry with me, but I try to solve it in another way.

CONTRIBUTION: You are inhibited from using the instrument that presents itself in the therapeutic situation, and you have to use another instrument that works.

GRINBERG: I think so. That different instrument exists as an important element in supervision and must be managed with patience and tolerance. You will say that it is a simple matter. I have had students who come with this attitude, conscious or unconscious; I try to deal with the situation, accepting their point of view and getting them to compare it with mine; I get them to see another way of tackling the material, from a different point of view. Sometimes they are right and I accept their criterion; sometimes they persist in their mistakes. When the situation becomes more difficult I try to make them see the need for their interpretations to be well based, and I seek comparison with the clinical material. In general I have not had problems.

CONTRIBUTION: A student has a certain level of tolerance and receives a certain quantity of information from his supervisor. Another student may have a different level of tolerance and a greater amount of rivalry, which may appear at the very moment when he is beginning to receive the information that he does not possess. To what extent can careful tempering of the quantity of new information, for a particularly sensitive person, be a 'therapeutic' element, so to speak, in the learning situation?

GRINBERG: I think the tempering of information can be as useful in supervision as the tempering of interpretations can be in the analysis of patients.

[Here there was a question that did not come out on the tape.]

GRINBERG: I generally use expressions that I find very useful, as, for example, the following: 'You need me to take on myself for *now* this situation that you are having such difficulty in bearing, until later on you can confront it and take it on yourself again.' In other words, I try not to give back to them their projection and deposit immediately. But when commenting on this type and similar types of formulation in supervision, I have had problems with some people who took my words and reproduced them literally with their analysands. For that reason I repeatedly advise them to work in their own way and to formulate their interpretations in the simplest language, using common sense.

CONTRIBUTION: With regard to the comment you made the last time about this initial informal dialogue with the student, which is often connected with the patient's material, I thought of the degree of identification between the analyst and his analysand. This may lead to an attempt to recreate a transference–countertransference relationship in the context of the supervision, which may be a very delicate matter because it involves the risk of intervening in the student's analysis. Nevertheless I believe it may be proper and even useful to show the student that certain of his interventions may be related to his own conflicts, and that they have to be distinguished from those of the patients.

GRINBERG: For my part I prefer to avoid that kind of demonstration. One of the greatest risks of supervision is that it may be confused with a therapeutic experience. I want to give a warning of the pressure that can be exerted by 'paratransference' and 'paracountertransference', increasing the tendency towards idealization. Given that there is potentially such a predisposition for transference and displacement of the therapeutic situation to supervision, any reference the supervisor makes to a personal problem of the student (even though he formulates it with the utmost care) runs the risk of approaching the danger zone, the 'powder keg' of treatment, and of being felt by the student as a type of interpretation. As you know, I usually work with projective counteridentification reactions, but I try to point this out as carefully as possible, and I always rely on the clinical material to show the student from whence it comes. To illustrate this with the session we are looking at today, I could tell Dr X, for example, that the patient tried to deposit in her the role of 'the lady who did not come to the wedding', so that she would act in accordance with her specific phantasy and that, due to the inoculatory character of that projective identification, she might be exposed to a projective counteridentification reaction, and might without realizing it, unconsciously, act with the characteristics attributed to that role by the patient. But I always try to differentiate these reactions from those corresponding to the personal history of the therapist. With regard to the latter, I do not intervene, and I do not mention them. Nor do I use the expression, 'see it in your analysis', because I consider it counterproductive. If the student says spontaneously to me that he has realized that a personal problem was involved, I prefer to keep silent and not add any other comment.

CONTRIBUTION: I should like to refer to another problem, that relating to the difference in schemes of reference between supervisor and student. To what extent can this cause conflict?

GRINBERG: I have never had problems of that sort. Sometimes I see it as a certain advantage because it could prevent the risk of submission to a fixed line of thought maintained by the supervisor. I am convinced, moreover, of the enormous benefit in the comparison of different schemes of reference, if this can be done without dogmatism or persecution. I do not deny, of course, that on certain occasions, and when there is a predominance in the student of persecution anxieties channelled through the phantasy of defending to the death his theory or scheme of reference, serious difficulties may arise in the common task. In such cases it is best to explain the situation with great care, to make clear that supervision is not intended to attack any scheme of reference, but to explain the meaning of the clinical material brought, and that this can be done from different points of view. I want to emphasize that it is a good thing that the student should have two supervisions, so that he can learn and compare two different styles. It may happen that he tends to identify mainly with one of these styles, until he has polished his technique and finally has achieved his own style.

Another aspect I want to add is the need to respect the internal *timing* of each student in the learning process of supervision. In this sense my attitude in the first period of work in common is to measure out the information I give and not hasten to show my own specific methods of tackling the clinical material. I try to get to know the way the student works and what his main difficulties are, and to help him to correct errors in captation, conceptualization, and so forth. I gradually begin to introduce my own approaches, always based on the clinical material. I try to bring out the importance of prognosis, but basically I insist on showing on what part of the material I am depending in making predictive hypotheses. I remember the particular reaction of some student in the face of the confirmation of certain predictions.

QUESTION: I should like to know how you tackle the problem of fees.

GRINBERG: Until a very short time ago I followed a sort of tradition that had reigned in our Institute for many years, charging the student the same fees as he paid to his training analyst. This was reasonable enough then, since relatively low fees, with a ceiling, had been fixed for young colleagues still in training. Unfortunately this arrangement was modified with time, and lately most of the supervisors have charged fees according to their own standards. Perhaps that has a certain advantage, if it can be called that, if it helps to discriminate between the two experiences, independently of whether the supervision fees are higher or lower than those for the training analysis. But I do still think that we should consider the tremendous expense of training for a young analyst who is beginning his career, and that it would be a very good thing to return to the criterion we had in the past.

QUESTION: Is the supervisor's time usually fifty minutes, or is some elasticity permissible?

GRINBERG: Usually each supervision is fifty minutes, but with sufficient flexibility to be able to prolong it if necessary. I have also held supervisions of two successive hours, which were very fruitful. In general these were supervisions of the 'consultative' or 'investigative' type, with very productive work on both sides. I see no reason why that time of two consecutive hours—with all its advantages—should not sometimes be applied to supervision with the students of the Institute.

QUESTION: What do you do to prevent the student from applying the indications he receives in supervision prematurely and inappropriately?

GRINBERG: I think this question is very important. This is precisely another of the aspects of the learning process to which I try to pay maximum attention. Very often I explain to the student that we are working on material that belongs to the past, to an experience that is already over, and one that probably has nothing to do with tomorrow's session. On the other hand, I explain to him that it is useful to formulate a working hypothesis, but that does not mean that it has to be immediately transformed into inter-pretations. I also insist on the need to know and understand as clearly as possible the elements of the manifest content of the material. If there is something obscure or confused, I advise asking so as to dissipate the doubt or confusion in the manifest content, and thus be able to make out the latent content more precisely.

QUESTION: I shall ask a question that will certainly give us all to think—one that involves a whole philosophy regarding the sense of the supervision. When does a supervision end?

GRINBERG: This question, too, I find extremely interesting. There are students who beg to continue the supervision when the two years that the Institute lays down as the official period of psychoanalytical training are over. They base their request on the wish to deepen their knowledge or to be able to be supervised with other patients and thus increase the benefit of the understanding of analytical work they have acquired during their experience of supervision. In reality there is always something to learn during the work of supervision. Strictly speaking, we could talk about 'interminable supervision' parallel to 'interminable analysis'. But my opinion is that both analysis and supervision have a cycle that must be completed and finalized in the best possible way. With the pretext that analyses are interminable (which is certain from the theoretical point of view, but not the practical), some analysts may ally themselves with their patients' resistance and break off the analysis prematurely and without sufficient working through, giving rise to bad terminations. I think, on the contrary, that it is a good thing to exhaust every possibility, so that the process can be carried through and a good termination can be arrived at. The same applies to the experience of supervision. Following the paral-lel with analytical treatment, I would say that as we try to help a patient to acquire the capacity for self-analysis, in our function as supervisors we should also reach the point where the students not only learn a technique and a method—with corresponding schemes of reference—but also learn to self-supervise their own work, to face and solve urgent problems in their patients' analysis, and to recognize their mistakes and be able to rectify them. I think these would be the basic conditions for considering the termination of a supervision. Of course I do not exclude the possibility of starting a new experience of re-supervision after a time, as is the case with re-analysis.

Perhaps I feel a little frustrated—and you may feel the same—because we cannot finish examining the material of the session. But on the other hand I feel greatly stimulated by this dialogue, which has enabled us to reflect on different aspects of the experience of supervision. I hope we shall have the opportunity to repeat this type of meeting in the future.

Thank you very much!

REFERENCES

Aberastury, A. (1958). 'La enseñanza del psicoanálisis'. Read at the Second Latin-American Congress, San Paulo.

Aberastury, A., et al. (1966). Adolescencia y psicopatia. Duelo par el cuerpo, la identidad y los padres infantiles. In: A. Rascovsky & D. Liberman (Eds.), *Psicoanálisis de la mania y la psicopatía*. Buenos Aires: Paidós.

Abraham, K. (1919). A particular form of neurotic resistance against the psycho-analytic method. *Selected Papers*. Reprinted 1979, 1988, London: Karnac Books.

———— (1924). A short study of the development of the libido viewed in the light of mental disorders. *Selected Papers*. Reprinted 1979, 1988, London: Karnac Books.

Abrams, S., & Shengold, L. (1978). Some reflexions on the topic of the 30th Congress: Affects and the psychoanalytic situation. *IJP, 59*.

Ackerman, N. (1953). Selected problems in supervised analysis. *Psychiatry, 15*.

Alvarez de Toledo, L. G., Grinberg, L., & Langer, M. (1966). Termination of training analysis. In: R. E. Litman (Ed.), *Psychoanalysis in the Americas*. New York: International Universities Press.

Anderson, A. R., & McLaughlin, F. (1963). Some observations on psychoanalytic supervision. *Psychoanal. Quart., 32.*

Arieti, S. (1967). *The Intrapsychic Self.* New York/London: Basic Books.

Arlow, J. (1963). The supervisory situation. *J. Amer. Psychoanal. Ass., 35.*

Ateneo de Psicoanalistas de Buenos Aires (1975). 'The identity of the psychoanalyst'. Panel held in Buenos Aires, December 1975.

Balint, A. (1943). Identification. *IJP, 24.*

Balint, M. (1948). On the psychoanalytic training system. *IJP, 29.*

—————— (1952). Genital love. In: *Primary Love and Psychoanalytic Technique.* London: Hogarth Press. Reprinted 1985, London: Karnac Books.

Balkoura, A. (1974). Panel: The fate of the transference neurosis after analysis. *J. Am. Psychoanal. Ass., 22.*

Baranger, M., & Baranger, W. (1961). La situación analitica como campo dinámico. *Rev. Urug. de Psicoanálisis, 4.*

Baranger, W. (1957). Interpretación e ideología. *Rev. de Psicoanálisis, 14.*

—————— (1960). 'El sueño como medio de comunicación'. Read at the 3rd Latin-American Psychoanalytic Congress, Santiago de Chile.

—————— (1968). El enfoque económico de Freud a Melanie Klein. *Rev. de Psicoanálisis, 25.*

Begoin, J. (1984). Presentation: Quelques repères sur l'evaluation du concept d'identification. *Rev. franc. de Psychanal., 48.*

Belmonte, L. O., del Valle, E., Kargieman, A., & Saludjian, D. (1976). *La identificación en Freud.* Buenos Aires.

Beres, D. (1960). Psychoanalytical psychology of imagination. *J. Amer. Psychoanal. Ass., 8.*

Bergeret, J. (1970). Les inaffectifs. Intervention in the discussion of A. Green's paper on 'L'affect'. *Rev. franc. Psychan., 34.*

Bianchedi, E. T. de, et al. (1978). Decisión de separación y terminación del análisis. In: Symposium S. Freud: Análisis terminable y interminable, 40 anõs despues. Associatión Psychoanalitica Provisional de Buenos Aires.

Bick, E. (1968). The experience of the skin in early object-relations. *IJP, 49.*

Bion, W. R. (1957). Differentiation of the psychotic from the non-psychotic personalities. *IJP, 38.* Also in *Second Thoughts,* London: Heineman, 1967. Reprinted 1984, London: Karnac Books.

———— (1962). *Learning from Experience.* London: Heinemann. Reprinted 1984, 1988, London: Karnac Books.

———— (1963). *Elements of Psycho-Analysis.* London: Heinemann. Reprinted 1984, London: Karnac Books.

———— (1964). The grid. In: *Two Papers: The Grid and Caesura.* Rio de Janeiro: Imago Editora. Revised edition 1989, London: Karnac Books.

———— (1965). *Transformations.* London: Heinemann. Reprinted 1984, London: Karnac Books.

———— (1966). Catastrophic change. *Scientific Bulletin of the British Psychoanalytical Society, 5.*

———— (1967). *Second Thoughts.* London: Heinemann. Reprinted 1984, London: Karnac Books.

———— (1968). Lectures given to the Argentinian Psychoanalytic Association.

———— (1970). *Attention and Interpretation.* London: Tavistock Publications. Reprinted 1984, London: Karnac Books.

———— (1971). *Brazilian Lectures.* Rio de Janeiro: Imago. Revised edition 1990, London: Karnac Books.

———— (1978). *Four Discussions with W. R. Bion.* Strathclyde: Clunie Press.

Bird, B. (1957). A specific peculiarity of acting out. *J. Am. Psychoan. Ass., 5.*

Bleger, J. (1958). *Psicoanálisis y dialéctica materialista.* Buenos Aires: Paidós.

———— (1965). Preface to G. Politzer's *Psicologia concreta.* Buenos Aires.

Blitzten, N. L., & Fleming, J. (1953). What is a supervisory analysis? *Bull. Menninger Clin., 17.*

Blitzten, N. L., Eissler, R. S., & Eissler, K. R. (1950). Emergence of hidden ego tendencies during dream analysis. *IJP, 31.*

Blos, B. (1962). *On Adolescence: A Psychoanalytic Interpretation.* New York: Collier Macmillan.

Brierley, M. (1951). *Trends in Psychoanalysis.* London: Hogarth.

British Psycho-Analytical Society (1967). The 1943 'controversial' discussions. *Sci Bull. Br. Psycho-Anal. Soc. & Inst. Psycho-Anal., 10.*

Brody, M. W., & Mahoney, V. P. (1964). Introjection, identification and incorporation. *IJP, 45.*

Brosin, H. W. (1955). Panel: Validation of psychoanalytic theory. *J. Am. Psychoanal. Ass., 3.*

Calef, V. (1968). Reports of discussion on acting out. *IJP, 49.*

Chasseguet-Smirgel, J. (1975). *L'Idéal du Moi. Essai psychologique sur la 'maladie d'idéalité'.* France: Tchou. *The Ego Ideal,* London: Free Association Books, 1985.

Chomsky, N. (1957). *Syntactic Structures.* The Hague: Mouton.

_____ (1968). *Language and Mind.* New York: Harcourt, Brace & World.

DeBell, D. E. (1963). A critical digest of the literature on psychoanalytic supervision. *J. Am. Psychoanal. Ass., 11.*

Deutsch, H. (1942). Some forms of emotional disturbance and their relationship to schizophrenia. In: *Neuroses and Character Types.* New York: International Universities Press, 1965.

Eissler, K. R. (1965). *Medical Orthodoxy and the Future of Psychoanalysis.* New York: International Universities Press.

Einstein, A. (1933). Letter to Freud on 'Why war?' *SE, 22.*

Ekstein, R. (1966). Termination of analysis and working through. In: R. E. Litman (Ed.), *Psychoanalysis in the Americas.* New York: International Universities Press.

_____ (1966). *Children of Time and Space, of Action and Impulse. Clinical Studies on the Psychoanalytic Treatment of Severely Disturbed Children.* New York: Appleton-Century-Crofts.

Ekstein, R., & Wallerstein, R. (1958). *The Teaching and Learning of Psychotherapy.* New York: International Universities Press.

Emch, M. (1955). The social context of supervision. *IJP, 36.*

Erikson, E. H. (1950). *Childhood and Society.* New York: W. W. Norton.

_____ (1956). The problem of ego identity. *J. Am. Psychoanal. Ass., 4.*

Etchegoyen, H. (1985). The vicissitudes of identification. *IJP, 66.*

_____ (1986). *Los Fundamentos de la Tecnica Psicoanalitica.* Buenos Aires: Amorrortu.

Fairbairn, W. R. (1952). *Psychoanalytic Studies of the Personality.* London: Routledge.

Federn, P. (1952). *Ego Psychology and the Psychoses.* New York: Basic Books; London: The Hogarth Press. Reprinted 1977, London: Karnac Books.

Fenichel, O. (1926). Identification. In: *Collected Papers of Otto Fenichel.* New York: W. W. Norton, 1953.

Ferenczi, S. (1909). Introjection and transference. In: *First Contributions to Psycho-Analysis.* London: Hogarth Press, 1952. Reprinted 1980, London: Karnac Books.

Firestein, S. (1969). Panel: Problems of termination in the analysis of adults. *J. Am. Psychoanal. Ass., 17.*

Fleming, J., & Benedek, T. (1966). *Psychoanalytic Supervision.* New York: International Universities Press.

Fliess, R. (1942). Metapsychology of the analyst. *Psychoanal. Quart., 11.*

——— (1956). *Erogeneity and the Libido.* New York: International Universities Press.

Flournoy, H. (1933). Le problème des hallucinations au point de vue psychanalitique. *Archives Suisses de Neurologie et de Psychiatrie, 32.*

Forman, M. S. (Ed.) (1931). *The Letters of John Keats.* London: Oxford University Press.

Frazier, S. H. (1965). Psychosomatic illness: A body language form of acting out. In: L. E. Abt & S. L. Weissman (Eds.), *Acting Out: Theoretical and Clinical Aspects.* New York/London: Grune and Stratton.

Freud, A. (1927). Introduction to the technique of child analysis. In: *The Psycho-Analytical Treatment of Children.* New York: International Universities Press, 1955.

——— (1936). *The Ego and the Mechanisms of Defence.* New York: International Universities Press, 1966. London: The Hogarth Press.

Freud, S. (1892–1899). Letters and manuscripts written to Fliess. *SE, 1.*

——— (1900a). *The Interpretation of Dreams.* SE, 4–5.

——— (1905d). Three essays on the theory of sexuality. *SE, 7.*

——— (1905e [1901]). Fragment of an analysis of a case of hysteria. *SE, 7.*

——— (1908e [1907]). Creative writers and day-dreaming. *SE, 9.*

——— (1909b). Analysis of a phobia in a five-year-old boy. *SE, 10.*

——— (1910d). The future prospects of psycho-analytic therapy. *SE, 11.*

_____ (1911b). Formulations on the two principles of mental functioning. *SE, 12.*

_____ (1911c [1910]). Psycho-analytic notes on an autobiographical account of a case of paranoia (dementia paranoides). *SE, 12.*

_____ (1912e). Recommendations to physicians practising psychoanalysis. *SE, 12.*

_____ (1913 [1912–1913]). *Totem and Taboo. SE, 13.*

_____ (1913j). The claims of psycho-analysis to scientific interest. *SE, 13.*

_____ (1914c). On narcissism: An introduction. *SE, 14.*

_____ (1914d). On the history of the psycho-analytic movement. *SE, 14.*

_____ (1914g). Remembering, repeating and working through. *SE, 12.*

_____ (1915b). Thoughts for the times on war and death. *SE, 14.*

_____ (1916–17 [1915–17]). *Introductory Lectures on Psycho-Analysis. SE, 15–16.*

_____ (1917d [1915]). A metapsychological supplement to the theory of dreams. *SE, 14.*

_____ (1917e [1915]). Mourning and melancholia. *SE, 14.*

_____ (1918b [1914]). From the history of an infantile neurosis. *SE, 17.*

_____ (1920g). *Beyond the Pleasure Principle. SE, 18.*

_____ (1921c). *Group Psychology and the Analysis of the Ego. SE, 18.*

_____ (1923a [1922]). Two encyclopaedic articles: (A) Psycho-analysis. *SE, 18.*

_____ (1923b). *The Ego and the Id. SE, 19.*

_____ (1923c [1922]). Remarks upon the theory and practice of dream interpretation. *SE, 19.*

_____ (1924d). The dissolution of the Oedipus complex. *SE, 19.*

_____ (1925d [1924]). An autobiographical study. *SE, 20.*

_____ (1926d [1925]). *Inhibitions, Symptoms and Anxiety. SE, 20.*

_____ (1927e). Fetishism. *SE, 21.*

_____ (1930a). Civilisation and its discontents. *SE, 21.*

_____ (1933a). *New Introductory Lectures on Psychoanalysis. SE, 22.*

_____ (1933b [1932]). Why war? *SE, 22.*

_____ (1937c). Analysis terminable and interminable. *SE, 23.*

_____ (1937d). Constructions in analysis. *SE, 23.*

_____ (1940a [1938]). Outline of psychoanalysis. *SE, 23.*

_____ (1940e [1938]). Splitting of the ego in the process of defence. *SE, 23*.

_____ (1941e [1926]). Address to the Society of B'nai B'rith. *SE, 20*.

_____ (1950a [1887–1902]). Project for a scientific psychology. *SE, 1*.

Frijling-Schreuder, E. C. N. (1970). On individual supervision. *IJP, 51*.

Frosch, J. (1976). Psychoanalytic contributions to the relationship between dreams and psychosis: A critical survey. *Int. J. Psychoan. Psychother., 5*.

Fuchs, S. E. (1937). On introjection. *IJP, 18*.

Gaddini, E. (1969). On imitation. *IJP, 50*.

Gear, M. C., & Liendo, E. (1973). *Semiologia Psicoanalitica*. Buenos Aires: Nueva Vision.

Giovacchini, P. L. (1960). On scientific creativity. *J. Am. Psychoanal. Ass., 8*.

_____ (1965). Some aspects of the development of the ego-ideal of a creative scientist. *Psychoanal. Quart., 34*.

Gitelson, M. (1962). The curative factors in psycho-analysis: The first phase of psycho-analysis. *IJP, 43*.

_____ (1963a). On the present scientific and social position of psycho-analysis. *IJP, 44*.

_____ (1963b). On the problem of curative factors in the first phase of psychoanalysis. *IJP, 44*.

Glover, E. (1935). *Bull. Int. Psychoanalytical Ass*. The Four Countries conference. *IJP, 16*.

Granel, J. (1970). 'Acting out, idealisación y creatividad. Estudio de su evolución en un tratamiento psicoanalitico'. Read at the Asociación Psicoanalitica Argentina.

Green, A. (1970). L'affect. *Rev. franc. Psychanal., 34*.

_____ (1971). La projection. De l'identification projective au project. *Rev. franc. Psychanal., 35*.

_____ (1977). Conceptions of affect. *IJP, 58*.

_____ (1984). 'The death drive, negative narcissism, the death objectalising function'. Symposium on the death-instinct, organized by the European Psycho-Analytical Federation, Marseilles.

Greenacre, P. (1953). *Trauma, Growth and Personality*. London: The Hogarth Press. International Psychoanal. Library, 46. Reprinted 1987, London: Karnac Books.

_____ (1957). The childhood of the artist. In: *Psychoanalytic Study of the Child*. New York, International Universities Press.

———— (1958). Early physical determinants in the development of the sense of identity. *J. Am. Psychoanal. Ass., 6.*

———— (1965). 'Problems of training analysis'. Read at the first Pre-Congress on Training in Amsterdam.

Greenson, R. (1966a). Acting out and working through. Comment on Dr. Limentani's paper. *IJP, 47.*

———— (1966b). That 'impossible' profession. *J. Am. Psychoan. Ass., 14.*

Grinberg, L. (1954). Sobre la depersonalización en el curso de la neurosis transferencial. *Rev. de Psicoanal., 20.*

———— (1955). 'Omnipotence, magic and depersonalisation in transference'. Presented at the 19th Psychoanalytical Congress, Geneva.

———— (1956). Sobre algunos problemas de técnica psico-analitica determinados por la identificación y contra-identificación proyectivas. *Rev. de Psicoanal., 14.*

———— (1957a). Perturbaciones en la interpretación motivadas por la contraidentificación proyectiva. *Rev. de Psychoanal., 14.*

———— (1957b). Si yo fuera usted. Contribución al estudio de la identificación projectiva. *Rev. de Psicoanal., 14.*

———— (1958). Aspectos magicos en la transferencia y en la contratransferencia. Identificación y contraidentificación proyectivas. *Rev. de Psicoanal., 15.*

———— (1962). On a specific aspect of countertransference due to the patient's projective identification. *IJP, 43.*

———— (1963a). *Culpa y Depresión.* Buenos Aires: Paidós.

———— (1963b). Psicopatologia de la identificación y contra-identificación proyectivas y de la contratransferencia. *Rev. de Psicoanal., 20.*

———— (1963c). Relations between analysts. *IJP, 44.*

———— (1963d). Relations between psychoanaytical processes. *IJP, 44.*

———— (1964). Two kinds of guilt: Their relations with normal and pathological aspects of mourning. *IJP, 45.*

———— (1965). Contribución al estudio de las modalidades de la identificación proyectiva. *Rev. de Psicoanal., 22.*

———— (1966). The relationship between obsessive mechanisms and a state of self disturbance: Depersonalisation. *IJP, 47.*

———— (1968). On acting out and its role in the psycho-analytic process. *IJP, 49.*

———— (1969). New ideas, conflict and evolution. *IJP, 50.*

_____ (1970). The problem of supervision in psychoanalytic education. *IJP, 51*.

_____ (1971). Sentimiento de identidad y elaboración del duelo por el self. In: *Culpa y depresion, estudio psicoanalitico*, 2nd ed. Buenos Aires: Paidós.

_____ (1972a). Psychoanalytical observations on creativity. *Isr. Ann. Psychiat., 10*.

_____ (1972b). Discussion of Dr. Lindon's paper, 'Supervision by tape: A new method of case supervision'. *The Psychoanal. Forum, 4*.

_____ (1976a). 'An approach to the understanding of borderline patients'. Presented to the Panel on borderline conditions. The Menninger Foundation, Topeka, Kansas.

_____ (1976b). L'identité du psychanalyste. A propos de l'exposé de Joseph & Widlöcher. In: *L'Identité du psychanalyste*. Symposium held at Haslemere, 1976. Paris: Presses Univ. France, 1979.

_____ (1976c). La identidad del psicoanalista. *Bulletin del Ateneo de Psicoanalistas de Buenos Aires*.

_____ (1978). The 'razor's edge' in depression and mourning. *IJP, 45*.

_____ (1979). Countertransference and projective counter-identification. *Contemporary Psychoanalysis, 15*.

_____ (1981). El 'filo de la navaja' en las depresiones y en los duelos. In: *Psicoanalisis: Aspectus teóricos y clinicus*. Buenos Aires: Paidós.

_____ (1982). 'Mas allá de la contraidentificación proyectiva'. Read at the Latin-American Psychoanalytic Congress, Buenos Aires.

_____ (1985). *Teoria de la Identificación*. Madrid: Tecnipublicaciones.

Grinberg, L., et al. (1967). Función del soñar y clasificación clinica de los suenos en el proceso analitico. *Rev. Psicoanal., 24*.

_____ (1973). *Introduction to the Work of Bion*. Strathclyde: Clunie Press, 1975. Reprinted 1985, London: Karnac Books.

_____ (1974a). La 'analogia', la 'simetria' y la 'polivalencia' en el uso de la 'interpretación-construcción'. *Rev. Bras. de Psic., 8*.

_____ (1974b). Utilización de los mitos como modelos para la comprensión del concepto de 'interpretación-construcción'. *Rev. Bras. de Psic., 8*.

Grinberg, L., & Grinberg, R. (1960). Los sueños del dia lunes. *Rev. Psicoanal., 17*.

_____ (1971). *Identidad y Cambio*. Buenos Aires.

_____ (1974). The problem of identity and the psycho-analytical process. *Int. Rev. Psychoan., 17*.

Grinberg, L., Langer, M., & Rodrigue, E. (1968). *Psicoanálisis en las Américas*. Buenos Aires: Paidós.

Grinberg, L., & Rodriguez-Perez, J. F. (1982). The borderline patient and acting out. In: P. Giovacchini & L. B. Boyer (Eds.), *Technical Factors in the Treatment of the Severely Disturbed Patient*. New York: Jason Aronson.

Grinberg, R. (1960). Los significados del mirar en una claustrofobia. *Rev. de Psicoanal., 17.*

———— (1961). Sobre la curiosidad. *Rev. de psicoanal., 18.*

Grotjahn, M. (1955). Problems and techniques of supervision. *Psychiatry, 18.*

Grotstein, J. S. (1985). A proposed revision of the psycho-analytic concept of death instinct. In: R. Langs (Ed.), *The Year Book of Psychoanalysis and Psychotherapy 1*, New Jersey: New Concept Press.

Guiard, F. (1978). 'Aportes al estudio de la transferencia y contratransferencia en el final del análisis y en el post-análisis'. Presented at the Soc. Cient. Argentina.

Guntrip, H. (1961). *Personality Structure and Human Interaction*. London: Hogarth.

———— (1967). The concept of psychodynamic science. *Int. J. Psycho-Anal., 48.*

Hartmann, H. (1955). Notes on the theory of sublimation. In: *Essays on Ego Psychology*. London: Hogarth Press.

———— (1958). *Ego Psychology and the Problem of Adaptation*. New York: International Universities Press.

———— (1964). *Essays on Ego Psychology*. London: Hogarth Press.

Hartmann, H., Kris, E., & Loewenstein, R. M. (1946). Comments on the formation of psychic structure. In: *The Psychoanalytic Study of the Child*. New York, International Universities Press.

Hartmann, H., & Loewenstein, R. M. (1962). Notes on the super-ego. In: *The Psychoanalytic Study of the Child*. New York: International Universities Press.

Head, H., & Holmes, G. (1911). Sensory disturbances from cerebral lesions. *Brain, 34.*

Heimann, P. (1950). On countertransference. *IJP, 31.*

———— (1952). Certain functions of introjection and projection in early infancy. In: M. Klein et al., *Developments in Psychoanalysis*. London: Hogarth Press. Reprinted 1989, London: Karnac Books.

———— (1974). Discussion of the paper of Ch. Brenner, 'Depression, anxiety affect theory'. *IJP, 55.*

Home, H. J. (1966). The concept of mind. *IJP, 47*.

Hook, S. (1959). *Psychoanalysis, Scientific Method and Philosophy*. New York: International Universities Press.

Hora, T. (1957). Contribution to the phenomenology of the supervisory process. *Amer. J. Psychotherapy, 11*.

Hug-Hellmuth, H. (1921). On the technique of child analysis. *IJP, 2*.

Hurn, H. (1973). Panel: On the fate of transference after the termination of analysis. *J. Am. Psychoanal. Ass., 21*.

Isakower, O. (1963). 'The analytic instrument'. Faculty meeting, 16 October and 20 November, 1963, New York Psychoanalytic Institute.

Jacobson, E. (1954). Contribution to the metapsychology of psychotic identifications. *J. Amer. Psychoanal. Ass., 11*.

———— (1959). Depersonalisation. *J. Am. Psychoanal. Ass., 7*.

———— (1964). *The Self and the Object World*. New York: International Universities Press.

———— (1967). *Psychotic Conflict and Reality*. London: Hogarth Press.

Jones, E. (1955). *The Life and Work of Sigmund Freud*. London: Hogarth Press.

Joseph, B. (1978a). Different types of anxiety and their handling in the analytic situation. In: *Psychic Equilibrium and Psychic Change: Selected Papers of Betty Joseph*. London: Routledge, 1989.

———— (1978b). Towards the experience of psychic pain. In: *Psychic Equilibrium and Psychic Change: Selected Papers of Betty Joseph*. London: Routledge, 1989.

———— (1984). 'Projective identification. Some clinical aspects'. Presented at the first Conference of the Sigmund Freud Centre of the Hebrew University of Jerusalem. In: J. Sandler et al., *Projection, Identification, Projective Identification*. London: Karnac Books, 1988.

Joseph, E. D. (1983). Identity of a psychoanalyst. In: E. D. Joseph & D. Widlöcher (Eds.), *The Identity of the Psychoanalyst*. New York: International Universities Press.

Kanzer, M. (1955). The communicative function of the dream. *IJP, 36*.

———— (1985). Identification and its vicissitudes. *IJP, 66*.

Kernberg, O. (1984). 'The influence of projective identification on countertransference'. Presented at the first Conference of the Sigmund Freud Centre of the Hebrew University of Jerusalem. In: J. Sandler et al., *Projection, Identification, Projective Identification*. London: Karnac Books, 1988.

Klein, G. S. (1966). 'Perspectives to change in psychoanalysis'. Read at the Conference of Psychoanalysts of the South-West, Galveston, Texas.

—————— (1976). Two theories or one? In: *Psychoanalytic Theory: An Exploration of Essentials*. New York: International Universities Press.

Klein, M. (1921). The development of a child. *The Writings of Melanie Klein, vol. I*, p. 1.

—————— (1923). Early analysis. *The Writings of Melanie Klein, vol. I*, p. 77.

—————— (1929). Personification in the play of children. *The Writings of Melanie Klein, vol. I*, p. 199.

—————— (1932). *The Psychoanalysis of Children. The Writings of Melanie Klein, vol. II*.

—————— (1933). The early development of conscience in the child. *The Writings of Melanie Klein, vol. I*, p. 248.

—————— (1940). Mourning and its relation to manic-depressive states. *The Writings of Melanie Klein, vol. I*, p. 344.

—————— (1946). Notes on some schizoid mechanisms. *The Writings of Melanie Klein*, vol. III, p. 1.

—————— (1950). On the criteria for the termination of a psycho-analysis. *IJP, 31; The Writings of Melanie Klein, vol. III*, p. 43.

—————— (1952). Some theoretical conclusions regarding the emotional life of infants. *The Writings of Melanie Klein, vol. III*, p. 61.

—————— (1955). On identification. *The Writings of Melanie Klein, vol. III*, p. 141.

—————— (1957). Envy and gratitude. *The Writings of Melanie Klein, vol. III*, p. 176.

—————— (1963). On the sense of loneliness. *The Writings of Melanie Klein, vol. III*, p. 200.

Klein, M., et al. (1952). *Developments in Psychoanalysis*. London: Hogarth Press. Reprinted 1989. London: Karnac Books.

Knight, R. P. (1940). Introjection, projection and identification. *Psychoanal. Quart., 9*.

—————— (1954). The present state of organised psychoanalysis in the United States. In: *Psychoanalytic Psychology and Psychiatry*. New York: International Universities Press.

Koff, R. H. (1961). A definition of identification. *IJP, 42*.

Kovacs, V. (1936). Training and control analysis. *IJP, 17*.

Kramer, M. K. (1959). On the continuation of the analytic process after psycho-analysis: A self-observation. *IJP, 40*.

Kramer, P. (1958). Panel: Problems of identity. *J. Am. Psychoanal. Ass., 6.*

Kris, E. (1938). *Psychoanalytic Explorations in Art.* New York: International Universities Press, 1952.

———— (1955). *Psicoanálisis y arte.* Buenos Aires: Paidós.

Kubie, L. (1958a). *Neurotic Distortions of the Creative Process.* Kansas: Kansas University Press.

———— (1958b). Research into the process of supervision in psychoanalysis. *Psychoanal. Quart., 27.*

Laing, R. D. (1960). *The Divided Self. A Study in Sanity and Madness.* London: Tavistock Publications.

Langer, M. (1963). Dificultades psicológicas del psicoanalista principiante. *Rev. Psicoanal., 20.*

———— (1968). El analizando del año 2000. *Rev. de Psicoanal., 25.*

Langer, M., Pujet, J., & Teper, E. (1964). A methodological approach to the teaching of psychoanalysis. *IJP, 45.*

Langer, S. K. (1942). *Philosophy in a New Key.* London: Oxford University Press.

Langs, R. (1979). The interactional dimension of countertransference. In: E. Epstein & A. Feiner (Eds.), *Countertransference.* New York: Jason Aronson.

Laplanche, J. (1984). 'The death drive in the theory of sexual drives'. In: Symposium on the death instinct, organized by the European Psychoanalytical Federation, Marseilles.

Laplanche, J., & Pontalis, J. B. (1967). *The Language of Psychoanalysis.* London: The Hogarth Press. Reprinted 1988, London: Karnac Books.

Lebovici, S. (1970). Technical remarks on the supervision of psychoanalytic treatment. *IJP, 51.*

Lewin, B., & Ross, H. (1960). *Psychoanalytic Education in the United States.* New York: W. W. Norton.

Lichtenstein, H. (1961). Identity and sexuality. *J. Am. Psychoanal. Ass., 9.*

Lindon, J. A. (1972). Supervision by tape: A new method of case supervision. *The Psychoanal. Forum, 4.*

Litman, R. E. (1966). *Psychoanalysis in the Americas.* New York: International Universities Press.

McDougall, J. (1979). Primitive communication and the use of countertransference. In: H. Feiner & L. Epstein (Eds.), *Countertransference.* New York: Jason Aronson.

Mahler, M. (1952). On child psychoses and schizophrenia: Autistic and symbiotic infantile psychoses. In: *The Psychoanalytic Study of the Child*. New York: International Universities Press.

———— (1958a). Certain aspects of the separation-individuation phase. *Psychoanal. Quart., 32*.

———— (1958b). Panel report: Problems of identity. *J. Am. Psychoanal. Ass., 6*.

———— (1963). Thoughts about development and individuation. In: *The Psychoanalytic Study of the Child, 18*. New York: International Universities Press.

———— (1965). On the significance of the normal separation-individuation phase. In: M. Schur (Ed.), *Drives, Affects, Behaviour*. New York: International Universities Press.

———— (1967). On human symbiosis and the vicissitudes of individuation. *J. Am. Psychoanal. Ass., 15*.

Meissner, W. W. (1970). Notes on identification, I. Origins in Freud. *Psychoanal. Quart., 39*.

———— (1971). Notes on identification. II. Classification of related concepts. *Psychoanal. Quart., 40*.

———— (1972). Notes on identification. III. The concept of identification. *Psychoanal. Quart., 41*.

———— (1974). The role of imitation social learning in the identificatory process. *J. Am. Psychoanal. Ass., 22*.

Meltzer, D. (1966). The relation of anal masturbation to projective identification. *IJP, 47*.

———— (1967). *The Psycho-Analytical Process*. Strathclyde: Clunie Press.

Institute of Psycho-Analysis.

———— (1984). *Dream Life*. Strathclyde: Clunie Press.

Meltzer, D., Bremner, C., Hoxter, S., Weddell, D., & Wittenberg, I. (1975). *Explorations in Autism*. Strathclyde: Clunie Press.

Menninger, K. (1942). Presidential address: The American Association. *Psychoanal. Quart., 26*.

Merleau-Ponty, M. (1957). *Fenomenologia de la Percepción*. Mexico: Fondo de Cultura Económica.

Milner, M. (1952). Aspects of symbolism in comprehension of the Not-Self. IJP, 33.

———— (1969). *The Hands of the Living God*. London: Hogarth Press.

Moore, B., & Fine, B.D. (1968). *A Glossary of Psychoanalytic Terms and Concepts*. New York: Amer. Psychoanal. Ass.

Noy, P. (1982). A revision of the psychoanalytic theory of affects. In: Chicago Institute of Psychoanalysis (Ed.), *The Annual of Psychoanalysis, X.*

Nunberg, H. (1950). *Teoria de las Neurosis Basada en el Psicoanálisis.* Barcelona: Pubul.

Oberndorf, C. P. (1934). Depersonalisation in relation to erotization of thought. *IJP, 15.*

Ogden, T. H. (1985). Discussion paper: Instinct structure and personal meaning. In: R. Langs (Ed.), *Year Book of Psychoanalysis and Psychotherapy, vol. I.* New Jersey: New Concept Press.

Pfeffer, A. (1959). A procedure for evaluating the results of psychoanalysis: A preliminary report. *J. Am. Psychoanal. Ass., 7.*

————— (1963). Panel: Analysis terminable and interminable: Twenty-five years later. *J. Am. Psychoanal. Ass., 11.*

Pfeiffer, E. (Ed.) (1972). *Sigmund Freud and Lou Andreas-Salomé, Letters.* London: Hogarth Press.

Piaget, J. (1969). Genetic epistemology. *Columbia Forum, 4.*

Pichon-Rivière, A. A. de (1958). 'La enseñanza del psicoanálisis'. Read at the Latin-American Psychoanalytical Congress, São Paulo.

Poincaré, H. (1967). In: R. Taton (Ed.), *Causalités et accidents de la découverte scientifique.* Paris: Mason & Cie.

Racker, E. (1958). Los significados de la contratransferencia. *Rev. de Psic., 1958.*

Racker, H. (1952). Observaciones sobre la contratransferencia como instrumento tecnico. *Rev. de Psicoanal., 9.*

————— (1953a). A contribution to the problem of counter-transference. *Int. J. Psycho-Anal., 34.*

————— (1953b). The countertransference neurosis. *IJP, 34.*

————— (1957). The meanings and uses of countertransference. *Psychoanal. Quart., 26.* Also in *Transference and Counter-transference,* London: Hogarth Press, 1968. Reprinted 1982, 1985, 1988, London: Karnac Books.

————— (1960). *Estudios sobre Tecnica Psicoanalítica.* Buenos Aires: Paidós.

————— (1966). Ethics and psycho-analysis and the psycho-analysis of ethics. *IJP, 47.*

Rallo, J. (1982). Les deux contenus latents du rêve. *Rev. Franc. Psychanal., 46.*

Rangell, L. (1966). An overview of the ending of an analysis. In: R. Litman (Ed.), *Psychoanalysis in the Americas.* New York: International Universities Press.

386   REFERENCES

Rank, O. (1932). *Art and Artist: Creative Urge and Personality Development*. New York: Tudor Publishing.

Rapaport, D. (1950). On the psychoanalytic theory of thinking. *IJP, 31*.

————— (1951). The conceptual model of psychoanalysis. *J. Personality, 20*.

————— (1953). On the psychoanalytic theory of affects. *IJP, 34*.

Rechardt, E. (1984). 'The vicissitudes of the death drive'. Symposium on the death instinct, organized by the European Psychoanalytical Federation, Marseilles.

Reichenbach, H. (1938). *Experience and Prediction*. Chicago: Chicago University Press.

Reik, T. (1927). *Wie man Psychologe wird*. Vienna: Inst. Psychoanal.

Richardson, G. A., & Moore, R. A. (1963). On the manifest-dream in schizophrenia. *J. Amer. Psychoanal. Ass., 11*.

Rickman, J. (1951). Reflections on the function and organisation of a psycho-analytic society. *IJP, 32*.

Rifflet-Lemaire, A. (1971). *Lacan*. Barcelona: Edhasa.

Rivière, J. (1936). A contribution to the analysis of negative therapeutic reaction. *IJP, 17*. Also in *Collected Papers of J. Rivière*, London: Karnac Books, 1990.

Robbins, W. (1975). Panel: Termination; problems and techniques. *J. Am. Psychoanal. Ass., 23*.

Rodrigué, E. (1969). The fifty thousand hours patient. *IJP, 50*.

Rodriguez Perez, J. F. (1985). 'Bases para una convicción psicoanalitica'. Lecture at the Madrid Psychoanalytical Association.

Rosen, V. (1960). Some aspects of the role of imagination in the analytic process. *J. Am Psychoanal. Ass., 8*.

Rosenfeld, H. (1947). Analysis of a schizophrenic state with depersonalisation. In: *Psychotic States*. London: Hogarth Press. Reprinted 1982, 1984, London: Karnac Books.

————— (1969). 'Contributions to the psychopathology of psychotic states. The importance of projective identification in the ego structure and the object relations of the psychotic states'. Paper presented at the International Colloquium on Psychosis, Montreal, November 1969.

————— (1978). 'Psychic pain and its relation to hypochondriasis and psychosomatic states' (unpublished paper).

Russell-Anderson, A., & McLaughlin, F. (1968). Some observations on psychoanalytic supervision. *Psychoanal. Quart., 32*.

Rycroft, C. (1968). *A Critical Dictionary of Psychoanalysis*. New York: Basic Books.

Sachs, H. (1951). The creative unconscious. *Studies on the Psycho-Analysis of Art*, 2nd ed. Boston: Sci-Art.

Sandler, J. (1960). On the concept of the superego. In: *The Psychoanalytic Study of the Child, XV*. New York: International Universities Press.

Sandler, J., & Sandler, A. M. (1978). On the development of object relationships and affects. *IJP, 59*.

Sandler, J., & Joffe, W. G. (1969). Towards a basic psycho-analytic model. *IJP, 50*.

Sanford, N. (1955). The dynamics of the superego. *Psychoanalytic Review, 62*.

Schafer, R. (1968). *Aspects of Internalization*. New York: International Universities Press.

Schilder, P. (1950). *The Image and Appearance of the Human Body*. New York: International Universities Press.

Schmideberg, M. (1930). Psychotic mechanism in cultural development. *IJP, 11*.

Schur, M. (1969). Affects and cognition. *IJP, 55*.

Searles, H. P. (1955). The informational value of the supervisor's emotional experience. *Psychiatry, 18*.

Segal, H. (1952). A psychoanalytical approach to aesthetics. *IJP, 33*. Also in *New Directions in Psycho-Analysis*, London: Tavistock, 1955. Reprinted 1977, 1985, London: Karnac Books.

———— (1957). Notes on symbol formation. *IJP, 38*. Also in *The Work of Hanna Segal*, New York: Jason Aronson. Reprinted 1986, London: Karnac Books.

———— (1962). The curative factors in psychoanalysis. *IJP, 43*. Also in *The Work of Hanna Segal*, New York: Jason Aronson. Reprinted 1986, London: Karnac Books.

———— (1964). *Introduction to the Work of Melanie Klein*. London. Reprinted 1988, London: Karnac Books.

———— (1977). Countertransference. *Int. Journal of Psychoanalytic Psychotherapy, 6*. Also in *The Work of Hanna Segal*, New York: Jason Aronson. Reprinted 1986, London: Karnac Books.

———— (1981). The function of dreams. In: *The Work of Hanna Segal*. New York: Jason Aronson. Reprinted 1986, London: Karnac Books.

———— (1984). 'On the clinical usefulness of the concept death

388   REFERENCES

instinct'. Symposium on the death instinct, organized by the European Psychoanalytical Federation.

Serebriany, R., et al. (1963).'La Asociación Psicoanalitica Argentina y sus miembros frente a un brote de antijudaismo. Resultados de una encuesta' (unpublished).

Sterba, R. F. (1946). Dreams and acting out. *Psychoanal. Quart. 15.*

Symposium (1937). On the theory of the therapeutic results of psychoanalysis. *IJP, 18.*

Symposium (1948). On the evaluation of therapeutic results. *IJP, 29.*

Symposium (1950). On the termination of psycho-analytical treatment and on the criteria for the termination of an analysis. *IJP, 31.*

Szasz, T. (1965). *The Ethics of Psychoanalysis.* London: RKP.

Taton, R. (1967). *Causalités et Accidents de la Découverte Scientifique.* Paris: Mason et Cie.

Tausk, V. (1933). On the origin of the 'influencing machine' in schizophrenia. *Psychoanal. Quart, 2.*

Thompson, C. (1958). A study of the emotional climate of psychoanalytic institutes. *Psychiatry, 421.*

Tustin, F. (1972). *Autism and Childhood Psychoses.* London: The Hogarth Press.

Wälder, R.(1955). The function and the pitfalls of psycho-analytic societies. *Bull. Philadelphia Assoc. for Psychoanal.*

Wagner, F. F. (1957). Supervision of psychotherapy. *Am. J. Psychother. 11.*

Wallerstein, R. (1977). Psychic energy reconsidered: Introduction. *J. Am. Psychoanal. Ass. 25.*

Weiss, E. (1947/48). Proyección, extrayección y objetivación. *Rev. de psicoanal. 5.*

Weissman, P. (1967). Ego regression and ego functions in creativity. *Psychoanal. Quart., 36.*

White, R. W. (1962). Identification as a development process. In: *Ego Reality in Psychoanalytic Theory.* Psychological Issues 3. New York: International Universities Press.

Widlöcher, D. (1970). Les processes d'identification. *Bull. de Psychologie, 23.*

———— (1983). Psychoanalysis today: A problem of identity. In: E. D. Joseph & D. Wildlöcher, *The Identity of the Psychoanalysts.* New York: International Universities Press.

———— (1984). Quel usage faisons-nous du concept de pulsion? In: 'La pulsion pourquoi faire?' Colloque de l'Association Psychanalique Française.

———— (1985). The wish for identification and structural effects in the work of Freud. *IJP, 66.*

Winnicott, D. W. (1955). Metapsychological and clinical aspects of regression within the psycho-analytical set-up. *IJP, 36.* Also *Through Pediatrics to Psycho-analysis.* London: Tavistock; New York: Basic Books.

———— (1958a). The capacity to be alone. *IJP, 36.* Also in *The Maturational Process and the Facilitating Environment.* London: Hogarth Press. Reprinted 1990. London: Karnac Books.

———— (1958a). *Selected Papers.* New York: Basic Books.

———— (1971). *Playing and Reality.* London: Tavistock. Reprinted London: Penguin Books.

Wisdom, J. O. (1961). A methodological approach to the problem of mystery, *IJP, 42.*

———— (1963). Comparación y desarollo de las teorias psico-analiticas sobre la melancolia. *Rev. Urug. de Psicoan, 2.*

Wollheim, R. (1969). The mind and the mind's image of itself. *IJP, 50.*